Violence in Children
and Adolescents

of related interest

Group Work with Children and Adolescents
A Handbook
Edited by Kedar Nath Dwivedi
1 85302 157 1

How and Why Children Hate
Edited by Ved Varma
1 85302 116 4
1 85302 185 7

How and Why Children Fail
A Study of Conscious and Unconscious Sources
Edited by Ved Varma
1 85302 108 3
1 85302 186 5

Forensic Psychotherapy
Crime, Psychodynamics and the Offender Patient
Edited by Christopher Cordess and Murray Cox
1 85302 240 3

A Practical Guide to Forensic Psychotherapy
Edited by Estela V. Welldon
1 85302 389 2

Challenges in Forensic Psychotherapy
Edited by Hjalmar van Marle
1 85302 419 8

Working with Offenders
Edited by Gill McIvor
1 85302 249 7

Violence in Children and Adolescents

Edited by Ved Varma

Jessica Kingsley Publishers
London and Bristol, Pennsylvania

First published in the United Kingdom in 1997 by
Jessica Kingsley Publishers Ltd
116 Pentonville Road
London N1 9JB, England
and
1900 Frost Road, Suite 101
Bristol, PA 19007, U S A

Copyright © 1997 Jessica Kingsley Publishers

Library of Congress Cataloging in Publication Data
Violence in children and adolescents / edited by Ved Varma
p. cm.
Includes bibliographical references and index.
ISBN 1-85302-344-2 (pb)
1. Children and violence. 2. Violence in children. 3. Juvenile
delinquency. 4. Adolescent psychotherapy. I. Varma, Ved P.
HQ 784.V55V53 1997
303.6'083--dc20 96-18256
CIP.

British Library Cataloguing in Publication Data
A CIP catalogue record for this book is available from the British Library

ISBN 1-85302-344-2

Printed and Bound in Great Britain by
Biddles Ltd, Guildford and King's Lynn

Contents

Introduction   1

1. The Emotional Impact of Violence on Children   2
    Sheila Melzak

2. The Backgrounds of Violent Young Offenders: The Present Picture   22
    Gwyneth Boswell

3. Psychiatric Assessment of the Violent Child and Adolescent
    Towards Understanding and Safe Intervention   37
    Susan Bailey

4. Psychological Assessment and Monitoring of Violent Children
    and Adolescents   48
    Kevin J. Epps

5. Psycho-Social Approaches to the Understanding and Reduction
    of Violence in Young People   65
    James McGuire

6. Roots of Sexual Violence in Children and Adolescents   84
    Colin Hawkes, Jill Ann Jenkins and Eileen Vizard

7. Violence in Adolescence   103
    Arthur Hyatt Williams

8. A Violent Child and his Family   111
    Richard Davies

9. Racial Violence and Young People   123
    Surya Bhate and Soni Bhate

10. Television and the Well-Being of Children and Young People   132
    Richard Sparks

11. Risk and Danger in Young People's Leisure   144
    Ken Roberts

12. Groupwork with Violent Children and Adolescents   157
    Kedar Nath Dwivedi

13. The Police Relationship with Violent Children and Adolescents   172
    Nigel Fielding

References   185

Contributors   205

Subject Index   208

Author Index   213

Introduction

Ved P. Varma

The Concise Oxford Dictionary defines violence as unlawful exercise of physical force. Our society is haunted by acts of mental and physical violence. Mary, aged 11, said 'murder isn't bad'! The roots of violence, sad to say, can often be traced to childhood. This book deals with violence against and by children. It also deals with how to understand violent people and how to cope with, manage and treat them.

The book was written by five forensic psychiatrists, two forensic psychologists, four psychotherapists, and five criminologists. All of them are recognized authorities in their fields. Accordingly, their views command every respect.

I would wholeheartedly therefore recommend this interesting and authoritative book to readers concerned with children and adolescents in any way. In particular, students and practitioners in psychiatry, psychology, psychotherapy, counselling, social work, criminology and education would find within it much to help them. Barbara Dockar-Drysdale (1990) says that people working with violent children have to learn a lot of painful things about themselves, if they are to be of use to children. For example, to be aware of violence in themselves. Do they know about these feelings in themselves? How do they contain these feelings: with a lot of pain? Their work and their personal lives will become enriched through analyzing experience. But the gaining of insight must always be a slow and painful process.

Ved P. Varma, London
March 1996

CHAPTER 1

The Emotional Impact of Violence on Children

Sheila Melzak

Introduction

The emotional impact of violence on children is organized by several factors which interact with each other in a dynamic way. The experience of violence may be traumatic and overwhelming; it may be strengthening; it may be challenging. It always has some effect. The child's age, the extent of the violence, the level of relationship of the child to the perpetrator, the meaning of the violence for the child in the long and in the short term, the extent to which the experience of violence is connected with loss and change and whether or not the child generalizes his/her understanding of the world from specific experiences of violence are all crucial factors. Many writers from psychoanalysis, from social psychology and from the systemic perspective agree that the experience of parental violence in a child's first five years may lead to violent thoughts and behaviour in adult life if the child has no opportunity to experience a positive secure relationship. There is also considerable agreement in recent writing that individual psychological explanations of 'anti-social' behaviour or political violence can result in inadequate solutions and perpetrate myths that children are not the socially active and interactive creatures that they are, and deny the effects of social factors, such as social position, social identity and public reputation (Dawes and Donald 1994). Writers such as Dawes and Donald (1994), Gilligan (1982), Punamacki (1987), Straker (1992) all treat the examination of social context with as much seriousness as their focus on internal experience and certainly conclude that political violence by children cannot be proved to generalize beyond the context in which it occurred (without denying its different effects on individuals).

I hope here to raise certain questions about the way in which violence is represented in children's minds, how these representations of violent relationships might link to behaviour, thinking and relating in a variety of contexts,

and how those representations of perpetrators and victims might be transformed, or isolated, in situations where they are linked to difficulties in living
that the child feels are problematic (rather than difficulties and problems defined
by adults in the child's social world, however significant).

Context

At the time when I began to think about writing this chapter (autumn 1995)
the newspapers, and in particular their front pages, all chose to give prominence
to reports of the trial of Rose West; someone who with her husband had
violently sexually abused and murdered a large number of young people
including some of their own children. There were analyses of the historical,
psychological and social roots of their behaviour and debates about good and
evil. After the trial two of the West's children were interviewed on television
and they made very clear that, in spite of their own complicated feelings
towards their parents, they wished simply that adults in their community with
whom they had shared the reality of their childhood abuse had been able to
hear what they were saying and to act to protect them many years before.
Allegations of abuse had been investigated and insufficient evidence had been
found to validate the children's disclosures.

During the same week that a life sentence was given to Mrs West for her
crimes it was reported in the press (much more briefly than the reports of the
West case) that a Law Lords ruling (*Professional Social Work*, Jan 1996) meant in
effect that children's evidence in abuse cases did not provide sufficient grounds
for social workers to take action to protect a child. This ruling has clear
implications 'for children who are being abused but where proof falls below
that necessary for criminal conviction' (*Professional Social Work*, Jan 1996).

At the same time as the British public, stimulated by the West trial, began
to think again about the widespread facts and causes of child abuse within
families, the British government proposed at their party conference a new
asylum law that would radically restrict the rights of refugees applying for
asylum in Britain. Thousands of refugee parents willing and able to work will
have difficulty in finding work and are unlikely to receive benefit in order to
care for their families, let alone be granted permanent refugee status. Families
may be divided (clearly against the best interests of children). Parents will be
under extreme stress and many will be forced to return to countries where their
lives are in danger. Families may feel helpless and overwhelmed. They may feel
violent. A society supposed to protect and care rejects and scapegoats some
groups. This law can be implemented even though Britain is a signatory of
many international treaties that seek to protect children in war and which agree
that schemes which facilitate 'rehabilitation, recovery and reintegration' of

children who have been exposed to organized violence and war are mandatory (Van Beuren 1994).

The proposed date of implementation of this asylum bill is mid 1996. Many children who are survivors of political violence and war will have no choice but to live in a situation of extreme uncertainty (and insecurity) where the principles of good child care (enshrined in concepts such as 'in the best interests of the child' (Goldstein, *et al.* 1986) which consider a child's developmental needs for parenting, for consistency and continuity of care and the child's idea of time and style of communication) are completely ignored by the authorities. The asylum legislation will have priority over serious child care principles that apply to other children in Britain via the Children Act.

These asylum law changes, which will affect thousands of children who have experienced state violence, scapegoating, loss and enormous change, were hardly reported in the press; yet these children have experienced human rights abuses, as did the West children.

These contradictory events occurring over the same brief period of weeks illustrate the Janus-like position of our society in relation to children, looking in two directions at once, having a sentimental approach to young vulnerable children and even laws to protect the best interests of children, our next generation, but in fact more often acting against children's planned long term needs and best interests, choosing to protect the rights of governments, the military and adults.

It is clearly hard for us to focus and think clearly about the effects of violence on children. We practise a form of gaze avoidance (described by Blom-Cooper (1985) in the Jasmine Beckford report) when we are faced with abused children in general, though our media becomes very excited by specific cases of perverse and abusive activity – as well as being horrified. Perhaps human rights abuses remind us of the worst possible aspects of human behaviour and we prefer not to acknowledge this potential in all of us, in other words that conflict in us all between being entitled and being expendable may lead to enormous resilience and enormous vulnerability, but may also lead us to scapegoat others and make them expendable in the pursuit of our own interests.

I intend here to address some questions about the individual, familial, social, community and cultural aspects of violent abuse of power and its effects. I do not think that one level of explanation is sufficient to address these questions adequately. Phenomenological, psychoanalytic, social, political, dialectical and cultural explanations are all important (Fanon 1966). In terms of treatment, a variety of treatment approaches in combination seem best to address the treatment needs of individuals, families and communities exposed to violence, including community models.

Violence – some figures

Violence is ubiquitous in our society. The child protection registers that British social services departments are required to keep record all children in each local area who are considered to be at risk of abuse. Many children who disclose abuse may not be recorded on these lists. Abused children, who were abused in the past and who are now well cared for, are also not on these lists. However, they do give some indication of the proportion of children in each area seen to be at risk. Children are recorded in one of five categories: neglect, physical injury, sexual abuse, emotional abuse, grave concern. The majority of these children are not on any kind of care or supervision order. Of the 34,900 children on the registers the majority of abuse recorded was physical abuse with neglect and sexual abuse categories being similarly high. Child abuse occurs at all ages. An average of thirty-two out of ten thousand children have recorded abuse (DOH 1995). As mentioned earlier, these recorded statistics are the tip of an iceberg representing the real number of children in our communities who have experienced abuse by adults (some of whom are outside the family). Perry (1993) in an article on children in America exposed to violence estimates that two million American youngsters are traumatized by exposure to violence.

Meanwhile at a different level of analysis the literature on children's experience of violence describing situations of state repression, war and urban life continues to grow.

In order to flesh out this numerical context a little and to illustrate children's widespread experience of violence I will quote two sources.

1. 'Sometimes it is hard to imagine the situations which we are dealing with. Across the world children are tortured, killed or unjustly imprisoned in order to force their parents' surrender or because they are seen as social or political threats. As a soldier said during a counter-insurgency operation in Guatemala in the early 1980s children are killed "because they have already heard the things their fathers say".' Pierre Sané, Secretary General of Amnesty International (from Childhood Stolen, Nov 1993)

2. 'In the past hundred years open warfare between sovereign states has, with notable exceptions, given way to internal armed conflicts often with covert support from outside the state. There has been a similar change in military strategy. Modern tactics seek to obscure the difference between those who fight and those who do not by camouflaging combatants within the overall population. In addition, there are increasing risks to children because many internal armed conflicts are perpetrated on a tribal or zonal basis with a result that any person outside that particular group is regarded as the enemy.

Consequently, the proportion of civilian casualties in armed conflicts has been rising. In the First World War only 5% approximately of all casualties were civilian. By the end of the Second World War this figure had risen to approximately 50% and continues to rise. Out of the twenty million killed in the 150 armed conflicts between 1945 and 1982, the majority of deaths were of women and children. In the past ten years alone internal armed conflicts have led to 1.5 million child deaths, 4 million children disabled as a result of war wounds and 5 million children living in refugee camps to escape conflicts.' (Van Beuren 1994)

Violence in relation to trauma, scapegoating, secrecy, loss and change

Students of the discipline of refugee studies usually deal with larger samples than mental health workers, but both show key similarities in their approach to the study of the effects of violence in individuals, families and social groups. There are also key differences in that even in the study of human rights abuses of children, refugee studies brings in phenomenological, sociological, historical, political and cultural frameworks in addition to the individual psychological perspective. In addition, the treatment solutions and perspectives deriving from refugee studies include more group and community based therapeutic interventions to address the therapeutic needs of children who have experienced violence than are usual in mental health programmes to address the needs of children who have been abused in the context of personal violence. In both disciplines exposure to violence is connected with loss, trauma and change and the child's age and stage of development and various mediating factors are crucial in determining an individual child's response to violence. At this point I think it would be helpful to address the potential issues in thinking about the effects of violence on children by exploring the territory of this subject.

1. Is the direct experience of violence always traumatic?

2. What are the differences between direct experience of violence to your own body and observation of violence to others?

3. What is the difference in effect between violence perpetrated by strangers and that perpetrated by close friends or family?

4. What are the different effects of violence on children at different ages and stages for development?

5. What are the mediating or protective factors that can act between the possible destructive action of violence and its effects?

6. Do children and adolescents who observe and experience the violence of adults sometimes identify with these actions in a long term way?

7. Do children and adolescents who observe and experience violence become passive and compliant?

8. Can therapeutic work enable children and adolescents to work through the effects of violence?

9. What forms of therapeutic work can enable children to work through the effects of violence?

I have written in other articles about the 'often polarised' debates about vulnerability and resilience that are carried out at conferences set up to discuss refugee issues (Melzak 1995). In an article entitled 'Resilience in the Face of Adversity' (Rutter 1985) the issue of resilience and vulnerability and psychological and social protective factors developed in the face of stressors was set out. Since Rutter's work, psychoanalysts such as Fonegy (1992) have developed these ideas in relation to the development of secure attachments, secure internal representations and other intrapsychic factors which can act as mediators in the face of extreme and even temporarily overwhelming stress. In general there is as much poor research from those clinicians who over-diagnose traumatization as in those who over-diagnose resilience. Dawes, Tredoux and Feinstein (1989) warned trauma investigators that theories of resilience among children could become as fashionable as the earlier damage thesis, leading researchers to underestimate the very real instances of psychological distress that occur in the context of violence.

Many writers have contributed to the arguments on either side of the debate: those who believe that all children who experience extreme violence are similarly and seriously affected, even traumatized; or the other polarity who write about enormous strength, resilience, and extraordinary coping strategies, to the extent that they seem to idealize refugees. The more balanced writers see the complexity of children's reactions to violence (Dawes and Donald 1994; Elbedour, Bensel and Bastien 1993; Richman 1992 and Straker 1992). The most thoughtful work comes in general from writers who have worked directly with children who have experienced both state and family violence and who use a mixture of empirical, psychoanalytic and social constructivist research models. This would include work in Palestine (El Sarray 1996; Punamacki and Suleiman 1989); South Africa (Dawes and Donald 1994; Gibson 1991; Straker 1992) and Northern Ireland (Frazer 1994; Fields 1975; Gilligan 1982). Dawes and Donald (1994) write in support of this approach:

> The social constructivist framework is a disturbing and disruptive alternative [to the dominant and powerful scientific discourses of positivist research which carries an ideology that children are only innocent and vulnerable rather than continuously and actively constructing and reconstructing their world] it challenges basic

assumptions about psychological functioning and how it develops. In so doing it breaks all sorts of prescriptions about how we study children. It recommends that we spend more time talking with them so as to unravel the sense that they make of things. It suggests that we pay more attention to the way in which adults produce forms of truth for children while they talk with them and interact with them in ways which signify what the social world is like. To do this we have to observe and talk with them in every day situations and in situations of violence [not simply by asking about their symptoms]. Shifting our approach in this way will improve our understanding of the short and longer term consequences of violence and displacement for children. It will also assist us to help them to overcome their trauma in more appropriate ways.

Conventional research will continue to have its place until the conventions change and because it answers certain important questions. It can speak an acceptable scientific language which is important in backing protests against human rights abuses with data. It also speaks a language to which those who offer aid and can relate. But, in order to improve our understanding of children in traumatic situations we have to recognize the limits of mechanistic formulations. It appears as though constructivist contributions offer a promising way forward.

A promising way forward is also offered by research and treatment approaches which are influenced by the developments in attachment theory and which make some effort to understand children's internal representations of violent experiences and abuses of power, in other words the relationships of perpetrator and victim, rescuer and survivor in the child's mind and to work through and around these internal maps (Bowlby 1953) which may have some neurological basis (Perry 1993) that needs to be acknowledged in treatment approaches. Communication of traumatic experiences is subtle and usually non-verbal. Traumatic experiences are recorded physiologically and in a form of memory that is not readily available to verbal expression. The therapeutic work of Hodges (1992) is very helpful here and relates to the theoretical and clinical developments of attachment theory covered by Main (1991) Crittenden (1988, 1992) and Zulueta (1993).

In order to illustrate something of the way I begin to assess and think about the effect of violence in children, I would like to introduce here two different case examples of children at different stages of their development from quite different contexts – Tom and Simon. The difficulty in assessment is always that of weighing up specific personal details against the generality of effects (e.g. fear, fight and flight reactions after overwhelming experiences) and external environment (e.g. disorganized, neglectful, ambivalent parenting or situations of organized violence) and the meaning of the violence to the child. Assessments take account of personal, internal and social, external factors and so the following nine concepts organized my thinking.

1.	Developmental issues	Relationships with carers and peers, level of thinking, e.g. magical, rational, development phase, e.g. infancy, adolescence.
2.	Social factors	Repressive society, presence of carers, poverty, connection to community or absence of a connection.
3.	Loss	of self – of others – has mourning begun? Is loss accepted or denied? Is loss temporary or permanent?
4.	Change	What changes has the child had to deal with? How flexible, rigid are they? Short term, long term effects.
5.	Trauma	Gross or subtle symptoms, defences, intrusive thoughts, dwelling in past, disconnection of memories and feelings, internal and external, past and present experiences. Difficulties in remembering.
6.	Violence	Personal, political, relationship to violence. Perpetrator, victim, survivor, rescuer bystander.
7.	Scapegoating	Who was in power? Why were you scapegoated? Position in family, gender, religious, political beliefs, skin colour.
8.	Secrecy	Are there personal, family, community, cultural secrets about violence and its effects?
9.	Culture	What aspects of culture lead to resilience, which to vulnerability? Does your culture *sensitize* you to effects of violence or *steel* you against the effects of violence, or both? Is there a sleeper effect of violence i.e. effects of violence invisible or absent even for years only to reappear a long time after the violent event/events? May be culturally syntonic or not.

In assessment and in any therapeutic work, that is, individual, group, family, community based work, the idea of secrecy is a helpful organizer. Many writers on sexual abuse (e.g. Bentovim 1992; Finklehor 1984, 1986, 1989) have underlined the fact that the pathogenic effects of childhood sexual abuse are considerably reduced when children are believed by the first adult with whom they share their experience. Children will tend to doubt their own experience of abuse by powerful adults, especially when they have no words to describe their actual experience and the extreme feelings connected with these experiences. Doubting their own experience can lead to physical and psychological difficulties in adult life that may interfere with work, relationships and their own sense of well being.

Any therapeutic work will be effective if therapists are sensitive to various subtle levels of communication; verbal, relational (transference and counter-transference) body language, non-verbal communication, artwork etc. and can acknowledge these in order to enable children and their carers to tease out and express the best story (reconstruction) possible. In successful family work the stories of parents and children that critically diverge on account of parental denial and children's conformity to parental denial can eventually be rewritten in their true complexity but giving each family member real respect (Bentovim 1991). Similar processes go on in effective group work. By secret in this context I mean in particular the gradual emergence of the aspects of children's stories that have either been forgotten (are unconscious) or which the child is unable to express due to anxiety, guilt, shame or simply through not having words and concepts for the expression of certain ideas. The child may also consciously withhold certain experiences out of loyalty to adults on whom they depend and to whom they are attached (even insecurely).

Tom

Tom lived with his mother in Britain. He came to the attention of social services as a result both of violence between his mother and her partner, and his own very aggressive behaviour in nursery school (hitting other smaller children). Tom's mother seemed to have a disorganized, ambivalent, avoidant relationship with Tom, clearly often leaving him to play alone while at other times exposing him to violent interactions. There is no evidence that he experienced physical abuse in her home.

A few days after the birth of an infant brother the baby was found dead with many broken bones. His mother was arrested, found guilty and given a prison sentence. She continued to blame Tom for the baby's death. Tom was placed with foster parents, who did abuse him physically, and eventually with a close relation who he had known since his birth.

Zulueta (1993) in her book makes links between insecure attachment, disorganized parenting and the representations of caring/abuse in the internal world of some violent adults. Though her ideas are interesting they simplify the complexity of the developmental process in that she does not look in sufficient depth at external social mediating factors that might act between these kinds of attachments and violence in adult life. Clearly any developmental process involves a subtle complex interaction between various events whose meaning may not be immediately obvious, for example the way in which internal representations can be transformed and adopted in ordinary loving relationships, not just with parental substitutes such as teachers, nursery workers and even idealized heroes and heroines of politics, sport and music and so forth.

When his mother was released from prison she wanted to resume parenting Tom but he remains with his foster carers.

Therapeutic work continued from the time Tom became settled with his familiar foster family. This work consisted of family work with various parts of the foster family as well as the whole. Tom attended for weekly, individual sessions. We had meetings with his school. A therapeutic group was desirable but not possible in the area where Tom lived. Tom sees his mother a few times each year. Tom is an anxious boy who in therapy flits from one topic to another and one play activity to another. He functions as a child much younger than his years as if his development became stuck at the age he was when his sibling died and is slowly becoming unstuck as a result of the combination of the therapeutic effect of consistent predictable care and developing trust and the therapeutic effect of clinic interventions.

Tom's foster carers were initially very reluctant to share with Tom any version of the truths of his past history. Family work explored all their reasons for this as well as his capacity to imagine worse realities than the terrible truth. Once convinced of the reasons to avoid both apparent secrecy and unrealistic elaborations the foster carers developed a sensitive style of dealing with Tom's anxieties, terrors, fantasies and specifically his tendency to live in a world of fantasy rather than the present real world.

Hodges (1992) demonstrates some themes in the internal world of children who have experienced violence within their homes during their first five years, for example extreme aggression, throwing out, denial or reversal of painful effect, bad/good shifts and their transformation.

> Attachment theory is an obvious theoretical framework for this work. It shares many assumptions with psychoanalytic object relations theories about the crucial role played by self and object representations. With 'attachment theory' Bowlby used a new metaphor, 'internal working models' which underlines the role of these representations in regulating expectations and interpretations of relationships. Working models of the

self and principal caregiving figures allow the interpretation and prediction of the behaviour of the attachment figure, and the planning of responses; Bowlby underlined the importance of reality experience, actual interpersonal transactions in the establishment of these models.

If we can gain access to these models of what relationships with carers have meant to a child until now. We can use these as a guide to their expectations of future relationships.

Once the models are organized, they tend to become automatic and hence to operate increasingly outside conscious awareness. New experiences are assimilated to existing models unless they are so discrepant that they cannot be made to fit in and a changed model has to be set up. This produces relative stability but also implies distortion of perception if external conditions have altered. Things are perceived in terms of the existing model if this is at all possible. Such models can thus have a powerful effect on how the individual perceives and reacts to new situations and relationships. (Hodges 1992)

This is relevant for Tom's relationship with new carers, and the way in which he experiences the present in terms of terrifying past relationships.

Tom began to feel more in control of his life and less a victim of fears of terrifying engulfing murderous others in his world as our work developed. He remains vulnerable though, as this interaction between Tom and myself illustrates. At the time of this session Tom had just begun a new class, after living with his foster parents for three years. When the new teacher shouted, Tom, who had persisting difficulties in learning, concentrating and in socializing in school, became paralyzed with fear and began to cry. He told his foster mother that the teacher reminded him of his mother and he believed she might destroy him (as he had believed his mother might). Away from his class Tom agreed with his foster mother that the teacher would not behave in this way but under the stress of the classroom it is not so easy for Tom to reflect on his own thoughts.

In our individual meeting following this experience at school Tom started to tell me about a family pet who had died some weeks before. He launched into an elaborate imaginative game in which I was asked to be the assistant surgeon and he operated on a plasticine body who transformed from the pet to his infant sibling. He agreed that he wished he had superpower and could bring them both back to life. He also agreed that he felt he had failed them both in not being able to bring them alive again.

We talked about the finality of death and how sad and empty he felt when his pet died recently and how he must have felt sad and empty when the baby died, but he did not have words then to talk about this. He retorted, 'My baby is always with me you know' and then looking at me, 'but I know he is dead and I am very sad not to have a little brother to play with and to see him grow up'. This was only after a lot of pretend play about skeletons, being with God, bone-land and finally he told me about fragments of various science fiction films he had watched where men were transformed into skeleton by machines. Tom said, 'It's the bones that are so scary.'

As Hodges describes, one of the central difficulties for this small boy is the transformation of good to bad and back to good especially under stress. In a therapy session or with his foster mother these transformations can be discussed and present reality can be discovered but Tom needs more work in order to be able to carry out this task for himself consistently, and to reflect consistently on what belongs in the past and what is present experience.

In his reality his mother transformed into a terrifying creature and back often and on one occasion his brother was killed. This internal representation can only be dealt with in the context of good experiences and the slow development of trust over a long time (Perry 1993).

These days, after telling me a long story about imaginary friends who make him feel less lonely, or about film monsters, heroes and transformations, I just need to look at him and raise my eyebrows and he will remark, 'I know that is just pretend! I don't think my baby is really with me or the ghosts!'

Simon

Simon also was present when someone (his father) was murdered. This murder took place in a different context completely and thus the consequences for Simon of this act of violence were completely different. Simon was ten when his father died. He comes from a loving close secure large family where he was the youngest son. His mother died from an illness when he was six and his eldest sister became a carer in the family working alongside Simon's beloved father. For Simon's two younger sisters, the eldest sister became like a mother but Simon had strong clear memories of his mother and had a very close relationship with his father to whom he could go with any personal problem or his difficulties with school work. It is likely that Simon's especially close relationship with his father was rooted in his being the youngest boy and very bright and successful in school.

Simon's family come from a central African country where a small group of people have taken power and money and govern the country in a repressive way. The government forces are violent and cruel and any resistance is punished with especial cruelty. Simon's father led a democratic resistance party against the autocratic leader of the country and his government. Simon understood his father's work and about the differences between different types of societies. There was a press in the family home and an anti-government newspaper was produced there. Simon remembers that when he was about eight his father was arrested, imprisoned and tortured. He had his legs broken under torture. Over the next two years the family were aware of violence in the area, fighting, murders and sometimes the children could not get to school. The day that Simon's father was murdered soldiers in army uniform came to the house and shot Simon's father directly. Simon and his small sisters hid when the soldiers knocked on the door, but Simon came out of the hiding place when he heard them leave. He saw his father's body and his oldest sister had fainted. His other brothers and sisters were not in the house. Some days later the soldiers returned and, as is common practice by government forces in this country, they forced the older brothers and sisters to have sexual intercourse with each other.

Simon was not present at the soldier's second visit. The brothers and sisters were very close to each other and Simon remembers that two in particular became very disturbed and were taken away by family friends. This is his version of the story and he feels they went out of their minds. The other older brothers and sisters ran away leaving the eldest sister and Simon and his two younger siblings to come to Britain eventually.

When I met Simon he was twelve. The family application for asylum had been turned down as the truth of their story had not been accepted by the Home Office. I was asked to write a report to support their appeal to remain in Britain. I met Simon and his family a few times separately and together and then the children began to attend separate therapeutic groups while the oldest sister (who had to be a mother with very little support to address her own needs as a parent and to mourn) began to receive individual counselling and casework support. In spite of huge material and practical difficulties the children have settled well in school (both in very caring attentive schools who knew the children's history and can offer them individual attention when necessary from pastoral staff).

Simon has friends, is learning well and is able to have fun with other boys his age. When I first met him his concentration, daytime thinking and dreams were interrupted by repeated strong images of his father's body, his disturbed siblings and himself being forced to return and then shot at the airport by soldiers. I felt this last was a realistic fear. All these intrusive thoughts subsided after some months and at this point the family still have had no decision on their appeal for asylum status in Britain. Simon is an anxious boy who is the most disruptive person in a therapeutic group for boys aged eleven to fifteen. In some ways he is the most resistant to shared activities in which the boys talk about pain and fear and anger in the past and in the present. This may be a mixture of real resistance and the culture into which boys from his country are socialized. With some clarity and firmness it is clear that Simon understands the aims of the group very clearly and he is always eventually thoughtful, honest and in touch with his feelings – for example, he talks with great sadness and respect about his father, and how much he misses him. Living as he does now in a female dominated family Simon has not had an opportunity to develop a new relationship with a man who he can respect and become close to. He also can talk articulately and in detail about how much he wants and needs to stay in Britain for his safety, for his education, and for his security. Simon is caring and responsible towards his younger sisters. He is able to play, to share, to have fun. In a recent group meeting he played very freely and when asked to mime something mimed a man with a shotgun, 'This is a soldier fighting for peace' he remarked.

For various reasons, though Simon showed some temporary problems as a result of his exposure to overwhelming violence and loss, he now seems to be able to use his intelligence and his early internalized representations of his relationships with caring adults, in order to cope and to develop further coping strategies.

It is impossible to know how Simon will develop, if the violence he experienced will sensitize him to later stress, if there will be a sleeper effect with difficulties emerging later. I hope he will be able to remain in Britain for us to see. At present he is an anxious boy, with a slight stutter, but neither his heightened anxiety and the stutter (both consequences of his experience of violence) seem to interfere with his self-perception or his relationships. He is subject to school based racism and bullying like all refugee children, but deals with incidents by both asserting and protecting himself wisely.

Though very different ages, these two case studies are intended to illustrate the complexity of issues determining the ways that children experience violence and come to understand the world after violent experiences. Both are affected by the context of violence and the violence, but clearly Simon can use his beliefs and understanding and his capacity to learn, socialize and have fun in order to cope. Tom has more serious interference with his learning, his ability to socialize and to trust adults. Simon has strong internal representations of good, trustworthy adults alongside those of violent soldiers. Tom's internal representations of trustworthy adults are in the process of development. For Tom the central theme of his therapy has been to help him to see his mother in a realistic way, whereas for Simon therapeutic work is focused around reducing isolation, developing his capacity to share and giving him time and space to acknowledge and integrate difficult and pleasurable experiences in exile and before, in order that he can retain and build on his cultural identity and integrate this with new identifications developed in exile.

Other refugee children with whom I have worked do not show Simon's internal security and motivation. Children coming from countries where war, poverty and repression have made school attendance impossible arrive in Britain, with or without parents, but without basic literacy and numeracy skills.

These youngsters provide a serious challenge to teachers who may struggle to find a non-humiliating curriculum for, for example, a fourteen year old Somali boy whose father is dead and whose mother is in a refugee camp in Kenya and who is living with an aunt in Britain. These adolescents become quickly frustrated and feel alienated with no serious access to a social position in exile. When these youngsters become violent in school or in the streets it is not because of violence they have observed or experienced in their own country, but because they do not have opportunities to access the education system in Britain, their one route to hope and security in the future. As one refugee father of four commented, 'You cannot survive in Europe without a large supply of Vitamin M' (money).

Useful concepts and treatment models

From the large body of research in this area there are a few particularly relevant and helpful concepts which can help us to think about the effects of adult violence on children. These include development of tolerance of risk (Garbarino 1992) and frustration (Freud 1966), children will flourish with the challenge of some risk and some frustration, the concept of home (Winnicott 1986), the connected subjects of moral development and moral reasoning in the context of the experience of violence, and abuse of power by authority figures, the idea of acute versus chronic difficulties, the idea of trauma and that of integration and adaptation. Children must adapt in some way to violent experiences and integrate them in order to move forward. Clearly, developmental harm arises when risk factors accumulate and overwhelm a child's capacity for coping. Garbarino (1992) and the ecological model of Elbedour *et al.* (1993) both emphasize psychological, social and community dimensions of coping and resilience. The child and the violence they experience both need to be contextualized.

Thus, we may include the following factors as leading to vulnerability (Melzak 1995)

1.	Exposure to violence	(a) direct
		(b) observed
		(c) to stranger
		(d) heard about
2.	Loss	(a) via death
		(b) via disappearance
		(c) via emotional unavailability

3. Difficulty in mourning and uncertainty about whether loss is temporary or permanent.

4. Inability to use natural healing processes such as dreams, play and community support. (Punamacki 1987)

5. Identification with the perpetrator of violence

and the factors leading towards resilience include

1. Having an active problem solving approach to difficulties and stress.

2. Being able to mourn.

3. Being able to develop an ideology that helps to explain and integrate past and present, social and personal experiences, including the integration of extreme events, and helps to reflect on past and present. This may include a religious or political belief system or philosophy.

4. Being able to use natural healing processes such as play, dreams and community rituals to celebrate life and to mourn losses.

5. Being connected to the community.

6. Having a parent or parental substitute, who can contain your anxieties and enable you to feel held.

Certainly the presence of an adult who can care for the abused child and make a secure relationship and link the child to community and society is a central mediating factor. The work of Keilson (1979), in a study following up over more than twenty years children who had both lost their parents and experienced enormous violence in the Holocaust, focuses again on the key mediating factor, which is the presence of a good substitute carer who can act as a mediator between the detrimental effects of war and the child at each of the developmental stages familiar to psychoanalytic theory. Loss of a parent was seen in this study to be a more significant organizer of psychological difficulties in adult life than exposure to violence. Good foster carers enabled the children to acknowledge their past while feeling secure in the present and in the transition from childhood to adulthood.

It is a truism of good child care practice that for most children who are attached to their biological parents, it is beneficial for children to work with these relationships rather than the child having to deal with separation and loss. The work of family systems therapists is important here. Bentovim (1992) describes work with family sexual and physical abuse. While he feels that only about a third of perpetrators are able to change he is clear that a process of therapeutic work with a system organized by trauma is worth beginning when perpetrators can acknowledge their actions, can consider the experiences of the victim and can be curious and genuinely interested in the roots of their behaviour. Only then is it worth beginning a process where entrenched family denial and the roles of victim, perpetrator and bystander are slowly acknowledged, challenged and undermined in the interests of all family members. In these situations it is clear that the perpetrator of this kind of family violence has experienced both insecure attachment and neglect and usually family violence in early childhood. In this type of family therapy family members are met separately and together in order that they might share and elaborate their own stories and develop new possibilities via acknowledging defences, myths and fantasies and relationships and position in society and feelings about those social identities.

These ideas of a 'containing', 'holding' parent and therapies that enable families to change, links again to the central concept of 'home' as a basis for the development of identity, and a fundamental link to social position.

Not all parents can remain emotionally available to their children when they are also under stress. Young children certainly equate home with family and research shows that young children cope well with stress when they retain a strong positive attachment to their family and when parents can continue to project a sense of stability, permanence and competence to their children (Freud and Burlingham 1943; Garbarino 1992). It is clearly those children who lose parents, those whose parents change radically during childhood to stop being parents and those who had an insecure, ambivalent or avoidant relationship with their parents before they experienced violence who are most vulnerable to traumatization and fixations and regressions in their development. Children with the attention of a warm reliable adult acting as a parental substitute are most likely to create a strong sense of their own identity and a positive social map (Garbarino 1992).

We need to think carefully about the meaning of care and family life in different cultures where extended family members can have equal importance to parents etc., especially for children who are isolated from their real extended family, but who have a rich internal world of relationships and expectations that may be thwarted by insensitive planning, for example by some social workers for unaccompanied children.

We would have too simplistic an approach if we did not look carefully at the separate effects of violence within the family and the effects of state violence. Certain Davar (1995) makes two very helpful points: (1) that the often temporary effects of political violence can look very similar to the more long term effects of early childhood abuse and neglect; (2) that the therapeutic task is to re-establish the internalized mother that has been temporarily lost or overwhelmed or that may have only partially developed and was overwhelmed by other more critical and destructive internalized relationships, linking again to the idea of 'home'.

The links between violence and traumatization and violence and moral development can be mediated by relationships with adults in the community who encourage communication, caring and democratic verbal ways to resolve conflicts (Fields 1973; Fraser 1974; Gilligan 1982). Certainly the idea that moral development is truncated by exposure to violence is contradicted by the work of Dawes and Donald (1994).

Traumatization implies overwhelming of physical and psychological ways of coping. Boundaries are broken between past and present, conscious and unconscious memories, internal and external experiences and memories and feelings. The central characteristic of trauma is disconnection with less energy for the present social and work demands as energy is caught up with the past and extreme emotions (Herman 1992). Any therapeutic process ideally combines psychoanalytic, cognitive and existential therapeutic techniques with cultural sensitivity to local belief systems and with the final aim of reintegrating disconnected experiences, feelings and memories including experiences that may have been somatised (Herman 1992; Melzak 1995; Straker 1994).

This reintegration is best done in a predictable relationship with one adult. It is our experience that for most children who have experienced violence the treatment of choice is a mixture of individual group and family work when this is possible; all these alongside a general culturally sensitive community approach. Family work can address family members' different experience of violence, whether the family system is organized by violence within the family or violence from outside the family (Bentovim 1992). Group work can reduce the isolation that children exposed to violence often feel and reflect on past and present memories, problems and pleasures and cultural issues.

The groups for children in the organization where I work deal with both political violence and the current racism and bullying that children experience in school. It also deals with issues of cultural identity, memories of home country and relationships, transitional identities and the difficulties of living either without familiar adults (unaccompanied children) or with parents transformed by their own experience of torture, loss and change. Groups provide a space in between home and school where internal worries, conflicts and dilemmas can be explored alongside issues of cultural and social identity. The central aim of each treatment model is to give children the opportunity to tell their own story in some detail and via the communication of the story to integrate disconnected experiences that are painful and hard to remember and think about as well as to find ways to communicate experiences that could not be conceptualized at the time they were experienced.

Individual treatment can focus on these more personal and private experiences connected with difficult emotions as well as unconscious feelings, fantasies and memories. Communities are resources of adults who can complement the care of traumatized parents. Also, work at a community level can explore violence in schools, at a policy level and in the curriculum, and can reinforce understanding and an exploration of new ways to deal with power imbalance, conflict resolution and authority, as well as developing identity by helping a child to feel at home in the community. At the same time schools can give care in more direct ways by making time for teachers to develop individual relationships with children under stress. Community projects dealing with children's experience of violence have strength when they include the child's construction of reality and perceptions and give these equal authority to the perceptions of experts (Pecnik and Stubbs 1994).

Here community workers and parents in Croatia, working with children who have experienced violence, make a plea for resources to develop their community rather than to pay for experts to make skilled diagnoses of the symptoms of trauma. These ideas certainly connect with the neurological perspectives of Perry (1993) and the implications he draws for the treatment of children who experience nightmares and intrusive thoughts, who are unable to concentrate and to live in the present and who may have developed a complicated defensive structure to deny pain, anxiety, fear and enormous anger. The only way to deal with this level of difficulty is by development of a close, trusting relationship where the difficult memories and extreme feelings from the past can be explored and integrated in order to develop new internal representations where children feel secure and in control. Hodges (1992) makes the important observation that children from the age of four can demonstrate the capacity to observe their own behaviour and responses. She gives clinical evidence of abused children who, in the course of a new close relationship with a non-abusing adult (in this case a child psychotherapist), gradually became able to comment on their own experiences of trauma. These are not worked through necessarily, but very young children can become able to recognize that their occasional experience of extreme feelings in the present can belong to past experiences of violence and not to the present relationships. This is certainly possible with older children who have experienced extreme violence, i.e. the development of an observing part of the self.

Conclusion

Given the ubiquity of children's experience of violence and in spite of a great deal of published research our knowledge of the following issues is limited

(1) What determines whether the experience of violence leads to short-term, temporary or long term effects (and can be transmitted through the generations).

(2) Whether violence is experienced as a challenge, as part of a solution or as a terrible threat.

(3) The way that violent relationships are represented intra-psychically.

(4) The way we might help children whose experience of violence has been traumatic and interfered with their basic trust of others.

(5) How we might solve conflicts without the use of physical violence.

The next generations may continue to use physical violence to assert power at a personal and a social level and not to share, co-operate and be democratic, about limited resources in the world. We have opportunities now to work with the next generation on these issues. As Elbedour *et al.* (1993) write in their conclusion, 'Even though most writers about war consider it to be 'normal' it is time to reconsider the myth and realize that few, if any, children experience war without some psychological residual effects.'

It is perhaps time to give higher profile to children's developmental needs and to take much more seriously the role of parents and the level of support this task needs in our communities. Ideas about privacy of the family being in the best interests of children have to be debated alongside ideas about alternative care and the provision of complementary care in which children's experiences are recognized and heard, so that children are not trapped in situations with adults who ignore or deny their developmental needs and serious parental responsibilities are shared.

I have raised here several questions about the relationships between violence and children's experience of violence during their development. Our society will show its commitment to children by making resources available to meet their developmental needs, if we are to transform our societies for future generations. Children's developmental needs span both the need for a good enough parent and the need for a place in society where they can work, feel involved and respected, respect themselves and have access to education, material comfort and freedom.

We certainly need to teach children to be more critical and more observant and to notice and challenge abuses of power and inequalities of opportunity.

CHAPTER 2

The Backgrounds of Violent Young Offenders

The Present Picture

Gwyneth Boswell

Introduction

This chapter concerns itself principally with a small but singular group of children and adolescents known as Section 53 offenders. This term derives from Section 53 of the Children and Young Persons Act 1933 which provides for the sentencing of children, aged between 10 and 17 years (inclusive), convicted on indictment by the Crown Court of murder or other grave crimes. This group differs from other categories of violent young people who may, for example, have been diverted into local authority or psychiatric care, in that its definition of violence is located in the list of crimes for which young offenders may be convicted under the 1933 Act. This list provides a continuum from intended to actual violence, ranging from various forms of assault and robbery, rape and arson, to manslaughter and murder. The chapter will discuss the author's research into the backgrounds of young people serving sentences for these crimes (Boswell 1995) and place this alongside other literature on the genesis of violence and violent offending. The research implications will be drawn upon to provide some pointers for criminal justice professionals in the processes of accurate assessment and effective intervention in the lives of these young detainees.

Legislation

Subsection (1) of Section 53 of the Children and Young Persons Act 1933 provides that a person between the ages of 10 and 17, convicted of murder, be detained during Her Majesty's pleasure in such place and under such conditions as the Home Secretary may direct. The length of this detention is indeterminate.

Subsection (2) (amended by the Criminal Justice Acts 1961 and 1991 and the Criminal Justice and Public Order Act 1994) provides that a person aged 10–17 years, convicted of an offence for which an adult may be sentenced to fourteen years' imprisonment or more, or for indecent assault on a woman, and for whom no other disposal is considered suitable by the Court, be detained in such place and under such conditions as the Home Secretary may direct. The period of detention (which may be for life) must be specified in the sentence, and must not exceed the maximum period of imprisonment with which the offence would be punishable in the case of an adult.

Population

The distribution of the Section 53 population as at 31st October 1994 is shown in Table 2.1. A breakdown is provided of numbers, age-range, sex and ethnic origin in the child care, Young Offender Institution (YOI) and Adult Prison

Table 2.1: Distribution of Section 53 population as at 31.10.94

Institution	Normal age range	Total number	Total Male	Total Female	Total White	Total Black
Child Care System						
Community Homes (open or secure accommodation)	10–18 years	101	89	12 (3 black)	82	19
Youth Treatment Centres	10–18 years	14	14	–	11	3
Sub-total		*115*	*103*	*12 (3 black)*	*93*	*22*
Prison System						
Young Offender Institutions	16–20 years	435	424	11 (2 black)	316	119
Adult Prisons	21+	231	223	8 (1 black)	196	35
Sub-total		*666*	*647*	*19 (3 black)*	*512*	*154*
Total		**781**	**750**	**31 (6 black)**	**605**	**176**

N.B.   The word 'black' is employed in these tables to denote people classed by the Home Office Statistical Division as follows: Black (African, Caribbean, other); South Asian (Bangladeshi, Indian, Pakistani); Chinese and other (Chinese, Asian other, other).

systems respectively. The longstanding convention surrounding allocation to institutions (which will be reflected in these figures, although the convention began a process of change in April 1995) has been broadly that youngsters under the age of sixteen years and six months would enter the child care system and those over this age a Young Offender Institution (YOI). Those already in the Child Care system will normally transfer to a YOI at the age of eighteen years and those still in custody at the age of twenty-one to an adult prison.

Table 2.1 shows that as at 31st October 1994, 666 Section 53 offenders were detained in the prison system (i.e. YOIs and adult prisons) and 115 in the child care system making a total of 781. This compares with 480 detained in the prison system and 135 in the child care system, making a total of 615 as at 1st February 1991 (Boswell 1991).

Table 2.2 depicts the sentence types within the Section 53 population and compares the 1991 and 1994 figures. Recall operates when an offender has been released on Parole Licence and has either committed a further offence or behaved in a way which may constitute a risk to the community.

Table 2.2: Types of Section 53 sentence

Sentence	1/2/91	31/10/94
Section 53(1)	212	253
Section 53 (2) Determinate	370	490
Section 53 (2) Life	26	28
Section 53 Recall (Prison System)	7	10
Total	615	781

Table 2.2 depicts an increase of the Section 53 (1) and a notable inflation of the Section 53 (2) populations over three and three-quarter years. In addition to its context within the 'prison works' policy of 1993 onwards, the rise in Section 53(2) numbers probably also reflects a continuing tendency during the late 1980s and early 1990s for sentencers to circumvent the one year maximum sentence for a Young Offender Institution, prior to its doubling with the implementation in 1995 of the Criminal Justice and Public Order Act 1994. It is also self-evident that violent crime by young people has increased during the first half of the 1990s.

The increase in the Section 53(1) population (the only sentence which can be passed for murder in the 10–17 age group) must, of necessity, indicate a rise in the prevalence of murder, but is also likely to reflect a reluctance, in the climate of the last two years, to release such offenders on parole so that they are being held in the system for longer. The current tendency for Home Office Ministers to increase the tariff dates (the earliest date at which such an offender *may* be released) set by trial judges, and for Home Secretaries not to endorse the parole recommendations which precede these dates, especially in the more notorious cases, is also liable to contribute to this situation.

Table 2.2 in addition shows that the Section 53(2) Life population, which has always been small, has remained more or less constant. It appears to be used with considerable restraint by judges who equally can and do pass Section 53(2) determinate sentences on young people convicted of crimes such as manslaughter, arson and rape. The Section 53 recall population, although showing a slight rise from 7 to 10, is negligible, indicating that this group of offenders is at low risk of reoffending in the community whilst on Licence. The post-release offending rate, in as far as it is known, confirms that Section 53(1) and Section 53(2) Life detainees have not, on the whole, reoffended. On the other hand, two thirds of Section 53(2) determinate offenders have done so, although many of them in a non-violent manner. A previous history of three or more convictions tends to be the key predictor of re-offending for the Section 53 group generally (Millham *et al.* 1988).

The breakdowns provided by Tables 2.1 and 2.2 show that the Section 53 population, notwithstanding the caveats outlined above, is relatively small but rising. This makes it all the more important to examine some of the background factors at work in the lives of these violent young offenders. During the course of an earlier study of the custodial experiences and needs of Section 53 offenders (Boswell 1991), the author had discovered an unanticipated category of hard evidence which was that 50 per cent of the offender sample had a background of some kind of child abuse (i.e. physical, sexual, emotional, organized/ritual or combinations thereof). Staff, familiar with the signs of abuse, estimated that the true figure could be as high as 90 per cent. The next obvious step was to survey a much higher proportion of cases to try to establish a reliable figure for the frequency of this phenomenon. In addition, the author had noted from the previous study an apparent prevalence of bereavement and other significant loss experiences, and decided to add this to the list of categories to be studied. Abuse and loss are separate phenomena and yet, at times, are not unrelated, especially where abuse is seen as a 'loss of trust' experience (although abuse has not been categorized as 'loss' in this survey); both constitute traumatic events for a child. The findings of this further study show that, in some instances, the two phenomena appear independently and that at other times they co-exist.

The prevalence of abuse and loss

The research method was to obtain the required data on approximately one third of the mid-1993 Section 53 population by (1) an examination of a random sample of 200 centrally held files, noting down evidence of abuse and loss and (2) where this evidence was partial or ambiguous to interview the offenders themselves to try and establish whether they had experienced a background of child abuse and/or loss.

Two hundred files comprising 78 adult prisoners, 59 YOI inmates and 63 Department of Health residents were scrutinized. Of this total, 12 were women and 48 were black, broadly reflecting their proportions in the wider Section 53 population. Ages ranged from 14 to 59, reflecting the very long sentences which many Section 53(1) and 53(2) Life offenders can actually serve. The five main categories studied were those of emotional, sexual, physical, organized/ritual abuse and loss. Confirmation of these phenomena by one or more trained professionals (e.g. doctors, psychiatrists, psychologists, probation officers, social workers) or by the recording of case conference decisions was also noted.

Where evidence on file was partial or ambiguous, interviews took place (32 in all) in 22 separate establishments with 21 adult male prisoners, 8 17–20 year olds (7 males in Y.O.I.s and one female in an adult prison) and 3 male D.O.H. establishment residents. Of these, five of the adults and three of the YOI males were black, again reflecting the high numbers of black males (approximately 25%) in the Section 53 population as a whole. At the beginning of the interview respondents were asked to complete a short questionnaire which entailed them ticking any of the headings listed which they considered applied to them. The questionnaire contained headings related to the five main categories stated above, but also included the broader heading of 'Problems in childhood' and an 'Other' category which respondents sometimes found less threatening to tick at the start than, say 'Sexual abuse' but with some drawing out might identify more specifically as the interview progressed. Each heading was then referred to verbally by the interviewer, whether ticked or not, to allow for second thoughts and for literacy problems.

Each interview took on average one hour. Although it might be expected that some respondents would seek to invoke or exaggerate traumatic childhood experiences as a justification for their violent offending the interviewers found, on the contrary, considerable initial hesitance to discuss deeply emotional and painful experiences. Indeed, it seemed likely to them that there were experiences of abuse, at least, which remained denied or undisclosed after their interviews. In addition, a minority of respondents identified significant abuse or loss experiences but were adamant that they would not wish to employ these as an excuse for their own unacceptable behaviour. Clearly, however, there will always be pitfalls to the personal corroboration approach, but its value in a study of this nature is to provide depth and authenticity at a different level to the framework of hard evidence and professional corroboration, and arguably both are appropriate and necessary ingredients in the broad picture which emerges.

Definitions and findings

For the purposes of this survey, the term 'abuse' was broken down into four categories based on inter-departmental guidelines (Home Office, Department of Health, Department of Education and Science, Welsh Office 1991) and adapted for ease of categorization and explanation to offenders. These were emotional, sexual, physical and organized/ritual abuse. Table 2.3 shows the frequency of these 4 categories of abuse in the backgrounds of the sample of 200 Section 53 offenders.

Table 2.3: Emotional, sexual, physical and organized/ritual abuse (N = 200)

Emotional Abuse:	Experienced by 28.5% of the sample
Sexual Abuse:	Experienced by 29% of the sample
Physical Abuse:	Experienced by 40% of the sample
Organized/Ritual Abuse:	Experienced by 1.5% of the sample
Combinations of 2 or more of the above forms of abuse (most often physical and emotional):	Experienced by 27% of the sample
Key Finding:	72% of the total sample had experienced emotional, sexual, physical or organized/ritual abuse, or combinations thereof.

The second phenomenon examined in this study was that of loss which for these research purposes was used to look at the prevalence of bereavement and other significant loss experiences as broken down in Table 2.4. The notion of loss derives from Bowlby's work on maternal deprivation (Bowlby 1951) and his own and Rutter's later adaptations of this thesis, centring around attachment and loss (Bowlby 1969, 1973, 1980; Rutter 1972). The emergent theory is that children who experience the permanent or semi-permanent loss of a significant figure to whom they are emotionally attached may suffer serious emotional disturbance as a result. Such disturbance is thought to be more likely when, as in many of the present cases, the children have not been effectively helped to understand and resolve their loss experiences.

The study described above showed that 72 per cent of Section 53 offenders had experienced one or more types of abuse, and that 57 per cent had experienced significant loss via bereavement or cessation of contact or both. In total, 91 per cent of the sample had experienced one or both phenomena; 35 per cent of the sample had experienced both, suggesting that the presence of a double childhood trauma may be a potent factor in the backgrounds of these young violent offenders. For there is little doubt that child abuse and childhood experience of loss, when no effective opportunity is provided for the child to make sense of these experiences, constitutes unresolved trauma which is likely to manifest itself in some way at a later date. This progression was fleshed out in the study with case examples of children who were beaten, bewildered, tortured and humiliated – who became depressed, disturbed, violent or all three. The profile of Robert, whose background contained most of these factors, follows.

Table 2.4: Experiences of loss (N = 200)

	Parent	Grandparent	Other Relative	Other Carer	Friend
Death of someone important	10%	6.5%	2.5%	1%	1%
Loss of contact with someone important	39.5%	1%	1.5%	–	1%
Total experiencing loss	49.5%	7.5%	4%	1%	2%

Childhood trauma and later violence: 57% had experienced significant loss via bereavement or cessation of contact and in some cases both.

Case study

Robert, now aged 32, was sentenced to Section 53 (2) Life, fifteen years ago for offences of Grievous Bodily Harm and Attempted Rape. His background contains almost every kind of abuse, but the experience which is most significant to him is that of the loss of his father, who had left home when Robert was three, for reasons which Robert did not understand; and they did not renew contact until relatively recently during Robert's prison sentence. The day his father left his mother beat Robert, and such beatings continued several times a week, until he was taken into care at the age of ten years. He has very little memory of his life between the ages of five and seven years. His older sister, however, tells him that he and she were both severely sexually abused by one of their mother's lovers during that period, and also that on one occasion Robert was nearly strangled. Robert himself has no memory of this incident but does know that he has panic attacks and on some occasions blackouts if anyone ever touches his neck. He also has nightmares about being strangled. One of his worst memories is of his mother locking him in the cellar of the house they lived in for two hours. The cellar contained rats and he recounts an experience of sheer terror as he tried to avoid them in the darkness.

Finally, at the age of ten, Robert was taken into care but again found himself being consistently physically, sexually and emotionally abused. At the age of fourteen he made the first of three unsuccessful suicide attempts. Long-serving staff at the Children's Home he was in have recently been convicted of abuse by the Courts, though social workers at the time did not treat his allegations seriously. At the age of fifteen Robert returned to his family home. He found work and spent most evenings out drinking so that he did not have to come into close contact with his family, particularly his mother and new stepfather, whom he strongly disliked. By this time Robert was seriously disturbed and depressed and in a state of mind which he, his probation officer, and one of his doctors all later considered had led to his commission of a violent offence. The doctor judged that the offence was a specific acting out of aggression against his mother. Robert himself has now made a deliberate decision to cease contact with her. However, his renewal of contact with his father has finally helped him to understand the reasons why his father left, an act which devastated Robert for years and removed from him the protection of an adult he trusted. During his fifteen years of incarceration there has been little sign of Robert receiving professional help to try and understand his violent behaviour and how he can avoid it in future. Instead he has turned to religion and believes that this has expiated his feelings of anger. A final ironic ingredient is that his newfound father is now dying of cancer.

The key research findings cited above would suggest that, at the very least, it is worth taking a closer look at the nature of the possible link between those sentenced under Section 53 and the high prevalence of abuse and/or loss in their earlier lives. Nevertheless, it must be emphasized that not all children who suffer abuse and/or loss will become violent offenders; and that not all violent young offenders will, as far as is known, have suffered abuse and/or loss. Strangely enough, however, whilst there is a plethora of published material on the effects of loss (in terms of failed or flawed attachment) and of child abuse (notably sexual), and plenty of literature on the genesis of violence and violent offending, historically there has been little attempt to review the evidence for a link between these phenomena. The succeeding paragraphs will endeavour to plug this gap somewhat with a view to outlining some of the implications for professional intervention.

Family stressors

Yule (1993) draws attention to the fact that 'Children are both victims and survivors of many violent acts...whether within the family or outside it' (p.153). Many writers have described the phenomenon of transgenerational (or intergenerational) violence in which abuse of one kind or another is transmitted across several generations (Herrenkohl and Herrenkohl 1981; Wolfe 1987; Rutter 1989). Widom (1989), indeed, describes this transmission as 'the premier developmental hypothesis in the field of abuse and neglect' (p.160). A variety of explanations is offered for this process: for example imitation of powerful adults by less powerful children; residual childhood anger from parents to their own parents being displaced onto their own child (their parents' grandchild); projection of parental conflict onto the child; expectation placed upon the child to fulfil parents' own unmet needs and violent reaction when they do not; the linking of parental stress and child abuse (Herrenkohl *et al.* 1983). Some or all of these may apply in different cases, but it is certainly arguable that 'many stresses on the family of origin may have elicited violent reactions in response to the frustrations generated, with violence then being incorporated by the children as a "coping strategy" for responding to stress in their current lives' (Herrenkohl *et al.* 1983, p.306). Whilst these kinds of deductions can be persuasive, it is nevertheless important, for a range of reasons, to approach them with some caution. First, it is necessary to bear in mind that any childhood abuse is difficult to research reliably because of the shame involved in revealing it. Second, many such studies are based on small, and sometimes unrepresentative, samples. Third, control groups have rarely been used, largely because of the difficulty of identifying and holding on to them. Fourth, large-scale longitudinal studies, which are the most likely reliably to test multivariate factors, are extremely thin on the ground; and finally specific gender-based research (particularly on sexually abused males) is still in its infancy.

A key factor in a child's reaction to parental abuse in the longer-term is likely to be the way in which s/he perceives and interprets the abuse and uses this interpretation to form a rationale for the nature of subsequent disciplinary encounters with her or his own children. Herzberger (1983) describes the differential between 'sensitization' (yelling and corporal punishment) and 'induction' (explaining, moralizing) discipline techniques and cites a study (Dienstbier *et al.* 1975) which showed that children falling within the second group tended to feel guilty and thus behave more responsibly, whilst those falling into the first group tended to feel shame and behave less responsibly. Sensitization (or 'power assertive' techniques) was associated with weak moral development in the child, whereas the employment of induction techniques was associated with strong moral internalization and social responsibility. The conclusion, cited below, would appear to constitute an additional risk factor in the later behaviour of those who have been physically punished and abused:

> To the extent that parents employ sensitization rather than inductive discipline, the parents do not encourage the development in their child of a tendency to reflect on his or her actions. Therefore, not only does an abusive parent provide a model for aggressive behaviour, but the parent may fail to provide the child with the cognitive ability to evaluate

the morality of his or her own aggressive and non aggressive behaviour.
(Herzberger 1983, p.325)

As well as constituting a further mechanism for transgenerational violence, this
'sensitization' discipline also provides support for the suggestion that those who
are regularly abused, in whatever form, become individuals with low empathy
who, if they later become abusive and violent in their own right, view their
victims as objects for whom they have no feeling (Goddard and Stanley 1994;
Wilson 1995). Such individuals clearly constitute a danger not only to their
own future children but within society at large.

The range of findings described above begins to suggest a connection
between children whose significant attachment figures abuse their positions as
trusted adults to create a domination/submission relationship, and some of
those children's later entry into that small but singular group of offenders who
commit grave and violent crimes, whether within their own subsequent families
or beyond. If their parental role models dominate in order to gain control then,
as time goes on, perhaps they too will find that part of their survival mechanism
lies in gaining their own form of control in keeping with that pattern. If they
have been denied their victim status by having no-one to confide in about what
has happened to them then it is possible that they will seek redress by finding
their own form of domination, sometimes within the family but, where this is
unfeasible, sometimes also as a 'displacement' activity beyond it. Thus a number
of issues are highlighted: the need for more effective mechanisms to enable
victims to report abuse; the assessment and intervention requirements for a
comprehensive understanding of the dynamics of domination and submission;
and the necessity of supplementing existing gaps in knowledge as to the
variables which intervene either to prevent or exacerbate the likelihood of
violent offending.

Gender factors

Perhaps the most obvious of the variables mentioned above is the sex of the
child since it is known, for example, that only slightly more than four per cent
of the current Section 53 population is female whilst slightly in excess of 95
per cent is male (Boswell 1995). In turn, 95 per cent of that population who
had experienced abuse and/or loss is also male. Cultural expectations of the
male as aggressor and the female as submissive recipient perhaps offer a key to
the suggestion that boy victims of abuse tend towards 'externalized' responses
in the form of later violent behaviour whilst girl victims tend towards 'internalized' responses in the form of psychiatric conditions, including depression
and self-harm (Carmen *et al.* 1984). The latter is fleshed out in a number of
women's accounts of their responses to abuse. For example:

I couldn't take my anger out on the people that really hurt me most. So instead I did bodily harm to myself (Armstrong 1978, p.221).

For if a child is forbidden to express her true feelings, observations and thoughts because only good, kind thoughts that are pleasing to God are permitted, then everything that has no place in this 'good' world is relegated to the realm of death. Käthe Kollwitz often dreamed she was dead: this was because the uncomfortable intense side of her nature was not allowed to live (Miller 1990, p.27).

These accounts would accord with the Diagnostic and Statistical Manual of Mental Disorders (DSM-III-R) framework which shows externalized disruptive behaviour disorders to be much more common in boys than girls whilst internalized anxiety and repressive disorders are either equally likely or more common amongst girls (American Psychiatric Association 1987).

Whilst much of the available literature refers to long-term effects in terms of sexual abuse it seems not unfeasible to deduce that similar effects may ensue from physical, emotional and organized/ritual abuse. In other words, as hypothesized earlier, those who have been victims, especially males, appear to reach a point where they experience the need to control and dominate and some do so in the very way which has been modelled to them by significant (usually male) adult figures in their earlier lives. In applying this notion to the boys who killed James Bulger, Jackson makes the following suggestion:

The effects on them of growing up in a culture that condones and even celebrates male violence and abuse towards women, children (as well as between boys and boys and men and men) is clear to see. It was the daily social practices of being brought up in an aggressive, male-dominated family, bullying, being bullied, having to face the pressures of the male peer group, learning to dump their pain and hurt onto other people, building fantasy heroes like Rambo and learning to emotionally detach yourself as a boy from the reality of other people's lives that socially produced the two boys who killed James Bulger. The appalling pain of the murder can't be separated from those devastating pressures on boys in Britain to be more aggressively manly, harder, stronger, more commanding and powerful than others. (Jackson 1995, p.40)

It should be remembered also that these two boys were prime examples of young people likely to be feeling bewildered by parental loss and separation, on the threshold of male adolescence, with male adulthood represented to them by partially or wholly absent fathers. In the sense that significant loss is a form of emotional abuse (albeit usually unintentional) because it has not been properly acknowledged and explained to the child, it seems possible that this too could constitute a form of internalized bewilderment and rage which in females progress towards self-harm whilst in males tends to surface later in the urge to take control and manufacture certainty. Fahlberg's work on the long-term effects of lack of normal attachment would certainly suggest that such developmental progressions are a possibility (Fahlberg 1994).

Predictors of violence

As highlighted earlier, the majority of studies carried out in recent decades on abuse, loss or delinquency have not, for the most part, made provision for examining a link between these phenomena and a violent offending outcome. However, Farrington and West's prospective study in delinquent development did identify a sub-group of 50 (out of 411) South London boys who were convicted of violent offences (Farrington 1989). They concluded that at age 8–10, the best predictors of violence included physical neglect by parent(s), harsh and erratic discipline by parent(s), and separation from parent(s) principally because of parental conflict. They did, however, also identify a number of other variables including low family income, unemployment, large family size and a parent with criminal convictions. More specifically, a New York State prospective study found that males who were the victims of physical punishment at age eight tended to commit violent offences up to the age of thirty (Eron *et al.* 1991). An important retrospective longitudinal cohort study by Widom (1989) also specifically focused upon the relationship between child abuse and neglect and later violent criminal behaviour. Avoiding the pitfalls of some earlier studies, Widom identified a large sample of substantiated cases of child abuse and neglect from twenty years previously and established a matched control group of non-abused children. She then determined the extent to which each group had engaged in officially recorded delinquent and adult criminal and violent criminal behaviour. This study produced a prediction that 'early childhood victimization has demonstrable long-term consequences for delinquency, adult criminality and violent criminal behaviour' (Widom 1989, p.164). In particular it found that physical abuse in childhood led significantly to later violent criminal behaviour when other variables such as age, sex and race were held constant. In addition, being neglected as a child increased the likelihood of later violent offending.

Significant and unresolved loss may in itself constitute a precursor of later violence, whether or not abuse is a recorded factor. A review of research studies on attachment, attunement, loss and deprivation leads one author to conclude that 'violent aggression may be the reciprocal manifestation of a damaged attachment system' (de Zulueta 1993, p.78). Other writers point to the unique difficulty for children in dealing with the interplay between grief work and trauma reactions following death or other significant loss because of their facility, by reason of age, for dealing in imagination, play and fantasy (Pynoos and Nader 1993). They cite cases where traumatic loss experiences affected some children's ego functioning to the extent that previously non-violent children became 'macho', aggressive, violent or murderous. Using an attachment framework, Wright, Birney and Smith (1995) found a group of disturbed 8–12 year olds less securely attached and more avoidant of emotion than control respondents. Their fears about possible separation from their carers tended to escalate into death and disaster fantasies and, in contrast with the control group they did not trust adults in their life to come to their aid. As a result, 'their internal working models of relationships gave rise to coping strategies which perpetuate their problematic interactions with others' (p.772). One possible manifestation of such interaction is violence, often as a defence against perceived danger. In common with experiences of abuse, De Zulueta (1993) argues that deprivation and loss 'can so deplete the self that defending itself becomes of paramount importance whatever the cost to the "other." This desperate need to bolster the self by whatever means contributes considerably to our understanding of the importance of the self in the origins of violence' (p.xii).

This brief review of prospective and retrospective research and literature which catalogues some of the variables at work in the lives of violent young offenders has highlighted the stress factors which are frequently in play. Many, such as abuse and loss, are of a traumatic variety, and others which exacerbate existing stresses may be of a structural variety, such as poverty and unemployment. The kinds of interventions which may be made in respect of the latter phenomena, whilst limited, are well known to 'helping' professionals. What is less known, because work is still only in its relative infancy, is the range of methods available to assist the identification and resolution of early childhood trauma.

Post-traumatic stress disorder in children

The emerging body of work on post-traumatic stress disorder (PTSD) (Pynoos and Eth 1985; Pynoos *et al.* 1987; Scott and Stradling 1992; Wilson and Raphael 1993) confirms that children suffer the after-effects of traumatic stress in a similar way to adults, and that one way in which unresolved fear or grief can manifest itself, particularly in males, is in later aggressive orviolent behaviour. (Women tend more frequently to be found in groups exhibiting psychiatric disorder, depression or self-harm.) Various studies have established modest links between early traumatic experiences and later violent/abusive behaviour, sometimes of the kind of which the offenders had themselves been victims (Dodge, Bates and Pettit 1990; Finkelhor 1987; Rutter 1989; Shepherd 1993; Widom 1989; Wolfe 1987). In 1980 PTSD, itself, was first identified as a category of the mental disorders listed in the Diagnostic and Statistical Manual of Mental Disorders (DSM-III, American Psychiatric Association 1980). A set of criteria to help establish whether an individual is suffering from PTSD was set out in a revised edition of this manual (DSM-III-R, American Psychiatric Association 1987) and constituted a response to rapid development in the field of traumatic stress studies during the 1980s. PTSD is frequently associated with catastrophe – warfare, earthquake, fire, transport disaster and so on – but perusal of its five criteria provides immediate pointers to the potential for its association with child abuse and traumatic loss.

First, the person must have witnessed or experienced a serious threat to their life or physical well-being. Provided the perceived threat to a child from experiences of emotional abuse or traumatic loss can be interpreted in this way, then 91 per cent of the Section 53 sample fall into this category. **Second**, the person must re-experience the event in some way, e.g. via dreams, intrusive thoughts, or flashbacks. This information was not sought from Section 53 respondents yet was occasionally referred to on file and sometimes spontaneously mentioned in interview. **Third**, the person must persistently avoid stimuli associated with the trauma or experience a numbing of general responsiveness. The researchers not infrequently found themselves reading or hearing about 'numbness', 'lost memory' or 'frozen emotion' in relation to Section 53 offenders. Johnson's work on the 'buried terror syndrome' also lends weight to the presence of this factor (Johnson 1993). **Fourth**, the person must experience persistent symptoms of increased arousal, e.g. irritability or outbursts of anger, and exaggerated startle responses. Clearly, those who have committed violent or murderous acts came into this category.

Finally, symptoms must have lasted at least a month – and those described as 'acute' sufferers have experienced symptoms for more than one but less than three months, whilst those described as 'chronic' have endured symptoms for more than three months. 'Delayed' sufferers do not develop symptoms until at least three months post-trauma. If there is, indeed, a link between childhood trauma and later violence then the respondents in the Section 53 study are likely to fall into one or both of the last two categories, although they may also have exhibited symptoms other than violence during the period between the trauma and the offence.

Overall, then, it is certainly arguable that the majority of Section 53 offenders studied (Boswell 1995) fall into the categories identified by the American Psychiatric Association; and would more clearly do so if some of those categories were slightly less rigid. Further to the DSM-III-R criteria, however, Young (1990) has developed a set of early maladaptive schemata to interact with unresolved PTSD symptoms. These schemata specifically allow for links between major childhood traumata, PTSD and what is described as 'psychological morbidity' in adult life. Of note, in relation to the Section 53 study, are those maladaptive schema which include subjugation, vulnerability to harm, emotional deprivation, abandonment or loss, mistrust and defectiveness or unlovability (often experienced by abused children). It seems entirely possible that such interactions at some point along the continuum between PTSD and psychological morbidity could manifest themselves in ways which include violent offending.

Summary

This chapter has sought to explain that the traumata of abuse and loss are significant factors in the backgrounds of violent young offenders. The diagnosis and treatment of post-traumatic stress disorder have been described in some detail as a recently emerging knowledge base, which is now beginning to be applied to the various forms of child abuse, but perhaps remains in embryo in relation to its application to traumatic loss. Little research has considered potential links between PTSD and violent offending, although when the literature on the effects of childhood abuse and loss is reviewed alongside its prevalence in violent young offenders, it is difficult to see why. Just as research by Craine, Henson, Colliver and MacLean (1988) showed that half their sample of hospitalized women psychiatric patients had been sexually abused in earlier life and that 69 per cent met the diagnostic criteria for PTSD but had not been identified as such, so it is possible that the same neglect of such characteristics in the lives of incarcerated violent youngsters has occurred. Child care and criminal justice professionals need to be alert to the fact that PTSD is not just a syndrome associated with dramatic disaster and to structure their enquiries accordingly:

> Unless the counsellor specifically inquires about whether they were sexually abused as a child this information is unlikely to be forthcoming. Regrettably such a question ought to be part of the counsellor's standard interview schedule. There is a need for counsellors to be attuned to the possibility of both dramatic and non-dramatic pathways to PTSD. (Scott and Stradling 1992, p.153)

It is clearly important that professionals keep themselves abreast of current research findings and cognizant of the potential links between abuse, loss, PTSD and violent manifestation so that, at the point of intervention, they can quickly identify salient features by the application of sensitive, systematic inquiry. Competent criminal justice management and crime prevention may well be the long-term outcome.

CHAPTER 3

Psychiatric Assessment of the Violent Child and Adolescent Towards Understanding and Safe Intervention

Susan Bailey

Violence occurs in context: one systemic, the other that of individual differences.

The phenomenon of violence is particularly subject to the hazards of rhetoric, which is borne largely out of factual ignorance and understandable fear. The evolution of violent behaviour involves loss of the sense of personal identifiability and uniqueness, loss of the sense of personal value, the child or young person engaging in their actions without concern for future consequences or past commitments.

Delinquency

Surveys of the general population show that over 90 per cent of boys admit to acts that could have led to appearance in court; however, most are minor in their nature. Delinquent acts by young children are less frequent, more likely to be associated with psychological abnormalities that are persistent and reflect both social dysfunction and individual psychopathology. However, the rate of grave offences of children and young adolescents has not risen to any significant event (McNally 1995). Nonetheless sadistic violent acts carried out by children bring with them a surfeit of public media interest and reaction – a response that at times risks becoming a voyeuristic end in itself.

Psychiatric disturbance in children and young people

In any one year up to one in five children and young people may experience psychological disturbance which is severe enough to warrant some form of professional intervention. Mental disorders in the young are more clearly defined, well established abnormal conditions which are more severe and may be long term or life long.

There are many types of severe mental disorder. Those beginning characteristically in childhood include, for example, childhood autism involving severe impairment in the development of personality; language and social relationships; and hyperkinetic disorder, characterized by extreme over-activity and lack of attention. Such conditions may continue into the adolescent years when other disorders can also emerge including manic depressive disorder, schizophrenia and conduct and personality disorders, where effects are likely to persist into adulthood.

Presentations vary according to the type of disorder but invariably affect several areas of the life of the child or young person. They can and do include disturbances of behaviour, mood and thinking, which may be difficult to understand or even frightening to observers, particularly if they extend to aggression, violence and destructiveness. The occurrence of these disorders during critical stages of maturation can cause major interference with normal psychological and social development, especially relationships with family and friends, impairment of school achievement, employment potential and work performance.

Precise diagnosis, particularly where there may be more than one co-existing disease, may be difficult during the early stages. There is a natural reluctance to diagnose psychiatric disorders owing to fears about the adverse effects of stigmatization through medical labelling. However, early diagnosis, particularly where the child presents a risk to others, is essential as early intervention can be crucial to successful treatment and minimization of risk to others.

Violence and childhood psychiatric disorder

There is a growing body of research literature describing the association of violence and suicidal behaviour with psychotic illness in adulthood (Taylor 1985, Noble and Rodger 1989, Lindquist and Allebeck 1990). However, little attention has been paid to these issues in psychotic older children and adolescents. Psychotic disorders presenting in late childhood and adolescence are undoubtedly among the most severe of psychiatric conditions (Parry-Jones 1984). In a study exclusively of hospitalized psychotic adolescents, Inamder *et al.* (1982) reported high prevalence rates of distorted behaviour, while recognizing that violence was not the defining feature of a psychotic adolescent but that socio-cultural factors mediated the expression of violence and psychosis in both children and adolescents.

In a study of admissions to a secure adolescent psychiatric unit (Bailey, Thornton and Weaver 1994; Kelsall, Dolan and Bailey 1995), a sub group of psychotic adolescents demonstrated a severity of disturbance with high levels of deliberate self-harm and acts of aggression including serious offence behaviour (including murder and attempted murder). The detection of psychotic illness in adolescence can be difficult. In our own series one third of chronic/relapsing cases had not been previously referred to a psychiatrist as the psychotic disorder had gone undetected. This failure can have serious consequences. Psychosis can be difficult to assess accurately in such young people particularly when conduct disturbance predominates the clinical picture. Unfortunately, failure to diagnose and treat psychotic disorder can have serious consequences of harm to others and unrecognized illness-driven behaviours leading to young people being inappropriately placed in social service provision or the penal system. The finding that the sample came from predominantely disadvantaged and disrupted backgrounds adds indirect support to the overall notion that socio-cultural factors play a mediating role in the behavioural expression of psychotic illness in this age group.

Previous studies did not examine the psychotic features associated with violent and suicidal behaviour. The high rates of paranoid ideation and elated mood in our own series are therefore of some clinical interest. These phenomena may represent particular risk factors in the generation of severely disturbed behaviour. It is therefore imperative that any perceived threats held by the paranoid adolescent and the degree of mood disturbance are rigorously assessed and the potential risk of violence and self-harm is monitored closely over time. Poor prognosis is associated with younger age of onset of schizophrenia and most serious offenders (Eggers 1978; Kydd and Werry 1982). In view of the severity of psychotic disorders in general and the multiple psychosocial problems associated with them, it is essential that there is available a fully integrated spectrum of mental health services to treat children and young people. This range of services needs to include secure, open in-patient unit and comprehensive community based provision. At present there are still marked deficits in the health care system (Kurtz, Thorne and Wolkind 1994).

General assessment of violence and risk of further violence

Scott (1977) suggested that the best criterion to establish whether an individual is likely to be violent is whether or not he/she has been violent in the past. The stages of assessing violence are: collection of information; examination of the child; and examination of the triad of perpetrator, victim and analysis of the violent behaviour.

Information

Sources of information include any police reports, witness statements, and medical reports of injuries to the victim(s). Previous health care records including birth notes, school reports, social or probation assessments and details of previous convictions need to be carefully studied in parallel with the essential discussion and detailed history taken from past and current primary carers whether parents, residential or community workers, or teachers.

Examination

The examination encompasses a study of the personal, developmental, social, educational, medical/psychiatric and family history of the child. The stressors, internal and external, leading up to the index offence must be teased out and the thoughts, feelings and perceptions and state of physical arousal of the child at each stage up to, during, and after the index offence must be elicited. It is important to test out the validity of young person's account against other sources and the attitude of the adolescent, including attitude to previous interventions, evidence of previous behavioural try outs however seemingly minor and the response of carers to such physical, verbal aggression and, as important, previous demonstrations of anger and in some cases pronounced features of hostility, characterized by feelings of jealousy, bitterness, oversuspiciousness, and distrustfulness.

Risk triad

Working specifically with the risk triad of the individual, the circumstances of the violent act and the actual and potential future victims, the following areas need to be reviewed. The nature of a specific disorder in the child and the relationship to violence and risk, the adolescent's explanation of the violent behaviour and the level of acceptance of the psychiatrist's understanding of the behaviour. Was the violent act a feature of the moment or carefully planned? Has the behaviour been modified by previous therapeutic intervention and if so is change measurable? An important feature is whether positive clinical change impacted on level of risk and if so, has real risk been minimized or, now the identified disorder is diagnosed, understood and treated, is risk of violence unchanged or even increased? Which factors are compounding and perpetuating future risk, e.g. emerging personality development, substance abuse, psychosexual development? How are these balanced by positive turning points such as reintegration back into education or constructive avocation, amelioration of family relationships and positive peer group interactions?

What is the accessibility to the adolescent's inner world; are his/her intentions to be less violent matched by the actual behaviour? What appreciation does the child and family have of the need for input from professionals?

Circumstances

Did situational factors contribute to the violent behaviour; if so which were they, and can they be identified and modified and how will they present in any new situation? What changes in circumstances will minimize the risk of violence? In an era of finite resources are desired changes in circumstances achievable, in terms of availability of suitable input and a willingness by agencies to provide and fund input? Will the system be able to monitor change?

Potential victims

Why the original victim and have the relationship issues been addressed? Could the relationship that led to violent contact be replicated and how much understanding does the child have of this?

Is there a risk of potential victims or their carers forming pathological collusive relationships with the violent child, thus excalating risk? Do family and carers understand the level of support and treatment needs and risk? Finally, what is the probability of achieving a therapeutic alliance with family carers and the multi-agency system?

Psychiatric assessment of the child's ability to distinguish 'right from wrong'

Where children and adolescents are concerned, despite the emphasis within the Children Act 1989 of the rights and voice of the child, there has emerged an increasingly paternalistic attitude towards children in court when making judgements about Consent to treatment matters. This contrasts sharply with the approach taken towards children who have committed grave acts of violence who subsequently face the Criminal Justice System.

The age of criminal responsibility in England and Wales is ten years old (eight in Scotland). Children between the ages of 10 and 13 years are presumed in law to be *doli incapax* (incapable of criminal intent). This assumption must be rebutted by the prosecution before the child can be convicted. In order to do this the prosecution must show beyond reasonable doubt that the child appreciated that what he or she did was 'seriously wrong' as opposed to merely naughty or mischievous. A child as young as ten can therefore find him or herself in the midst of an adversarial legal system in either the Youth Court or in more serious cases the Crown Court.

Whilst political and social debate continues (Bullock, Little and Millham 1991) the clinician has to assess the child's capacity to distinguish right from wrong. Although psychological, emotional and educational levels of functioning can be measured, the task of gaining a true understanding of the child's level of moral development is far more problematical. Key factors that need to be fully explored are the child's appreciation of time sequences, the influence and vulnerability of the child to same age or older co-defendants, the child's sense of permanence and, with younger adolescents, issues of rationality, identity, autonomy and, critically, for all ages, cause and effect in relation to their own behaviour.

In cases of grave violence where a victim has been irreversibly injured or has died, it is critical to gain from the child their level of understanding of the four major concepts of death, irreversibility, finality, (non-functionality) causality and inevitability (universality). The age of acquisition of the three most studied concepts (irreversibility, finality and inevitability) in children is between five and seven but in some cases is not fully evolved at the age of ten.

Some children younger than 12 demonstrate elements of the ability to generate hypotheses and weigh up different options. However, in clinical practice the difference in this capacity between younger and older children is relative rather than absolute.

Relatedness and connection aspects of the difficult concept of emotional maturity form an integral part of the moral identity of the individual child. All the above factors should be taken into consideration in offering an opinion to the court about a child's capacity to distinguish right from wrong – a decision that in the final analysis is made by the court itself.

Understanding children who commit offences of extreme sadistic violence

Psychodynamic explanations of adolescent aggression (Glover 1960) in particular homicidal aggression (Bender and Curran 1940; Satten, Menninger and Rosen 1960; Easson and Steinhilber 1961), have related the murderous act to a powerful sense of unconscious guilt, primarily Oedipal in origin (McCarthy 1978), and to early experiences of deprivation leading to an underdeveloped ego vulnerable to outbursts of violence. Contributory sociocultural factors (Walsh-Brennan 1974) have included severe physical abuse (Lewis *et al.* 1985), sexual abuse (Ressler, Burgess and Douglas 1985; Lewis *et al.* 1988) exposure to repetitive or extreme violence (Pfeffer 1980), parental mental illness (Hellsten and Katila 1965) and gang participation (Busch *et al.* 1990).

More recently increasing concern has centred both in the United States and United Kingdom on the quantity and level of exposure of children to media violence (Heath 1986). Neurological abnormalities have long been associated with adolescent murderers, Lewis in 1988 stressing the prevalence of major neurological impairment in this population, head injury, EEG abnormality, current and past seizure disorders and soft neurological signs.

Violent adolescents often fulfil the criteria for conduct disorder (Myers and Kemph 1990) with associated, learning difficulties and language delay (Hays, Solway and Schreiner 1978). Psychotic disorder is reported as unusual but paranoid ideation not uncommon (Cornell, Benedek and Benedek 1987).

Substance abuse, in particular of alcohol, is common (Labelle *et al.* 1991). Although impaired moral reasoning has been described in delinquent adolescents (Hollin 1990), this has not been reported specifically in homicidal adolescents.

Insecure attachment (Bowlby 1973) may be an important risk factor in the development of antisocial behaviour in childhood and as such is more deserving of attention in the specific area of adolescent violence and homicide. When parental behaviours are chronically inconsistent or rejecting the child is almost constantly in a state of uncertainty about the physical or emotional availability of the parent, resulting in the experience of frequent and intense anger. Over time the child learns a model of relationship in which anger and insecurity become core features. Unchanged, these hostile angry models of relationships place the child at heightened risk of problem behaviour including aggression. In addition, as they enter adolescence the young person may view him/herself as incompetent and less in control. In contrast competent adolescents are able to seek autonomy in ways that both meet their needs and respect the needs of others. Whatever the adolescent's underlying risk status that risk is ultimately expressed in the social context.

Pointers from adulthood

The adult literature (MacCullock *et al.* 1983) points to antecedent history in late childhood and early adolescence of behavioural try outs for a final violent sadistic act. Often because not overtly sadistic or violent the significance of apparently trivial components of stealing had been overlooked, for example, conduct disordered youngsters engaged in burglaries retaining keys and photographs, using these as a focus for developing sadistic fantasies. Failing to make such connections the thinking patterns and early fantasies of these youngsters had not been explored, with later grave consequences. Liebert (1985) has pointed out the resistance among both criminal investigators and clinicians to uncovering the sexual basis for grave acts committed by young people, particularly when conventional evidence for a sexual motivation may be lacking at the scene of the crime. In a series of child and adolescent murderers (Bailey 1996) it became apparent that a third had been sexually abused; males described uncertainty about emerging sexuality and identity, negative experiences of sexual experimentation with age similar peers and inappropriate sexual experience with older females and males. In a third of cases there was both a sexual and sadistic motivation to the offence but, more important, undetected and previous 'offence' behaviour of a violent, sadistic and sexual nature. In a series of 121 sex offenders (Dolan, Holloway and Bailey 1996), a third had used physical violence or threats. Their sexual offences were not isolated incidents involving normally developing adolescents and many had a previous record of similar or less serious offences. The psychiatric interview of young sex offenders in the case of non contact as well as contact type offences should always include an enquiry into the presence of rape fantasies and other concurrent violent behaviours in addition to the paraphilias.

The evolution and role of fantasy

Fantasy has its origin in day dreaming, defined by Singer (1966) as any cognitive activity representing a shift of attention away from a task. The fantasy itself is characterized as an elaborate thought with great preoccupation and anchored in emotion. The young person may be aware of images, feelings and internal dialogue, and the fantasy provides a normal way for a child, or young person to obtain and maintain control of an imagined situation. In violent children rate of fantasy development and frequency differ considerably and may either substitute or, critically for some, prepare for action (Beres 1961). How many young people activate sadistic fantasy and in what context remains uncertain (Crepault and Couture 1980). Once a fantasy builds to a point where inner stress is unbearable, action may follow (Schlesinger and Revitch 1980). Early expression of fantasy development is clearly seen in children's play, and in adolescence thinking patterns emerge from and are influence by earlier life experiences. As a child matures his use of language increases with the fantasy which is usually both positive and seems to promote the child's learning through repetitive thinking and rehearsal of actions.

In violent and sadistic children, particularly in the latency period, they start to demonstrate repetitive acting out of the core aggressive fantasy, persistent themes emerging in their own play or in play with others. Secondary attempts at mastery and control over others appear in set situations when the repetition can often become a direct expression of an original assault either against or witnessed by the younger child. A high degree of egocentricity evolves in both fantasy and play and gradually other children, family, and significant adults merge to become extensions of the child's inner world.

Adult sadists often report an absence of positive fantasies in their early life, whether never present or lost in very negative experiences is unclear, but what emerges is the overwhelming importance of the secret reality of the fantasies to the individual in adolescence. The early aggressive behaviours serve to displace anger onto the victim but clinically, as fantasies elaborate, the displayed aggression whether still in play or against an individual, occurs with diminishing fear or anxiety about adult disapproval. Each subsequent act serves to allow increasingly intense emotions to be incorporated into their imaginations, in turn allowing the intensity of violent thoughts to escalate.

During adolescence the nature of the first sexual experience which is followed by orgasm may be crucial in determining sexual deviation and the sexual component to subsequent sadistic acts. Early general difficulties in social relationships are epitomized after puberty by an inability to make any sort of appropriate approach to their preferred sex. In contrast through the pattern of fantasy in which the young person controls their inner world he/she becomes the success they would like to be but are unable to control in the real world. Fantasy of successful control and domination of the world becomes the key which unlocks the increasing probability of its own reoccurrence by the relief which it gives from a previous sense of failure. The stage is thus set for the violent sadistic act.

A key issue emerging from our own work with the 40 child and adolescent murderers and 121 child and adolescent sex offenders centres on longstanding cumulative risk factors reaching a crescendo as they enter the physical stage of puberty. Critically over a short period of weeks their social interactions prior to the sadistic act deteriorate, when issues of trust, emerging patterns of verbal, physical aggression, feelings of hostility and paranoid reactions towards peers and adults reach a climax. Even where the child has gained a sense of power and pleasure from organized behavioural try outs accompanied by sadistic fantasies they still at the eleventh hour expect an adult intervention, positive or negative, to occur. If the cues presented to the outside world of both adults and peers goes unheeded their rage explodes onto a fragile victim in a chaotic, disorganized sadistic act (McCarthy 1978).

Towards safe intervention

The debate on the rights and wrongs of how young people are currently dealt with by the Criminal Justice System in their career routes through secure care, Young Offender Institutions and adult custody continues (Bullock *et al.* 1994; Little 1990), with a simplistic tendency to attribute all blame and criticism to one part of the system serving as an easy but often counterproductive route to follow.

Realistically, therapy with young people who have committed sadistic acts of violence has to be tailored to the demands of the external environment and has to be approached cautiously. Motivational dynamics are complex and the monitoring of ongoing level of risk critical, especially if the young person remains within the community and with their family. The emergence of a sense of guilt involves the appreciation for negative outcomes resulting from an act of omission (often a key agenda where two or more youngsters have been involved in a sadistic act) or commission. A sense of shame is associated with negative feelings on the basis of a self-perception of being unworthy or bad (often a characteristically poorly defended feelings state the youngster has wrongly held about him/herself for much of their existence). Thus given the frequent distortion of perception of self and others the emergence of a true sense of guilt and shame can and often is a slow, difficult, painful and angry process.

Detention itself can provide allowance of time for further neurodevelopment, cognitive and emotional growth, allowing the adolescent to gain better control of his or her emotional and aggressive impulses. Irrespective of the available, if any, treatment model provided by the care or custody institution the parallel process of education, vocation, avocation, consistent role models and continued family contact are of critical importance. This parallel process is best facilitated in a milieu characterized by warmth and harmony, with clear organization practicality and high expectations, allowing for the establishment of positive staff–adolescent, staff–staff and adolescent–adolescent relations (Harris, Cole and Vipond 1987).

The majority initially dissociate themselves from the reality of their act, but gradually experience a similar progression of reactions and feelings akin to a grief reaction (Hambridge 1990). Their grief is initially about their own loss of freedom, enforced separation from family and lastly they grieve about their victim. The effect on the young person's family can be as devastating as on the victim's family (Macleod 1982). Against the inevitable waxing and waning of outside pressure the child has to move safely through the process of disbelief, denial, loss, grief anger/blame and now increasingly recognized post traumatic stress disorder, arising from the participation in the sadistic act either directly or observing the action of their partners in the act or arising from the past personal abuse.

Our own service has found, in working with the sadistic children and adolescents referred to us over 12 years, that a combination of cognitive behavioural psychotherapy and non verbal therapies have most to offer those who have committed sadistic acts. Qualities such as previous frequent and severe aggression, low intelligence and a poor capacity for insight, weigh against a positive safe outcome. The clinician has to remain alert to the possibility of emerging formal mental illness, in particular depression (Stewart, Myers and Burket 1990).

In understanding the role of violence in the youngster's life it is necessary to understand the depth of their sensitivity and reaction to a perceived threat, seeing threat and ridicule in many day-to-day events. A related theme is saving face. As the youngster starts to discuss their sadistic act, they have to face past loss trauma and abuse, disclosing fears of being vulnerable, that therapy many bring about change they do not like and above all cannot control.

Burgess, Hartman and Hawe (1990) described the use of drawing, painting and sculpture with juveniles in accessing memory of sadistic acts, allowing further insight into the motivational dynamics. Since 1990 I have been fortunate to be able to work in conjunction with an art therapist (Aulich 1994) making easier the task of enabling the young people to face the most sadistic elements of their own acts and past abuse, particularly in those cases where the spoken word has become such a painful and destructive reminder of how systems have dealt with them. The drawing series has given a potentially non invasive way of providing information and, critically, has allowed the youngster to make contact with gaps in their own emotional state. Both can then help direct intervention that will diminish rather than escalate future risk.

In our own series of cases a range of motivational dynamics have become apparent: victim provocation, the victim as a physical threat and role reversal of victim and offender with often gross size distortion. Victim and offender will often merge and the drawings show a remarkable variation in use of detail and colour some, critically, showing clear attribution of blame and emotional expression.

The exposure of the distortions through non verbal images can represent the first therapeutic effort to separate out causal constraints that another person is the cause from being responsible for one's own rage. This can help the young person come to terms with their own behaviour and their sense of needing to seek revenge on vulnerable people.

Thus in the psychiatric assessment of violence in children and adolescents it is essential always to take an holistic view of the individual, to view their behaviour in a developmental context and with other professionals to remain alert to the existence of formal mental illness.

If a risk factor model is adopted with respect to practices policy and research it will help to understand and then act upon influences that may have had a small but cumulative impact on the child's violent behaviour. In the individual multiple influences may have combined to increase the likelihood of a violent outcome or may as importantly have interacted to influence outcome.

The purpose of accurately assessing and then reducing risk factors in a group of potentially or violent children is not to remove the problem in its entirity but to ensure a positive palpable impact in the work carried out by multi-disciplinary and multi-agency teams involved in the jurisdictions of health, care, education and criminal justice.

CHAPTER 4

Psychological Assessment and Monitoring of Violent Children and Adolescents

Kevin J. Epps

Drawing from the research and clinical literature, and from clinical experience, this chapter aims to provide an introduction to the psychological assessment of violent children and adolescents. It suggests a structure and methodology for organizing, managing and undertaking clinical assessments.

Theoretical approach

The task of assessment involves asking questions and collecting information about a particular problem. Inevitably, the type of information collected depends on how the problem being assessed is conceptualized. A cognitive-behavioural approach is advocated in this chapter. This approach provides a structured methodology for analyzing aggressive and violent behaviour. Violent behaviour is seen as the outcome of an interaction between psychological characteristics of the individual, especially cognitive factors (i.e. perceptions, thoughts, attributions), and his or her surrounding social and physical environment. The model recognizes that, through social learning, certain behavioural and cognitive styles may develop which increase the potential for aggressive and violent behaviour. Research carried out in the United States, for example, suggests that the experience of childhood physical abuse may lead to chronic aggressive behaviour by having an impact on the development of social information-processing patterns (Dodge, Bates and Pettit 1990). Compared to nonphysically harmed children, the children who had experienced physical harm were significantly less attentive to relevant social cues, more biased toward attributing hostile intent, and less likely to generate competent solutions to personal problems. Dodge *et al.* (1990) argue that the experience of severe physical harm is associated with later violent behaviour through the 'acquisition of a set of biased and deficient patterns of processing social provocative information' (p.1679).

The cognitive-behavioural model suggests a number of broad areas pertinent to the assessment of aggressive and violent behaviour in children and adolescents, shown in Table 4.1.

Table 4.1: Assessment areas

1. **Organic factors**
   Including: hereditary conditions, hormonal influences, acquired brain damage, temperamental characteristics, and intellectual impairment.

2. **Previous learning experience**
   Including: previous exposure to aggression and violence (actual and vicarious), and parental response to familial aggression and violence.

3. **Contemporary influences**
   Including: 'macro factors' such as culture/subculture, economic factors, education, family functioning, and the influences of the peer group; and 'micro factors' such as the current situation, cognitive style, the influence of fantasy, emotional state and the role of physical factors (e.g. tiredness, illness, effects of alcohol/drugs).

The model allows for a violent incident to be broken down into its constituent parts. Thus a violent behaviour (B) can be analyzed in terms of its antecedents (A) and its consequences (C). The relationship between the setting or antecedent events, the behaviour, and the consequences is called a *three-term contingency* (Skinner 1953). A detailed analysis of the factors helping to trigger and maintain aggressive and violent behaviour in the current environment is especially relevant to the development and implementation of cognitive-behavioural intervention programmes.

Antecedents can include unobservable phenomena, such as thoughts (i.e. cognitions) and feelings (i.e. mood states), in addition to information regarding observable behaviour. One advantage of this approach lies in its ability to combine information about historical influences (i.e. distal antecedents) that served to increase the potential for aggressive and violent behaviour, with information about more recent events (i.e. proximal antecedents) that helped to *trigger* a particular act of violence. For example, certain inherited temperamental characteristics combined with childhood physical abuse may contribute to the development of a belief system and cognitive style which supports the use of physical aggression and violence, whilst a reprimand from a disliked schoolteacher may act as the trigger for a violent assault.

Through the application of this model, each episode of violent behaviour is construed as a unique event, the result of the coming together of a particular set of factors at a certain moment. Clearly, some young people find the consequences of their aggressive or violent behaviour rewarding, thereby increasing the probability that they will go on to perpetrate further acts of violence. Over time, a young person may develop habitual styles of violent behaviour, responding to particular situations with well-learned forms of violent behaviour. As such, their violent behaviour may become more predictable to those who know them well. Research suggests that, once established, habitual patterns of aggressive and violent behaviour can be resistant to change (Olweus 1979).

Assessment

The term assessment has been defined in various ways. Essentially it refers to the *process* of gathering information for making informed decisions about a client. Before the process of assessment begins it is important to be clear about what decisions need to be taken. In other words, what is the problem that is being assessed? Who wants a solution to the problem? What are the possible outcomes? The value of an assessment lies in the extent to which it leads to constructive problem solving. Often, however, assessments are carried out, sometimes at great expense, with no clear goals in mind. Frequently, much of the information that has been collected is redundant, having no relevance to the process of decision making.

The process of assessment can be broken down into several stages, shown in Table 4.2. The amount of time taken to complete an assessment is determined first by the nature of the problem being assessed, and second by the kind of assessment requested by the referring agency. Complex problems require complex assessments, usually at greater cost. Assessment frequently performs the role of excluding particular contributory factors, such as the presence of psychiatric or physical illness, therefore helping to direct the assessment toward other, more useful areas of investigation. However, a referring agency may request that the assessment is focused on only a specific aspect of the presenting problem.

Having established the aims and boundaries of the assessment, it should take no longer than is necessary to find the most effective solution to the problem. Assessment is, after all, only a means to an end, not an end in itself. For example, the assessment may indicate that the best way to proceed is for the young person to attend a programme aimed at improving anger management.

It is important that the assessment process is well organized and managed. Assessments are frequently undertaken by multi-disciplinary teams. Information will need to be shared among involved professionals, usually involving report writing and formal, minuted meetings. Issues surrounding confidentiality will need to be clarified early on. Team members also need to be clear about their respective roles. One of the advantages of multi-disciplinary teamwork is that it draws on the strengths of different professional approaches.

Table 4.2: Stages of assessment

1. **The referral.** Who is asking for help? Is the referral appropriate? Should the assessment proceed?

2. **Initial assessment.** How urgent is the problem? Is the young person currently being adequately managed or should he or she be moved to another setting? Are specialist skills or tests likely to be required?

3. **Setting the agenda.** Gathering archival information. Identifying key players. Defining the problem to be assessed. Setting assessment goals. Establishing rapport with the young person. Setting priorities for further assessment, taking into account time and resource factors.

4. **Broad assessment screen.** Establishing a global picture of the young person, including personal, family and cultural factors.

5. **Focused behavioural assessment.** Targeting the referral behaviour of aggression and violence, establishing the settings in which it occurs (places, times, people present), identifying specific triggers, and quantifying the frequency, intensity and severity of the behaviour.

6. **Cognitive and emotional assessment.** Examination of perceptions, thoughts, and feelings associated with aggressive and violent behaviour.

7. **Formulation and recommendations.** Summarizing and interpreting the assessment findings. Identifying intervention strategies.

8. **Intervention, monitoring and follow-up.** If indicated, applying interventions, checking on progress and outcome.

Psychological assessment

Traditionally, psychological assessment has emphasized the use of *objective methods* of data collection and hypotheses testing in the form of tests, ratings, or structured interviews and observations. Assessment should be multi-modal, drawing from a variety of information sources using a range of different assessment methods. This helps to ensure that important information is not overlooked. It also provides a way of checking on the accuracy (reliability) of information. For example, information obtained from interviewing the young person (self-report) can be compared to that obtained from interviewing other relevant individuals (e.g. parents) and from behavioural observation.

Methods of gathering information

A variety of methods are commonly used by psychologists for collecting information about aggressive and violent behaviour exhibited by children and adolescents. These are summarized in Table 4.3. Information is required about each of the three areas shown in Table 4.1. The accuracy (reliability) of information is enhanced if more than one method is employed, drawing from a variety of sources. Careful attention should also be given to the psychometric properties (especially validity and reliability) of any paper-and-pencil tests that are used, including questionnaires, inventories and checklists.

Table 4.3: Assessment methods

Information from the young person (self-report)

Archival sources
Interviewing
Self-monitoring
Inventories
Tests of intellectual functioning
Psychophysiological assessment

Information about the young person (third party)

Archival sources
Interviewing
Inventories
Direct behavioural observation
Role-play

Before formal assessment begins, it is important to define operationally the problem being assessed. This helps to focus the assessment, facilitates communication between everybody involved, and ensures that the correct assessment methods and measures are selected. Labels such as 'aggressive', 'violent', or 'sadistic' should be avoided. Whilst global terms such as these provide a convenient shorthand, they are emotionally loaded and often 'stick' to the young person, even after there has been an improvement in behaviour. They are also imprecise and uninformative. For example, a boy in residential accommodation who has assaulted staff on one occasion over a six month period can just as easily be called 'aggressive' as one who has assaulted staff sixty times over the same period of time. Examples of well defined and poorly defined problem behaviours are shown below:

POORLY DEFINED PROBLEM

John is an aggressive 16-year-old boy. He has assaulted a number of care staff since his admission to residential care.

John is a 16-year-old boy. He was first admitted to residential care two years ago. Since then, he has had four different placements. During this time he has physically assaulted both male and female care staff on 14 occasions. However, 12 of these assaults have occurred over the last two week period, following the death of his father. Eight of these have been directed towards the same person. Most of the assaults seem to occur in the evening, when he appears low in mood. Usually they begin with John verbally threatening a member of staff over a minor incident. He then begins to push the staff member, followed by an attempt to punch him or her in the face. Fortunately, he has been prevented from causing physical harm.

Archival sources

Access to historical information is important in helping to build up a picture of the development of aggressive and violent behaviour. Clearly, the quantity and quality of archival information will vary from case to case. Information can be obtained from previous reports (e.g. medical, psychiatric, psychological, social work, educational), from personal contact with previous carers (e.g. foster parents), and, in the instance of more serious forms of violence, from victim and witness statements. Information about early childhood development and medical conditions is especially important where organic factors are suspected of playing an important contributory role. In the case of school-aged children it is useful to have access to school reports. It may be necessary to write to the heads of the schools attended by the child for further information, particularly relating to the child's social behaviour and peer relationships. Aggressive and violent behaviour is sometimes restricted to specific contexts, whilst in other cases it is more generalized, occurring in a wide range of settings.

When assessing children and adolescents convicted of serious violent offences, perhaps resulting in death or serious injury (e.g. murder, manslaughter, grievous or actual bodily harm), it is particularly important to obtain copies of victim and witness statements. Information obtained from these can be compared to the young person's account of the offence. Discrepancies can then be clarified through interviewing. Frequently, it is in the young person's interest to minimize the seriousness of the offence and to avoid responsibility for his or her actions. Overcoming denial and other forms of cognitive distortion constitutes an important component of cognitive-behavioural intervention programmes.

Interview

Essentially, an interview is a conversation with a purpose. Traditionally, clinical assessments have taken for granted the reliability of information obtained through interviewing. Psychologists in particular have emphasized the need to corroborate information obtained via self-report, ideally through direct behavioural observation (Herbert 1987), although the interview technique can also be used to obtain information from third parties, such as family members, school teachers and friends.

Despite its potential limitations, interviewing still remains the most commonly used method of assessment. It is especially useful for collecting information about the young person's personal experience of aggression and violence, especially how they think and feel in particular situations. It can also prove useful when trying to gain some degree of understanding of the young person's inner fantasy world which, in some instances, can play an important contributory role in helping to shape and determine violent behaviour. Several psychologists have argued that an act of violence can only be understood by reference to the social context and the meaning of the violence to the perpetrator (Felson 1978).

Interviewing can be used to explore the various types of perceptual and cognitive distortion commonly found among young people with an extensive history of aggression and violence. For example, clinical and research evidence suggests that some young people, perhaps as a consequence of their own learning experience, more often perceive the actions of others as hostile and threatening (Dodge and Somberg 1987). Social interactions are often viewed with suspicion, as an opportunity to attack or be attacked. It is not difficult to see how an adolescent who has for many years been physically abused, emotionally manipulated, and exploited, may come to view the world in this way.

Another cognitive deficit frequently found in aggressive and violent children is the ability to produce cognitive and behavioural solutions to social problems. D'Zurilla and Goldfried (1971) identify a number of processes which influence the problem-solving process. These include: being able to recognize problematic situations when they occur; resisting the temptation to act impulsively; generating possible courses of action; choosing the course of action most likely to produce a positive outcome; acting upon the decision; and checking to see whether the outcome was successful. Cognitive self-control intervention strategies have been used with some success in helping to reduce aggressive and violent behaviour in delinquent adolescents (Camp 1977; Camp, Blom, Herbert and van Doorninck 1977; Snyder and White 1979).

In addition to thinking about the content of the interview, it is equally important to pay attention to the interview process. Children and adolescents are often reluctant to talk about their aggressive and violent behaviour even after effective rapport has been established. Resistance is especially likely to occur if the young person is ashamed or embarrassed about his or her behaviour. In contrast, some seasoned aggressive delinquents actually enjoy talking about their exploits, which in itself may serve as a source of reinforcement. However, they may be vague and imprecise in their account, and fail to see the relationship between their thoughts, feelings, and situational events (i.e. setting conditions) and the effect these have on their behaviour. It is not unusual for delinquent adolescents to state that the incident 'just happened'.

A useful strategy for helping to overcome resistance, avoidance, and vagueness is to focus on the most recent episode of aggression or violence. The incident can be explored in detail, beginning with a discussion of the events leading up to the behaviour (i.e. antecedents). The young person may identify particular stressful life-events that occurred several months or weeks before the incident (i.e. distal events) as being significant in helping to set-up a chain of events culminating violence. For example, parental divorce, examination failure, and bullying. More recent (i.e. proximal) events can then be explored, building-up to the final minutes and seconds before the incident. When appropriate, the young person can be prompted to identify his or her thoughts and feelings at particular points in time, with a view to assessing the extent to which they contributed to the incident. The same process can be used to explore the actual incident and the events occurring afterwards (i.e. consequences). Whilst it is useful to vary the style of interviewing, particularly the extent to which the interview is directed and structured, it is important that the interviewer remains in control and collects the required information.

Young people with a long history of aggression or violence may identify a pattern to their behaviour. Specific clusters of antecedents may serve to trigger aggression and violence on successive occasions. For example, there is a relationship between alcohol use and offending in some juvenile delinquents (McMurran and Hollin 1993). A study looking at the relationship between alcohol consumption and criminal behaviour in young people found that most young offenders were of the view that alcohol directly influenced their behaviour (McMurran and Hollin 1989).

In some cases, there may be a specific situational or behavioural trigger. For example, in clinical practice I have encountered a number of delinquent adolescents who are extremely sensitive to criticism of their mother, physically attacking anybody who they perceive as attempting to degrade her.

It is also important to distinguish between aggressive and violent behaviour occurring as a result of emotional over-arousal and loss of self-control, and that which takes place in a more deliberate, planned manner, perhaps in accordance with internal fantasies or 'rules' (i.e. rule-governed behaviour). Whilst both types of behaviour may occur in response to specific triggers, the latter is often marked by an absence of emotional over-arousal, with aggression and violence being purposefully and intentionally used to achieve a particular goal. For example, an adolescent boy in a residential unit may have a 'rule' which dictates that any male member of staff who confronts him deserves to be physically assaulted. He may decide to disclose this rule during assessment interviews. If not, it may take the staff team several weeks of observational assessment and episodes of assaults on male staff before the rule is identified, thereby allowing effective management procedures to be adopted. Anger management interventions (Feindler and Ecton 1986) aimed at helping the young person to more effectively manage intense feelings of anger may prove less effective when dealing with rule-governed violence. Alternative approaches to intervention are required, such as 'Aggression Replacement Training' (ART), (Goldstein and Glick 1987). Drawing from empirical research, ART consists of a programme of structured learning skills, aimed at the cognitive and behavioural dimensions of aggression and violence, in addition to the emotional component of anger.

Self-monitoring

It is often helpful to ask young people to record actual incidents of aggression or violence as soon as possible after they occur, when recall of events is more accurate. The most common technique is the 'anger diary' or 'hassle log', whereby the young person takes a couple of minutes to complete a structured pro-forma (Feindler and Ecton 1986). The diary can be used to elicit information under various headings such as: time of day; location; other people present; nature of incident; what happened immediately before the incident; and what happened immediately after the incident. One advantage of this form of assessment is that it allows the young person to report freely his or her side of the incident, something which most adolescents are usually keen to do. This in itself can have therapeutic potential, allowing the young person to view the sequence of events more objectively, enhancing awareness of the role he or she played in the build-up the incident.

Inventories

A variety of checklists and questionnaires have been designed for the assessment of problem areas which, either directly or indirectly, contribute to the development and maintenance of aggressive and violent behaviour. Some of these have proven psychometric properties, providing valid and reliable data and enabling comparison with selected groups of young people. For example, the Spielberger State-Trait Anger Expression Inventory (STAXI) (Spielberger 1991) provides normative data on college and high-school students. Most inventories are administered to the young person to obtain self-report. Clearly, their use is restricted to young people who are willing and able to complete them.

Other inventories are designed to be administered to third-parties, such as school teachers or parents. Some inventories, such as the Conners Teacher Rating Scale (Conners 1969) and The Child Behaviour Problem Profile (Achenbach 1978) provide a profile of overall adjustment and problem behaviour. Others, such as the Social Situations Questionnaire (Trower, Bryant and Argyle 1978) and the Children's Anger Inventory (Finch and Eastman 1983) focus on specific problem areas. Information obtained from these, however, should never be used in isolation. Rather, it should be used to supplement information collected in other ways.

Tests of intellectual functioning

Other types of psychometric tests are often used by psychologists in addition to inventories and questionnaires, especially those concerned with intellectual functioning and educational attainment. The two most commonly used tests of intellectual and cognitive functioning are the Wechsler Intelligence Scale for Children-Third Edition UK (WISC-III) (Wechsler 1992) and, for young people aged 16 years and over, the Wechsler Adult Intelligence Scale-Revised Edition (WAIS-R) (Wechsler 1981). Information obtained from these tests can make an important contribution to the assessment of aggressive and violent young people.

First, they provide a global indication of the young person's overall level of intellectual and cognitive functioning. The term learning difficulty is used to identify those children whose overall level of intellectual functioning is two standard deviations or more below the mean for their age-group. Young people with severe and moderate learning difficulties will be slower at processing socially relevant information which may contribute to their feelings of anger and frustration. Interventions will need to be suitably adapted to take into account the degree of learning difficulty. For example, young people with learning difficulties will require more time to learn new strategies for dealing with their aggressive and violent behaviour. Further, they may be unable to grasp abstract concepts such as 'cognitions' and be unaware of the relationship between their thoughts, feelings, and environment.

Second, testing can provide information about the pattern of functioning, indicating areas of relative strength and weakness. Learning problems in young people of otherwise average or above-average intelligence are referred to as specific learning difficulties. Such children frequently have difficulty with reading and arithmetic, which may remain undetected even into adolescence. Consequently, they may not be able to meet the academic demands placed on them. Young people who are struggling to achieve under pressure from parents and school are more likely to feel angry and frustrated. They may also become sensitive to criticism and use aggression and violence as a way of protecting their crumbling self-esteem. Specific learning difficulties are commonly found in juvenile delinquents, many of whom score lower than nondelinquent adolescents on intelligence tests (Hirschi and Hindelang 1977; Quay 1987; Wilson and Herrnstein 1985). There is also some evidence to suggest that juvenile delinquents with a history of violence are more likely than nonviolent offenders to display evidence of neuropsychological and neurological impairments (Lewis, Shanok, Grant and Ritvo 1983; Lewis, Shanok, Pincus and Glaser 1979; Spellacy 1977), especially those detained in custody for serious violent offences (Tarter, Hegedus, Winsten and Alterman 1987). Quay (1987) has presented considerable evidence that there is a substantial discrepancy between the performance and verbal IQs of delinquents, and that the association between delinquency and IQ is the result of the relatively low verbal IQs of juvenile offenders. In addition, research into adult offenders has found a strong association between poor verbal skills and convictions for violent crimes (Holland, Beckett and Levi 1981). Henggeler (1989) suggests that, in addition to disrupting educational attainment, poor verbal abilities may delay the development of higher-order sociocognitive processes such as moral reasoning, empathy and problem-solving. Deficits in these areas will undoubtedly contribute to the development and maintenance of aggressive and violent behaviour.

Direct behavioural observation

This assessment method provides a way of obtaining relevant information about a young person's aggressive and violent behaviour in real-life situations, such as in the classroom, at home, or in the peer group. Although other methods of assessment such as interviewing and psychometric testing provide necessary and useful information, nothing compares to the quality of information obtained from direct behavioural observation.

TARGETING BEHAVIOUR

A target behaviour is one that has been clearly specified as the focus of behavioural assessment and, if appropriate, intervention. Behaviours targeted for observation need to be clearly defined. This is especially important in residential settings, where more than one observer may be involved. For example, targeting 'violent behaviour' is of little use: it is not clear what is meant by the term violence. Does it include violence to the self, such as self-injurious behaviour? Or threats of violence? Or violent acts causing damage to property? Any practitioner who has been involved in setting-up an observational programme, whether involving parents, schoolteachers or residential staff, will appreciate the importance of helping the observers to arrive at a clear, unambiguous definition of the target behaviour. Failure to do so results in wasted time and effort spent collecting irrelevant information. It can also lead to destructive arguments among observers, adding to their sense of frustration in their attempts to deal with the problem behaviour.

MEASURING BEHAVIOUR

Having targeted a behaviour for observation, it is necessary to decide how it is going to be measured. To some extent this depends on what is being measured.

Frequency. In clinical practice most observation programmes are initiated to assess how often a particular behaviour occurs and the extent to which frequency varies in response to environmental and situational change. Observers simply count, or check-off, the number of times the targeted behaviour occurs within a specific period of time. It is especially useful for assessing single, discrete behaviours that do not occur at too high a frequency, thereby making recording difficult.

Duration. Some behaviours do not easily lend themselves to frequency measurement. For example, behaviours which occur infrequently but, when they do occur, last for a long period of time. Take, for instance, a child's destructive, aggressive temper tantrums. Frequency measurement may show them to occur only once or twice each day, suggesting that they are not as problematic as the mother indicated. However, when they do occur, they may last for over an hour. In such a case, it makes more sense to measure the duration of each tantrum.

Establishing a baseline. The practice of measuring a targeted behaviour to establish its frequency and, if necessary, its duration, before an intervention is applied, is known as establishing a baseline. The extent to which an intervention reduces the frequency or duration of the behaviour below baseline level serves as measure of its effectiveness. Baselines are especially important when applying complex, expensive interventions, where programme continuation is subject to evidence of positive behavioural change.

The establishment of a baseline is important in helping to establish the true extent of a problem behaviour. This process can in itself have therapeutic benefits. Take, for example, a mother encountered in clinical practice who complained that her seven-year-old son was 'always fighting' with his older sister. An observational programme, targeting various forms of aggressive behaviour and conducted over the course of a typical week, found that only five fights occurred. The mother was relieved to find that the problem was not as severe as she had initially thought. She was later engaged in an intervention programme aimed at helping her to manage her children's behaviour more effectively.

The technique of baselining is also useful in helping to assess the extent to which a behaviour varies across situations. For example, within the context of school a child may display a much greater level of disruptive and aggressive behaviour in the playground than in the classroom.

BEHAVIOURAL RECORDING TECHNIQUES

A number of techniques exist for observing and recording targeted behaviour, each with different advantages and disadvantages. It is not possible, or necessary, to observe continuously the behaviour of a young person. As such, some form of *sampling* is required. The aim of sampling is to collect samples of behaviour that are representative of the young person's behavioural repertoire. The design of sampling programmes varies according to the amount and type of information that is required, the amount of time that can be devoted to observation and recording, and accessibility to recording technology, such as portable computers.

There are two main types of sampling. The first, *event sampling*, involves keeping a record of the frequency of the target behaviour. No other information is recorded, except perhaps the date, time, and place. This technique is useful when collecting information about relatively infrequent behaviours. For example, staff in a residential children's home may be asked to record the number of times a particular young person requires physical restraint as a result of aggression and violence.

Event sampling becomes problematic when attempting to record behaviours that occur more frequently, especially if information is also required about situational variables. The technique of *time sampling* helps to overcome such problems. Various types of time sampling can be used, each requiring the observer to make observations and recordings according to a predetermined time schedule. Separate time intervals are set aside for observing and recording, thereby overcoming the problem of how to record and observe at the same time. Several variables can be manipulated to design methods of time sampling suited to particular tasks. First, the *observation interval* can be varied. For example, the observer may observe for one minute, followed by a period of time to record the behaviour that occurred within the minute. Second, the *recording interval* can be varied. This is the length of time allowed for recording observations. Simple frequency counts may necessitate brief recording intervals. On the other hand, the recording of multiple target behaviours will necessitate longer periods available for recording. The observation interval plus the recording interval is termed the *observation occasion*.

The third variable that may vary in time sampling procedures is the *inter-occasion interval*. This refers to the length of time between occasions of observation. The reliability of the data is increased with the frequency of observations. When designing observation programmes, careful consideration should be given to the frequency and pattern of observation. It is also important not to restrict observation to one setting or situation. This limits the extent to which it is possible to generalize the findings beyond the situation observed. For example, if all the observational data on a boy exhibiting various forms of disruptive behaviour were collected in the classroom, it would be unfair to make assumptions about his behaviour in other settings, such as in the home.

Finally, the type of information that is collected may be varied. Some assessments require simple frequency counts, described earlier, focusing on specific target behaviours. Others, however, demand the collection of more complex information, looking at the interaction between the young person and environmental events. The use of video-recording equipment facilitates the recording and analysis of complex sequences of behaviour. Video-tapes can be viewed at leisure, making it possible to collect various types of information about several different target behaviours. Reliability can be enhanced through the use of more than one observer, with each observer rating behaviour according to strict operational criteria using specially designed coding systems. However, this can be very time-consuming and is often feasible only as part of a research project.

However, where video equipment is unavailable or inappropriate, other techniques can be used, such as non-specific narratives. This technique involves observing the young person in a variety of settings whilst making a continuous written or audio-taped narratives. The aim is to obtain a complete picture of how the young person behaves in a variety of situations. An example is shown in Table 4.4. This technique has several advantages. It has the potential to allow for a great deal of information to be collected, including observations about the relationship between behaviour and environmental events.

Table 4.4: Example of a non-specific narrative

Date: 10/09/1994
Time: 6.30–6.45pm
Present: Mrs C and Michael C.
Observer: T.E.

Mrs C is alone in the kitchen preparing supper on work surface. At 6.38pm Michael walks into the kitchen without speaking. Mrs C looks up but makes no comment. Michael walks over to where she is standing. He reaches past her, knocking her arm, causing her to spill some milk. Mrs C shouts at Michael 'watch what you're doing'. Michael kicks Mrs C in the leg, saying 'Don't shout at me you stupid old bag'. Mrs C slaps Michael across the head, ordering him to go to his room. Michael kicks her again, then runs out of the kitchen and through the front door. Mrs C calls upstairs to Mr C asking him to go and find Michael.

It is always desirable to collect behavioural information through observing behaviour in real-life, naturalistic settings. However, it is not always possible to do this. Whilst it is quite feasible unobtrusively to observe small children playing in the school playground, it is more difficult to blend in to a group of delinquent adolescents whilst they go about their daily business! Although any departure from observations in naturalistic settings reduces the validity of the data collected, it is sometimes necessary to create artificial situations. Role-play assessments have been used successfully with groups of adolescents (Beck, Forehand, Neeper and Baskin 1982). Semi-structured scripts are used to create situations which the young person is asked to deal with. For example, a situation could be arranged to assess how the young person deals with interpersonal conflict. One advantage of this technique is that it allows the practitioner to remain in control of the situation. It also has therapeutic value, allowing adolescents to explore new ways of responding to situations. Caution is needed, however, in generalizing observations from this type of assessment strategy (Bellack, Hersen and Lamparski 1979).

Formulation

When sufficient information has been collected, or there is no time to collect further information, it is necessary to summarize and interpret the assessment findings into a formulation. This can be a difficult task, especially if some of the assessment findings appear contradictory. Nevertheless, it is essential if the assessment findings are to inform effectively the development and implementation of effective management and intervention strategies.

The formulation is a hypothesis specifying the factors that appear to instigate and maintain aggressive and violent behaviour in any one case, suggesting possible strategies for intervention. There will always be more than one possible hypothesis. The aim is to begin with the one that is most plausible, one which best summarizes the assessment findings. This can then be used as the basis for developing intervention plans. The technique of *functional analysis* is especially useful for formulating behavioural problems, such as aggressive and violent behaviour (Hollin 1990). One of the main concerns of functional analysis is to identify the contingencies that help to maintain a particular behaviour, using the A:B:C model discussed earlier in this chapter. The analysis aims to specify the extent to which the individual finds particular behaviours rewarding, in the sense that the behaviour produces consequences that he or she finds desirable. Such behaviours are more likely to be repeated. It seems important to point out that a behaviour which the individual experiences as rewarding may, to an observer, appear to produce largely unpleasant consequences. Take, for example, a boy with a history of violent behaviour who violently assaults another boy whilst being watched by several of his peers. As a result of this behaviour he may receive a variety of unpleasant consequences. Thus, he gets battered and bruised, experiencing physical pain; his clothes are torn and muddied, for which he is reprimanded by his parents; and he is apprehended by a teacher, receives a detention, and therefore misses out on some of his leisure time. However, if in the eyes of his peers he won the fight, the positive consequences arising from enhanced kudos and self-esteem may well outweigh all of the undesirable consequences. As such, he is more likely to go on to fight again. It is easy to see how a vicious cycle of events may be set in train, with adults becoming more punitive in their attempts to stop the boy fighting, but having little or no success. Eventually, in desperation, the boy may be expelled from school, perhaps serving to exacerbate the problem.

This is not say that a functional analysis, followed by an intervention programme, will always produce behavioural change. What it will do, however, is help to identify potentially useful management and intervention strategies, generate creative solutions to the problem, and increase the possibility of a positive outcome. Functional analysis is particularly ideal for developing individualized interventions, recognizing the unique set of factors that contribute to the development and maintenance of an individual's aggressive and violent behaviour.

Monitoring and follow-up

One of the consequences of adopting a scientist-practitioner approach to assessment and intervention through the use of functional analysis, is that the intervention is construed as a form of hypothesis-testing. If the hypothesis is incorrect or inaccurate, the effectiveness of management and intervention strategies will be reduced. As such, it is important to monitor and evaluate the young person's response to the intervention. Monitoring also helps to ensure that the intervention is delivered as planned, referred to as *treatment integrity* (Kazdin 1987). Even if the hypothesis is correct, an intervention programme will only be successful if it is rigorously and properly implemented. In practice, however, it appears that few intervention programmes are evaluated (Blakely and Davidson 1984).

Monitoring is also important when no intervention is implemented but where concern exists that the young person's behaviour may further deteriorate, becoming more aggressive and violent. Take, for example, a child displaying aggressive behaviour within the context of school. Following an assessment the decision may be taken to allow the child to continue attending the same school, providing his or her behaviour does not deteriorate. Failure to monitor the child's behaviour would allow such a deterioration to go undetected, thereby placing other children at risk.

Monitoring also serves an important role within large institutions, such as schools, where bullying can be a significant problem (Smith and Sharp 1994), residential facilities (Gentry and Ostapiuk 1989), and secure settings (McDougall, Clark, and Fisher 1994). Efforts to reduce the number of violent incidents can only be effective if information is available about the frequency, type and pattern of incidents. Systems of record-keeping should be developed so that an overview of incidents can be maintained. Changes in organizational policy and practice can then be evaluated. For example, Epps (1990) showed that the implementation of organizational policies and practices for the management of violent behaviour within a Youth Treatment Centre helped to reduce the severity of injuries sustained by staff as a result of violent assault.

CHAPTER 5

Psycho-Social Approaches to the Understanding and Reduction of Violence in Young People

James McGuire

The extent of aggression and violence

Society appears to find it very difficult to retain a reasonable sense of proportion concerning the problem of juvenile crime. Over recent years, a small number of highly publicized cases of serious or persistent offending by young people has created an atmosphere of considerable alarm. The most notorious incidents have involved juveniles who are reported to have committed large numbers of property crimes (mainly car theft) over a short period, on the one hand; or relatively rare instances of extremely violent crimes on the other. Seized upon as an issue of acute public anxiety by the media, these reports have in turn led to concerted justifications for 'firm' government action.

Examination of official statistics and of more systematic research, however, suggests that there is not, as has been implied by the media, an epidemic of lawlessness amongst the young. Indeed in the decade between 1981 and 1991, there was a steady decline in rates of juvenile crime in both absolute and relative terms. Between these years the total number of recorded crimes for the 10–17 year age group fell from 230,700 to 149,000 for males and from 42,200 to 33,500 for females (Home Affairs Committee 1993). Only a proportion (approximately half) of this decline could be attributed to demographic changes. Turning to still more recent figures, the offending rate per 100,000 population for young males fell from 7700 in 1985 to 5300 in 1993; that for females fell from 1700 to 1400 (Gulbenkian Foundation 1995). Between 1985 and 1993 the number of known offenders in the 10–17 age group fell by 39 per cent for males and 25 per cent for females (*op cit*).

However, running counter to these trends, there does appear to be a worrying rise in violent crime by juveniles. Within the age group 10–17, the rate per 100,000 rose from 267 in 1985 to 324 in 1993. In the latter year, violence against the person constituted 9 per cent of offences committed by young males, and 12 per cent of those committed by females. James (1995) has calculated that the proportion of all offences against the person committed by juveniles rose at an accelerating pace, particularly during the period 1987–93. Note that for all offences including violence there is a marked gender differential, males outnumbering females in a ratio of approximately 5:1; physical violence is largely, though not exclusively, a male preserve.

The evidence of the Home Affairs Committee (1993) demonstrated that there are some young offenders who commit sizeable numbers of crimes. For example amongst 17-year-olds, a mere 1 per cent of those born in 1973 was responsible for 60 per cent of crimes. Figures such as these have been used to support the view that 'selective incapacitation' of a small number of high-frequency offenders could yield a substantial reduction in the age-related crime rate. It may, however, be that the fraction of total crime which is attributable to a recidivistic minority has been over-estimated. Recent work by Hagell and Newburn (1994) illuminates this issue. These authors examined a sample of 531 young 're-offenders' arrested three or more times during 1992, and attempted to identify the most 'persistent'. Three separate definitions of the latter were used: (1) simple frequency of arrests over a one-year period; (2) frequency of known and alleged offending over a single three-month period; and (3) individuals aged 12–14 who had committed three imprisonable offences, one of them whilst under supervision (proposed Home Office criteria for 'secure training orders'). Focusing on 193 young people from a Midlands-based sample, comparisons were made for the extent of overlap between definitions. While 36 young offenders were 'persistent' according to one or other of the criteria, only three were common to all definitions. There was no difference between these sub-groups and the main sample in terms of types or seriousness of offending; they were no more likely than their peers to have committed offences of violence.

Statistics like these are essential for furnishing an overall picture of the extent of unlawful behaviour. However, in attempting to understand the potential problems of aggression and violence amongst the young, it has been argued that a focus on delinquency statistics alone will result in a misleading picture. A number of research studies have turned attention, for example, towards school bullying, violence in families, or serious conduct disorders shown amongst clinical populations. Thus Farrington (1994) has argued for examining 'official' delinquency alongside, or as only one manifestation of, other forms of anti-social behaviour amongst the young. Recorded offences of violence are thus best viewed, in developmental terms, in the context of general conduct problems which may be present in children and adolescents prior to any onset of known illegal activity *per se*.

The psycho-social perspective

In this chapter, a perspective is offered for the understanding of youth violence which draws upon social-cognitive learning theory. This is a coherent framework within which aggressive behaviour is approached primarily as a learned phenomenon (Bandura 1973). Recently, the original behavioural basis of this framework has been augmented by a growing body of research on the role of cognitive factors (Crick and Dodge 1994; Eron 1986). The chapter will be divided into two principal sections, the first on understanding violence amongst young people. The second will present a survey of research on treatment approaches.

Before proceeding, it will be helpful to clarify the meaning of some frequently used terms as there are often confusions in this field due to the interchanging use of words whose meanings are best kept distinct. It is difficult to find any terms in this area which do not carry moral or value-laden implications. Usage of words also differs according to the standpoints of perpetrators, victims, and observers of actions. To complicate things further, words are often used both as descriptions of behaviour and of assumed underlying thoughts or feelings.

Here, use of the word *violence* is reserved to denote '...the forceful infliction of physical injury' (Blackburn 1993, p.210), though others have used it in a broader sense to include '...behaviour by people or against people liable to cause physical or psychological harm' (Gulbenkian Foundation 1995, p.10). The word *aggression*, by contrast, is used more loosely to describe harmful, threatening or antagonistic behaviour and its accompanying mental attitude and emotional state. It is customary to subdivide it into two main sorts: *instrumental*, where threats or injury facilitate achievement of non-injurious goals, as, for example, in robbery; and *expressive*, in which harm to a victim reduces an unpleasant internal emotional state in the aggressor (Berkowitz 1993; Blackburn 1993). Note, however, that the two often co-exist. *Aggressiveness* is then conceptualized as '...a relatively persistent readiness to become aggressive in a variety of different situations' (Berkowitz 1993, p.21).

Understanding adolescent aggression

Adoption of a psycho-social perspective on aggression and violence has a number of advantages, principally in the opportunities it creates for integrating evidence from sociologically-based and psychologically-based research. Regrettably, these have often been pursued in largely segregated traditions. Within the social-cognitive-learning perspective an emphasis is placed on key environmental and socialization factors, but more explicitly on their impact on the developing individual's patterns of adaptation and adjustment, interpersonal perceptions, and social-interactional style.

One major source of information concerning child and adolescent aggression has been research in the field of developmental psychopathology and criminology. This is an attempt to account for adult distress or proscribed behaviour in terms of background histories and developmental processes (Loeber and LeBlanc 1990). There are now numerous studies which have tracked the formation of anti-social behaviours by following a cohort of children or families over periods ranging up to thirty years. Several sets of results are available from longitudinal studies of this kind conducted in various parts of the world (Farrington 1995a).

For the most part, those factors which are associated with manifestation of aggressiveness are similar to those associated with offending behaviour in general. Most individuals who are repeatedly convicted of crimes are 'non-specialists' in that they commit a variety of types of offence. In the Cambridge Study of Delinquent Development, for example, '…the causes of aggression and violence were essentially the same as the causes of persistent and extreme antisocial, delinquent and criminal behaviour' (Farrington 1995a, p.945). For this reason most accounts of aggression are set in the context of the wider study of anti-social behaviour.

Stability of aggressiveness

A central question in this field concerns the relative stability or continuity of patterns of aggressiveness between infancy, middle childhood, adolescence and adulthood. Some of the strongest evidence pertaining to this has been assembled by Olweus (1979, 1988) who reported a review of 16 longitudinal studies examining levels of consistency in aggressive behaviour over periods ranging from one to 21 years. The dependent variables in these studies were based not on self-report, but on nominations or ratings of aggressiveness by peers, teachers or other observers. A total of 24 correlation coefficients was extracted and their inter-relationships plotted on a regression line. The results showed an impressive degree of consistency of observed aggressiveness over time, though inevitably the correlations decreased with increasing time-intervals. For example mean correlations across one year were 0.76; two years, 0.69; but in one 21-year follow-up, 0.36.

For intermediate time-intervals of say ten years or so, childhood aggressiveness appears to be indicative of likely future problems. For example, the presence of aggressive classroom behaviour at an early age has been shown to be a good predictor of delinquency in the teenage years (Spivack and Cianci 1987). Across a more limited time-span of five or six years, studies have shown that aggressive behaviour in middle childhood is strongly predictive of conduct disorder in adolescence (Farrington and West 1993; Loeber and Stouthamer-

Loeber 1987) especially if coupled with peer rejection (Coie, Lochman, Terry and Hyman 1992).

Other evidence concerning the continuity of aggressiveness has come from studies of the so-called 'HIA' syndrome (Hyperactivity-Impulsivity-Attention Deficit). This is a cluster of apparently inter-related problems shown by a small proportion of children, who appear restless, have problems in attention-concentration, are prone to daring and risky activities, and whom parents describe as difficult to manage (though it should be noted that the inter-connectedness of these problems as a classifiable 'syndrome' is a matter of some controversy). Continuity of these difficulties and their links to later conduct disorder have been difficult to interpret, as some features of HIA are also features of conduct disorder (Farrington 1995b). However, there is evidence that HIA is associated with later involvement in delinquency independently of concurrent behaviour disorders (Farrington, Loeber and van Kammen 1990). Factors present in HIA have also been shown to be associated with aggressiveness, though these patterns are not firmly established (Farrington 1995b).

On the basis of these findings, it can be concluded with reasonable confidence that there is evidence of some continuity of patterns of aggressiveness from childhood through adolescence into young adulthood. Such findings raise the prospect, if key operative variables can be isolated, of early identification and prediction of future vulnerability and risk, with potential implications for preventive work. The limitations of this have been recognized, as the power of predictive methods does not always improve satisfactorily on chance (Loeber and Dishion 1987). However, a more recent review has shown that some factors prove better than others in this regard, and that when a number of factors are combined in a prediction scale, '...predictive efficiency increases dramatically' (Loeber 1990, p.8).

Given the above observations of a certain degree of stability in aggressiveness, the question has naturally arisen as to whether such patterns are inherited. Some authors such as Wilson and Herrnstein (1985) favour a sizeable role for constitutional and genetic factors in crime. This view has been disputed by Gottfredson and Hirschi (1990) who assert instead that the role of heritability is '...substantively trivial' (p.61).

In the field of developmental psychopathology, a consensus has emerged on this point. The possible role of inherited characteristics is acknowledged, but few researchers accept that they play a direct causal part in the development of criminality. Instead, it is considered that what is inherited may be a set of dispositions collectively called 'temperament'. This refers to a number of quite basic features of behavioural and emotional responsiveness, such as activity level, attentiveness, adaptiveness to new situations, quality and intensity of mood expression, distress-proneness, or distractibility (Chess and Thomas 1990; Rothbart, Derryberry and Posner 1994). It has been argued that one form of inherited temperamental variable, 'impulsive unsocialised sensation seeking', underpins the development of antisocial personality traits in adulthood (Zuckerman 1994). That individual differences in some of these variables are apparent very soon after birth and prior to any significant learning experiences is beyond doubt, and there is evidence that they are maintained into the first few months and perhaps first few years of life. But for such differences to remain consistent, environmental factors probably play a decisive facilitatory role. For example, these patterns, in conjunction with poor-quality parenting, are associated with poor school attainment and troublesome behaviour in later childhood and early adolescence. Calkins and Fox (1994) have put forward a tentative model of relationships between biologically-driven temperamental patterns and socialization processes in behavioural development.

Thus, while findings such as those of Olweus (1988) regarding the consistency of aggressiveness over time are fairly striking, evidence for the long-term consistency of features of temperament, even using a relatively global 'easy-difficult' continuum, is less cohesive and convincing (Chess and Thomas 1990). The part played by biological roots notwithstanding, by far the bulk of evidence currently available supports the general contention of '...the superiority of social over genetic explanations of delinquency and crime' (Gold 1987, p.67).

Family interactions

A substantial body of research now links observed patterns of continuity in aggressiveness to socialization experiences within families (Rutter 1985). These processes themselves are almost certainly influenced by large-scale environmental factors, including social deprivation. In the Newcastle Thousand Family study, Kolvin, Miller, Fleeting and Kolvin (1988) found that there was a strong association between multiple deprivation in childhood and later criminal conduct. 'Multiple deprivation' was defined as a cluster of factors including overcrowding and economic dependency, marital instability and poor parental care. The interactions of such external and internal pressures are themselves complex, but their combination places families under stress and so leads to increased risks of difficulty in child socialization. Levels of deprivation were associated with numbers of convictions, particularly in the mid-teenage years. These results notwithstanding it must be remembered that by no means all of those who grow up in adverse circumstances later break the law. For example, just under 50 per cent of those designated 'multiply-deprived' in the Newcastle study were *not* later recorded in the criminal statistics; and even within the most deprived group the rate of violent offending was just 3 per cent.

The predominant factors *within* families which contribute to the development of longer-term aggressiveness and the risk of violence are in child-rearing and parenting processes (Farrington 1995a, 1995b; Gulbenkian Foundation

1995; Snyder and Patterson 1987). Against a general background of social deprivation, low income and poor housing, indices identified in the studies can be considered as forming several clusters. The first includes the presence of criminal parents and of siblings with behaviour problems (which are themselves likely to be causally interconnected). The second relates to the everyday behaviour of the parents or care-givers. Parental conflict, poor or inconsistent supervision, and physical or emotional neglect are associated in general terms with later overall risks for delinquency. There is also evidence that some parents provide little reinforcement of children's pro-social behaviours, whilst at the same time giving direct reinforcement of coercive behaviours. Thus children progressively learn that their own aversive behaviour 'works' in terminating unwanted intrusions by parents (Patterson and Yoerger 1993). This may serve to explain why assaultive adolescents have been found to have significantly lower rates of positive communication with their families than do other adolescent groups, and why their relations with peers are so relatively aggressive in nature (Blake et al. 1989).

The third cluster is more expressly associated with later aggressiveness, and includes cruel and authoritarian discipline, use of physical methods of control, and shaming and emotional degradation of children. Findings collated by the Gulbenkian Foundation (1995) are virtually unanimous in this respect: research '…emphatically confirms that harsh and humiliating discipline are implicated in the development of anti-social and violent behaviour' (p.134). These findings are concordant with others concerning the long-term impact upon young people of childhood maltreatment, and the extent to which there is inter-generational continuity in patterns of physical and sexual abuse. Research on relationships between early experiences of harsh discipline or physical abuse and later aggressiveness has been reviewed by Lewis, Mallouh and Webb (1989). While results of some studies have been equivocal concerning such a connection (see Widom 1989), the balance of available findings suggests that '…a childhood history of severe abuse and of witnessing family violence is significantly associated with ongoing violent behaviors in adulthood' (Lewis et al., p.710).

All of the above findings are consistent with a psycho-social model which posits direct experiences and learning processes as fundamental in the growth of tendencies towards anti-social, and especially aggressive, attitudes and behaviour. The family is the most powerful single agent of socialization in this respect. As Loeber (1990) has stated, '…factors in the family are among the best predictors of later delinquency in offspring…' (p.17). Other important influences come from adolescent peer-groups and the media, but neither of these approaches family environment in the strength of its effects.

There is tentative evidence that patterns of anti-social behaviour linked to aggressiveness make an earlier appearance than other more 'socialized' forms of delinquency. Some research has distinguished separate pathways leading to different types of offending (Loeber 1990; Stattin and Magnusson 1995). What is known as the 'aggressive-versatile' path begins earlier, with conduct problems appearing in the pre-school years, more evidence of impulsivity, poor peer relationships, and later delinquency more likely to include offences of violence. The 'non-aggressive' path appears in later childhood or adolescence, and is characterized by individuals who are less impulsive, better integrated socially, and with more specialized patterns of property or drug-related offences.

The studies cited so far have reported on factors which in some way serve to elevate the risk that an individual will become aggression-prone. A portion of research, however, has focused instead upon the role of 'protective' or 'resilience' factors. For example, it is known that even in unfavourable circumstances, a proportion of the exposed individuals will not resort to antisocial behaviour. Important protective factors identified in longitudinal studies have included being first-born, coming from a small family, high IQ, a high level of caretaker attention, and good maternal health. However, protective factors are not always simply the inverse of risk factors, and the interactions between the two may be quite complex. For example, social isolation may be a protective factor against some forms of offending though not against other kinds of social dysfunction (Farrington 1995b). Furthermore, the route from delineated risk factors to the actual occurrence of violent acts may not be a linear one and may not be uni-directional; reversals may occur along the pathway (Lösel and Bliesener 1994; Rutter 1989).

Models of differences between individuals' proneness to discrete types of aggression are still at an early stage. Concerning adolescents who commit sexual assaults for example, cross-sectional comparative studies appear to indicate that they may have experienced more violence from parents than other groups of aggressive juveniles (Ford and Linney 1995). They are also reported to be more isolated and to have poor social relationships with both family and peers (Vizard, Monck and Misch 1995). Provisional models have been forwarded to account for this specific form of assaultive behaviour in adolescents (e.g., Becker and Kaplan 1988) but to date this remains a relatively unexplored area. One question often asked is whether sexual abusers have themselves been victims of abuse; this is certainly not uniformly found and the issue remains unresolved (Vizard *et al.* 1995).

All of this highlights the crucial importance of individualized assessment of young people in difficulty. The results of longitudinal studies are invaluable in having mapped out the types of factors and processes implicated in the development of aggressive behaviour and some of their causal inter-relationships. But in attempting to work with any single young person who is acting aggressively or has committed a violent offence, we must still investigate why *this* individual has behaved in *this* unique fashion on *this* occasion.

Situational and cognitive factors

The studies discussed so far demonstrate the existence of some continuities in socialization which are linked to the appearance of aggression and violence in young people. To obtain a fuller understanding of such behaviour, this background must be supplemented by information on immediate precursors of aggression. This has come from laboratory and field research in social psychology (Berkowitz 1993). That work shows that there is an enormous range of situational influences upon aggression: including basic stimulus conditions such as heat and noise, a wide array of personal frustrations and stressors, as well as definitive events like provocations or threats. (Note, however, that some authors have expressed scepticism concerning laboratory research and insist that it is futile to attempt to distinguish a propensity to aggression from other forms of criminality (Gottfredson and Hirschi 1993)). Onto these must be superimposed audience or self-image enhancement effects, group norms concerning aggression, and wider cultural values promoting violence for example through glamorization of a 'macho' image.

However, studies of this kind still tell us little about the processes within individuals which make the emergence or maintenance of aggressive behaviour more likely. Few external events lead uniformly to aggression. It is now widely recognized that an individual's cognitive appraisal of an event, and the meaning which he or she attributes to it, is a prime determinant of the subsequent behavioural response. The component mechanisms of this have recently been elaborated in an information-processing model of social maladjustment and aggression-proneness (Crick and Dodge 1994). In this model, reactions to an external event are analyzed in terms of a sequence of cognitive processes, comprising six stages: encoding, representation, goal clarification, response construction, response decision, and enactment. Research reviewed by Akhtar and Bradley (1991) and by Kendall (1993) shows that aggressive children when compared with non-aggressive controls, (1) encode a narrower range of environmental cues; (2) selectively attend to aggressive cues; (3) attribute hostile intent to others, especially in ambiguous situations; (4) more readily label internal states of arousal as anger; (5) generate fewer potential alternative solutions to problems; (6) select action-oriented rather than reflective solutions; (7) possess a more limited range of interactional skills; and (8) manifest an 'egocentric' perspective in social problem-solving. Patterning of these deficits will vary between individuals, and it is unlikely that all of them will be present in any one person. It is vital to identify which if any of these processes is involved in individual patterns of aggressiveness. The precise implications of this model, while they appear highly promising, await verification from further research.

On the basis of this accumulated evidence it is possible to build a working theory of the development of aggression, which is conceptualized not in terms of direct causal factors but of risk factors. The presence of such factors is thought to have a cumulative and interactive effect, though the nature of this may not be simply additive. Risk factors may interplay with each other and with protective factors in as yet not fully understood ways. Integrative models of this kind have been proposed for example by Patterson (1986, 1992; Patterson and Yoerger 1993) and by Loeber (1990). It is postulated that the causal patterns detected in the longitudinal studies have a developmental impact on the child's cognitive appraisals, social-cognitive skills and typical modes of construing and problem-solving in interpersonal relationships.

But once again it must be emphasized that all of the above research findings, however useful, result in generalizations. Whatever the extent of empirical support, the effects are discerned usually across very large samples. Any single individual may display a pattern which departs markedly from observed trends, and this must be borne in mind when undertaking assessments, planning interventions or delivering services to young people or families in difficulty.

Management and treatment

The research just summarized indicates that a major role in the causation of aggression and violence in young people must be assigned to factors of psycho-social origin. One fairly direct implication of such a viewpoint is the possibility that it may therefore be feasible to rectify such behaviours by psychosocial interventions. The remainder of this chapter will be devoted to a brief survey of methods for the reduction of aggressive tendencies amongst young people. A standard conceptual framework for interventions is to classify them either as *primary* (population-based and preventive), *secondary* (focused on high-risk groups) or *tertiary* (treatment-centred) (Guerra, Tolan and Hammond 1994). Evidence will be considered here in three sub-sections which overlap but depart slightly from this tripartite scheme. The first will focus on individu-ally-targetted interventions; the second on the role of parent and family-based work; and the third will turn to the allied question of long-term prevention.

Two general points are worth noting in advance. The first is that there is now fairly robust evidence concerning the efficacy of psychological therapies for amelioration of a wide spectrum of behavioural and psychological problems. This conclusion draws upon the findings of Lipsey and Wilson (1993) who surveyed the results of a total of 302 meta-analyses of outcome studies of educational and psychotherapeutic interventions. Regarding the effectiveness of psychotherapy in reducing the problems of young people, a recent major review also provides strong support for its value (Kazdin 1994a).

The second point, restricting attention to delinquency, is that there is also a substantial quantity of evidence for the effectiveness of a variety of interven-tions for reducing criminal recidivism (Garrett 1985; Hollin 1993; Lipsey

1992, 1995). The approaches which show the largest and most consistent effects in these reviews are those employing behavioural, cognitive, and multi-modal cognitive-behavioural methods.

Prior to implementing any form of intervention, of course, it is essential to undertake as comprehensive as possible an assessment of any child or adolescent. This must include collecting background information on family and other social relationships; and developmental information on problem behaviours, personal distress, and involvement of child-care and other health and social services agencies, as well as police contacts. Assessment must include direct interviews with the young person, and part of this should focus, subject to the collaboration of the client, on characteristic incidents and their patterns over time. Where feasible and agreed, family members or other influential figures in the young person's life should also be seen. This exploratory work must be complemented by reports of other professionals involved. It can also be extended and supplemented by use of a range of structured assessments, including problem checklists, self-rating scales and questionnaires, or other psychometric inventories. A massive range of these is now available for both general assessment purposes, and also, for example, to assess impulsiveness, hostility, anger experiences, self-control, self-esteem, interpersonal problem-solving, social interaction skills, or socio-moral reasoning (for other examples see Kazdin, 1994b).

Individual

Psychosocial interventions for reduction of aggressiveness have taken several forms: (1) social skills training to enhance abilities in positive social interaction; (2) self-instructional training for reduction of impulsivity; (3) problem-solving training directed towards social-cognitive processes thought to be conducive to aggression; (4) anger control training; and (5) programmes combining two or more of these components. In addition, some less well researched interventions, such as moral reasoning training, have yielded favourable results (at one-year follow-up) with groups of young people presenting mixed problems including aggressiveness (Arbuthnot and Gordon 1986).

Social skills training is a behaviourally-based sequence of procedures for enabling individuals to increase their abilities and effectiveness in selected interpersonal situations. It includes instructions, modelling, roleplaying, coaching and feedback. As such it has potential usefulness in work with young people as they learn to cope with new social encounters, and especially if there is evidence that they have difficulties in this area. Research suggests this is often the case with those who in some circumstances resort to violence. The value of such methods has been shown in a number of studies with young offenders (Chandler 1973; Sarason 1978). Elder, Edelstein and Narick (1979) used the approach with four adolescents with histories of aggressiveness. Training focused on behaviours in selected situations where aggression had previously occurred. The clients showed improvements both in these skills and in their general social behaviour, and three of the group maintained these changes at a nine-month follow up.

Goldstein (1986) reviewed 30 studies of psychological skill training with aggressive young people and concluded that there was clear evidence of effectiveness for increasing interactive skill. It was less clear at that stage, however, that enhanced social skills transferred to other situations or led to reductions in aggressiveness.

More recently, Bierman, Miller and Stabb (1987) described the results of a social skills programme for boys aged six to eight who acted aggressively and who were rejected by their peers. The children were randomly assigned to three conditions. One consisted of instructions on social skill alone. In the second, adherence to rules was reinforced by a system of tokens. The third was a combined 'instructions plus prohibitions' condition. Whereas the first condition improved pro-social behaviours but did not affect negative behaviours, the second decreased negative behaviours but had no impact on positive skills. The combined condition achieved both objectives of increasing pro-social and reducing aversive acts; this was maintained at a one-year follow-up.

Self-instructional training is a form of work designed to modify the 'things children say to themselves': the automatic cognitive events which play a regulatory role in everyday behaviour. The importance of incorporating methods which address cognitive factors in the design of rehabilitation programmes is underlined in a meta-analysis by Izzo and Ross (1990). This showed that intervention programmes containing cognitive ingredients, which centred on the thinking of participants, had significantly better outcomes than ones which did not.

Acquisition of new cognitive skills is a pivotal method in the cognitive-behavioural approach, and a number of different techniques have been evaluated for this purpose, including self-instructional training. The use of modified self-talk to reduce the impulsiveness of children was demonstrated in an early experiment by Meichenbaum and Goodman (1971), though their results were very task-specific. Reviewing the early literature in this field, Kendall and Braswell (1985) noted that there was encouraging evidence of treatment effectiveness, but that procedures needed to be adapted to the age, verbal ability level, and other features of individual children. A combination of self-instructional and problem-solving exercises was used by Lochman, Burch, Curry and Lampron (1984) to achieve short-term reductions in disruptive and aggressive behaviour in 11-year-old boys, though results were more mixed at a 7-month follow-up (Lochman 1985; Lochman and Lampron 1988). More successful outcomes were reported by McCullough, Huntsinger and Nay (1977) who described a single-case study of the treatment of an aggressive 16-year-old boy. Snyder and White (1979) obtained positive results with a group of behaviourally-disturbed adolescents; decreases in impulsiveness were maintained at a six-week follow-up.

Social problem-solving training is a more elaborate form of cognitive intervention, in which an attempt is made to foster interpersonal problem-solving skills believed on the basis of background research to be conducive to avoidance of conflicts and to reduce risks of aggression. A 12-session programme of this type was tested by Guerra and Slaby (1990). This well-designed study employed random assignment and blind rating by social supervisors. The clients were 15–18-year-old offenders (n = 120, equally divided by gender), incarcerated for offences of serious violence. Significant changes were found in problem-solving skills, beliefs supportive of aggression, and in aggressive, impulsive, and inflexible behaviour for the treatment group. This group also had the lowest rate of parole violation at a 24-month follow-up, but the difference was not statistically significant.

Overall, in the majority of studies in this area, interventions have typically been of relatively brief duration, comprising only a few (e.g. 6 to 12) sessions. It has been recommended that more intensive interventions are required, and that they should also contain procedures for promoting generalization (Michelson 1987). Reviewers of this area have also proposed that amalgamating methods in a 'multi-modal' package will produce superior outcomes (Hughes 1988; Kendall 1993; and see below).

A systematic review of 64 outcome studies utilizing these methods showed beneficial effects of cognitive-behavioural treatments for a variety of maladaptive behaviours including aggression; though the impact was more marked for personality and cognitive variables than for behaviour (Durlak, Fuhrman and Lampman 1991). Nevertheless, there was evidence that impulsiveness and aggressiveness can be significantly reduced. These authors also endorsed the view that '…cognitive process appear critical in determining treatment responsiveness' (*op cit*, p.210). A recent less technical review of methods in this area with useful case illustrations is provided by Kazdin (1994c).

Anger control training is one of the most widely-used variants of cognitive-behavioural work. It employs self-instructional methods but they are conjoined with relaxation training in a model referred to as 'stress inoculation'. Individuals experiencing difficulties in self-management of angry aggression are given assistance to recognize its onset, and to retain control through simultaneous self-regulation of cognitions and levels of physiological arousal.

Initially encouraging though limited results with aggressive adolescents were presented by Schlichter and Horan (1981). More convincing evidence was provided by Dangel, Deschner and Rasp (1989) who worked with aggressive, emotionally disturbed children aged 10–17 in a residential treatment centre. Their package, though fairly minimal (six hours duration), had observable effects on nine out of twelve participants. The potential value of this approach has been endorsed by other results from work with young offenders convicted of serious assaults. McGuire (1995) found that poor self-control of anger was a feature of their offences in a majority of cases; though hostile attitudes, condoning aggression, also played a part.

The most extensive trials of anger-control training with adolescents have been conducted by Feindler and her associates (Feindler and Ecton 1986; Feindler and Fremouw 1983; Feindler Marriott and Iwata 1984). In a series of both single-case and group-comparison studies these authors have applied this training in a variety of settings. The best results reported, however, with aggressive adolescent in-patients exhibiting severe behaviour disorders (Feindler, Ecton, Kingsley and Dubey 1986), were obtained when anger-control sessions were combined with assertion and social skills training. Thus reductions in aggressive responses were paralleled by increases in appropriate social behaviours. Follow-up information indicated that 90 per cent of participants were successfully discharged.

Combined programmes. Evidence has gradually accumulated that single-component interventions, while effective, are usually restricted in their impact to those 'treatment targets' on which they are focused. A favoured strategy, therefore, has been to assemble a number of methods in integrated or 'multi-modal' intervention programmes. For example in a small-scale study Hains (1989) worked with four youths aged 15–17 with convictions for violent offences. A ten-session programme was run which contained elements of self-instruction and problem-solving training. Outcomes were measured in terms of problem-solving abilities, self-reports of conflict management, and recorded institutional behaviour (episodes of room confinement). Substantial gains were made for three of the participants providing convergent evidence of the effects of the training.

On a much grander scale, possibly the most complex and advanced approach to reduction of violent behaviour in young offenders to date is the Aggression Replacement Training (ART) programme of Goldstein and his colleagues. The rationale for the development of this work is based partly in a recognition of the growing problem of juvenile gang violence in the United States (Goldstein and Soriano 1994). ART is a synthesis of three types of methods: social skills training ('skillstreaming'), self-instructional/anger-control training; and moral reasoning enhancement. The programme is organized in a curriculum of ten weekly three-hour sessions but this format has evolved over time (Goldstein and Keller 1987; Goldstein *et al.* 1989; Goldstein *et al.* 1994). Its effects have been evaluated in separate experiments in institutions and in the community. In the latter, participants were compared with a control sample on re-arrest rates over a six-month period; the corresponding figures were 30 per cent and 43 per cent. However, ART is conceptualized not simply as an individually-focused form of work, but also as having a broader remit in work with families. In another condition, parents and siblings of ART clients also took part in sessions. The six-month re-arrest rate in this case was 15 per cent. The programme has also been run with members of intact violent juvenile gangs in New York. Re-arrest rates for ART participants and a control group over an eight-month tracking period were 13 per cent and 52 per cent respectively.

Family-based interventions

As indicated previously, family variables, especially those associated with child socialization and parenting styles, are suggested by research to be probably the most powerful contributory causes of later aggressiveness. Some of the findings just described exemplify the potency of involving parents in interventions; or indeed of making parent behaviour itself the principal focus of interventive work.

Parent training. The possibility of training parents in improved child management skills has been explored in a number of studies since the early 1970s. Using single-case methodology with two families in which parents had been physically abusive towards their children, Denicola and Sandler (1980) trained the parents in self-control and coping skills. Changes were obtained both in the parents' behaviour and that of the children, showing more pro-social and less aversive behaviour which was sustained at a three-month follow-up. Working with a larger sample (34 mother–child pairs) and a much longer time-frame, Baum and Forehand (1981) evaluated the effects of a training programme which taught parents constructive and non-abusive child management skills. Improvements were obtained in quality of parenting, and in attitudes to children; for the children, compliance with parental requests increased and deviant behaviour decreased. These gains were maintained at follow-up intervals ranging from one year to 4.5 years. The study did not, however, include a control-group.

By far the most extensive work in this area has been undertaken by Patterson and his colleagues at the Oregon Social Learning Center (Bank *et al.* 1991; Bank, Patterson and Reid 1987; Reid and Patterson 1976). In this long-term project, parents are taught improved family management skills in a social learning approach which employs a mixture of behavioural management techniques, problem-solving and negotiation. The average length of training was 18 sessions. Outcomes have been evaluated using observation methods, parent reports and, for older children, law violations, in a series of studies using follow-up periods of up to three years, with generally positive results including reduction of child aggressiveness. Similarly positive findings were obtained in a community-based replication of the OSLC studies by Fleischman and Szykula (1981), though it should again be noted that in this study there was no control group.

Functional Family Therapy. One of the most effective intervention studies to date for reduction of delinquency in general was that reported by Klein, Alexander and Parsons (1977). These authors described the results of a form of 'behavioural-systems' or functional family therapy which involved determining which were the commonest sources of conflict between parents and children. Parent–child pairs were then trained in a cycle of problem-identification, negotiation and conflict resolution skills. In a controlled experimental design, this intervention proved effective for lowering levels of conflict in families, and for significantly reducing delinquency amongst juveniles, over two-year follow-up periods. In a longer-term follow-up, Gordon, Graves and Arbuthnot (1995) have reported lasting effects of the intervention, resulting in reduced criminal behaviour in adulthood (recidivism rates of 8.7% for experimentals, and 40.9% for controls). While only a small proportion of this sample had initially committed violent offences, this programme draws upon essentially the same skills-training and problem-solving methods as have been utilized in other studies summarized here. The methods employed in these studies and details of their implementation have been described by Gordon and Arbuthnot (1987; see also Morton and Ewald 1987). Miller and Prinz (1990) categorized the foregoing methods and others under a general heading of 'social learning family interventions', and recommended them as '...the treatment of choice for changing debilitating coercive parent–child interactions typically observed in families with conduct-disordered children' (*op cit*, p.301). They also advocated a number of directions for improving treatment compliance and effectiveness. A recent overview of the applicability of these methods with family violence is provided by Feindler and Becker (1994).

Evidence that a consolidated individual-plus-family approach is superior to either alone has come from a study by Kazdin, Siegel and Bass (1992). Here problem-solving skills training and parent management training were compared with the two combined in a random-assignment experiment with 97 children (all but two of them boys) aged 7–13 who had been referred to a psychiatric clinic for aggressive and antisocial behaviour. The work was conducted by specially trained clinic staff who were provided with a manual for the purpose, but session contents were adapted to meet the needs of each client. Significant improvements were obtained in both child and parent functioning, and at one-year follow-up the problem behaviours of a majority of the children were reduced to within a normative 'non-clinical' range.

More impressive findings still, and with a longer follow-up period averaging four years, have been reported by Borduin *et al.* (1995) for the effects of 'multisystemic therapy'. This consists of a multi-faceted treatment approach involving cognitively-focused sessions with individual adolescents, combined with work on social relationships with family, peers and school. This intervention was compared with individual therapy in random-allocation design with a sample of 176 high-risk juvenile offenders aged 12 to 17, many of whom had committed violent assaults. At post-test there was significant improvement in family functioning and reductions in interpersonal conflict. At follow-up the 'multisystemic' group had a significantly lower recidivism rate than the comparison group (22.1% against 71.4%), and when arrested had committed significantly less serious offences; in particular, they were much less likely to have committed offences of violence.

Prevention

Individual and family-focused work of the sort just surveyed is invaluable for work with adjudicated young offenders or for other problems of aggression in young people. Resources for it should be expanded accordingly. However, its provision inevitably occurs after problems have developed, and ample evidence indicates that early intervention and prevention strategies may hold out the prospect of avoiding development of problems in the first place.

A number of successful preventive programmes have been mounted, including the Seattle Social Development Project (Hawkins *et al.* 1992) and the Montreal Longitudinal-Experimental Study (Tremblay *et al.* 1992). In the former, a school-based innovation (in which teachers were trained in new methods of classroom management and teaching styles) was combined with problem-solving training sessions for children, and parent training sessions within families. Two hundred children placed in this programme were followed over a four-year period (between the ages of 10 and 15) and contrasted with a large control sample. There were significant differences at the end of this time in children's views of school and family, and significantly less involvement in under-age drinking and in delinquency. In the Montreal project, groups of high-risk boys were followed between the ages of six and twelve. Between the ages of seven and nine, a randomly-assigned proportion of these boys took part in an intervention programme consisting of (1) parent training along the lines of the Oregon Social Learning Centre, outlined above; (2) social skills training sessions provided in schools. The programme was evaluated by means of self-reports and teacher and parent ratings. By age 12, the experimental-group boys had significantly better academic performance, lower levels of fighting, fewer personal difficulties, and lower rates of involvement in delinquency, than the comparison group samples.

Recently Yoshikawa (1994) has undertaken a comprehensive review of intervention studies in the area of early identification and prevention. This was focused on 'chronic' general delinquency rather than on aggression and violence as such, but the findings are invaluable for placing the methods described in the present chapter in context. The most effective programmes for long-term prevention of delinquency addressed multiple-risk factors. They included components which responded to the economic plight of families through provision of family support and education. Intervention took place in the pre-school years. Confirming some of the studies itemized above, the best strategy was a dual one of delivering services both in schools and at home, and focusing both on parenting and on cognitive variables.

Conclusions and implications

Any appraisal of existing knowledge in this area is ineluctably driven towards important questions which still need to be researched, for instance on risk prediction; the practicalities of assessment; evaluation of interventions; relationships between individual, family, and community-based work. Large-scale studies have been of immense value in this field but there is no direct mapping of causal factors discovered in cross-sectional or longitudinal research onto face-to-face work in the individual case. The question of how to bridge that gap remains unanswered. One urgent requirement is a clearer understanding of dynamic risk factors over medium-term periods between childhood and adolescence, and the development of guidelines for those working with vulnerable young people in this age-group.

It is paradoxical that in principle we already have enough knowledge to have a meaningful impact on levels of aggression, and to reduce its continuation amongst many of those for whom it has become a problem. Yet a number of damaging myths and misconceptions prevail concerning it. As regards practice, few individuals at work in the relevant professions have training in the required intervention methods. There are sizeable gaps and inadequacies in provision of appropriate services. As regards policy, at present there seems to be a lack of administrative and ultimately political will to use research findings as a basis for new departures.

This situation is not incommutable. It may be that there is now an increasing awareness of the possibility that the goal of reducing aggression and violence and the distress and suffering they create is attainable by positive means. The proposals of recent non-governmental commissions, for example by the American Psychological Association (Becker, Barham, Eron and Chen 1994) and by the Gulbenkian Foundation (1995) could yet generate a new momentum and fresh priorities for the creation of a non-violent society.

CHAPTER 6

Roots of Sexual Violence in Children and Adolescents

Colin Hawkes, Jill Ann Jenkins and Eileen Vizard

Introduction

Although the topic of sexual violence in adult males has had much professional attention the roots of sexual violence in children and adolescents has not received the same degree of interest or analysis.

This chapter will review the theoretical perspectives developed for both adult and adolescent populations in relation to the roots of sexual violence. The authors will then present a new model for understanding the origins of child and adolescent sexual violence, the *YAP Integrated Perspectives Model*. The *YAP Integrated Perspectives Model* takes into account existing models of aetiology, information from research and adds a developmental perspective unique to children and adolescents.

Definitional issues will be discussed and a suggestion will be made about a new diagnostic category for sexually aroused and abusing young people. Our model is based on the experience and data collected at the Young Abuser's Project (YAP) in London. The YAP subject sample will be described briefly.

Definitional issues and shared characteristics of sexually violent children and adolescents at the YAP

Clinically accepted definitions for sexual violence in children and adolescents have not been described in formal classificatory systems such as those developed by the American Psychiatric Association 1994 (known as DSM IV) or the International Classification of Diseases 1992 (known as ICD 10). According to DSM IV, 'Certain of the fantasies and behaviours associated with Paraphilias may begin in childhood or early adolescence but become better defined and elaborated during adolescence and early adulthood' (p.524).

Although some sexual violence is recognized as starting during the developmental years of childhood and adolescence, diagnosis of a pedophilic disorder is only possible for adolescents over 16 years and adults. Nor does the ICD 10 classificatory system acknowledge that children under the age of 16 years may have a sexual arousal disorder. Therefore, it appears that there is no formal way in which the existence of chronic sexual arousal towards other children can be described in young people under 16 years of age. This is particularly anomalous, since it is quite recently that other sexual problems in young people, for example Gender Identity Disorder of Childhood (ICD 10 1992), and Gender Identity Disorder in Children/Adolescents (APA 1994) have been acknowledged.

Clinical experience with sexually aroused and abusing children under 16 years of age suggests that an appropriate way of describing this maladaptive behaviour needs to be found urgently, since many cases are not being identified until they are in their late teens. It is our proposal, therefore, that a new diagnostic category 'Sexual Arousal Disorder of Childhood/ in Childhood' (ICD 10/ DSM IV) should be created in order to give an acceptable name to what is an unacceptable type of behaviour.

As far as clinical definitions are concerned, the concept that sexual abuse of children by older children includes any sexual interaction between an adolescent and a much younger child, whether or not force is used, appears satisfactory. For younger children, sexually abusive behaviour as discussed by Bremmer (1993), in her conceptualization of a 'continuum' of sexual problems appears to be particularly helpful with children. Bremer's (1993), developmental perspective moves from normative to inappropriate to hypersexualized to orgasm-orientated sexualized behaviours. For further discussion on the definitional issues surrounding child and adolescent sex offenders, see Vizard *et al.* (1996).

Thirty-two boys have been assessed so far at the Young Abuser's Project, ranging in age from eight to nineteen at the time of referral with a mean age of 15.25 years. The great majority of young people assessed at the YAP have been traumatized via abuse (91%:29 boys). Of our total sample (N =32) 75%: 24 had been sexually abused 47%:15 had been physically abused 47%:15 had been emotionally abused 37%: 12 had been neglectfully abused and 6%:6 had been sexually, emotionally, and physically abused.

Overall, therefore, the YAP sample is a seriously traumatized group with few non abused cases referred. Of the three non abused boys in this sample, all had experienced other adverse life events such as several changes in placement, loss of attachment figures or serious physical illness.

Two notable shared characteristics were observed in the young people sampled to date: a high percentage of learning disability, and a high rate of experience either of being bullied or bullying. Approximately half of the young adults, on referral, were identified as having a learning difficulty (53%:17). A large proportion (78%:25) of the sample were involved in bullying one way or another, of whom ten young people (31%) reported being bullied, whilst 13 (41%) reported bullying others. A smaller proportion (6%:2) were known to have been bullied and to have bullied others.

The most common DSM-III-R diagnosis, found in half of the subject sample (50%: 16) was Conduct Disorder. Of these 16 cases, 37% (12) received a diagnosis of 312. 00 Solitary Aggressive Type, and the remaining four subjects (12%) received a diagnosis of 312. 90 Undifferentiated Type. Almost half of the subject sample received a diagnosis of Pedophilia (47%:15). However, this diagnosis could only be given to subjects over the age of 16; such data should be viewed cautiously since many much younger boys showed some or all of the required characteristics for Pedophilia but, because they are under 16 years of age, cannot be described in this way. Other shared DSM III-R classifications can be seen in Table 6.1.

Table 6.1: Shared characteristics of young sex offenders (N=32)

DSM III-R	Disorder	n	%
302.20	Pedophilia	15	46.9
312.00	Conduct Disorder Aggressive Type	12	37.5
312.90	Conduct Disorder Undifferentiated Type	4	12.5
312.00 and 312.90	Total Conduct Disorder	16	50.0
302.84	Sexual Sadism	7	21.9
309.89	Post Traumatic Stress Disorder	9	28.1
311.00	Depressive Disorder	1	3.1
312.33	Pyromania	6	18.8
302.90	Zoophilia	3	9.4
	3 or more disorders	12	37.5
	2 or more disorders	21	65.6

Theoretical perspectives

The potentials for violent behaviour and for sexual arousal are qualities which have helped ensure the survival of the human species. As societies have developed, rules to govern the expression of these qualities have emerged. In general the linking of violence and sexual behaviour is, cross culturally, controlled by both informal and formal rules, such as taboo, tradition and legislation. There are times, however, when sexual violence takes place in a systematic or ritualized way and such controls are ignored or sexual violence is even legitimized, for instance in times of war. Such behaviour can be perpetrated by individuals or carried out by groups. Organizations of adults who share a pleasure in inflicting and receiving physical pain, usually in a sexualized way, have defended their right to do so (Reg. V Brown 1993).

In Western society sexual violence is the selling point of a financial empire, based on books, magazines, films and television, all of which focus on images of rape, sexual assault and murder. In particular, fictional accounts of sexual violence against women or material based on the activities of murderers, such as Jack the Ripper, Geoffrey Dahmer or Ian Brady and Myra Hindley now form an identifiable genre. It is evident that a large proportion of the population is interested in and aroused by such material. Nevertheless, the behaviour of groups or individuals who carry out sexually violent acts as opposed to those who obtain a vicarious pleasure from reading about or watching representations of such acts is regarded as deviant from the norm and wrong. This behaviour has been the subject of comment and analysis from many different perspectives (discussed below), both general and specific, which have sought to provide an understanding of and explanation for it.

The Theoretical Classifications Diagram (Figure 6.1) offers a format in which to view the many current theoretical models available to those investigating the etiology of sex offending. The Theoretical Classifications Diagram will be utilized throughout our description of current theoretical models to assist the reader.

The Theoretical Classifications Diagram requires the reader to visualize the models of sexual violence as fitting neatly into a nest of boxes. At the centre (level one) are theories based on the individual characteristics of the perpetrator (i.e. psychodynamic, medical, trauma, cognitive, and behavioural theories). Within the next box, level two, are those models which take into account the effect of family on sexual violence. These in turn are contained within level three, which holds models commenting on the impact of peer group. In level four are those models which analyze the influence of the more formal structure of society and culture which define and provide cultural norms on taboo and 'normal' sexual conduct. Finally, in level five, the outer box contains those perspectives which consider the effect of wider influences such as the media, public opinion and so on.

The Theoretical Classifications Diagram is a framework and different theoretical models do not necessarily fit neatly into any one level. However, it does give the impression of the flux of influences and avoids a polarized, confrontational presentation of different explanations. Although models are represented somewhat hierarchically they should not be viewed as having rigid

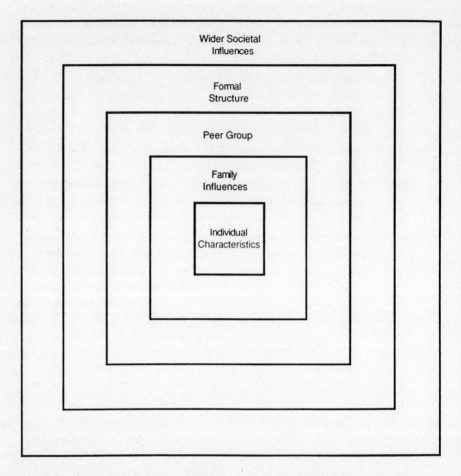

Figure 6.1: Theoretical Classifications Model

boundaries as many do indeed overlap. For example, although psychodynamic theorists would pay very important attention to initial bonding processes (level 1) they would also look at family systems and dynamics (level 2).

Level I: Explanations centred on the individual

The central box of the diagram, which focuses on the individual, is explored from a number of standpoints, including medical, psychodynamic, trauma, behavioural and cognitive theories.

(1) Medical theorists have long sought to uncover a genetic, biological or physical determinant for sexual violence. Lombroso (1874) analyzed skeletal characteristics and skull shape to identify atavistic individuals

who behaved in ways no longer appropriate in communal societies. Other theorists have suggested through animal and human research that sexual violence may be due to an imbalance of various neurotransmitters (Funkenstein 1955; Welch and Welch 1969) or hormones (Allee, Collias and Lutherman 1939; Hamburg 1966; Levy and King 1953; Moyer 1971). Others have found food allergies (Moyer 1971), chromosomal disorders (Court-Brown 1967; Price 1967; Shah 1970a and b; Turpin and Lejeune 1969; Valentine 1969); and brain trauma to the limbic system (Bard and Mountcastle 1948; Dicks, Myers and Klings 1969; Egger and Flynn 1963; Kluver and Bucy 1937; Plotnik 1968) as etiologically to sexual violence. More recently researchers have sought to identify a genetic factor which links sexual violence cross-generationally in a number of families, while American research, published by Ann Moir and David Jessel (1995), has suggested that dysfunction in the prefrontal lobe of the brain has a significant influence on sexual violence and other behavioural problems.

The work of Perry (1994), looking at the neurobiological sequelae of childhood trauma and their links to PTSD in children has suggested traumatic events may leave a lasting effect on the neurophysiological functioning of the individual. In other words, it is suggested that childhood trauma may have a permanent effect on brain function. Other work (Le Doux 1994) suggests that emotional memories brought about by fear conditioning may be relatively permanent. Le Doux (1994), suggests that 'changes in behaviour can be brought about by controlling the fearful response rather than by eliminating the emotional memory itself', a comment which has direct implications for clinical practice. Perry (1994) points out that 'Severe trauma during childhood can have a devastating effect on the development of the brain and on all functions mediated by this complex organ – emotional, cognitive, behavioral and physiological' (p.249). Perry (1994) goes on to say that PTSD must be considered within the broader concept of the diathesis-stress model of mental illness whereby a genetic or developmental predisposition for a specific psychiatric disorder depends on the degree of biopsychosocial stressors. In other words, Perry (1994), is suggesting that the severity of the trauma as experienced by the child will be relevant for the development of PTSD as well as any predisposition towards psychiatric disorder.

The recent research (Perry 1994; Le Doux 1994) into trauma, brain chemistry, memory and neurological pathways has originated in work with trauma victims. However, to date, no research has been undertaken with traumatized, aroused abusers to discern whether and how the lasting effects on the brain of sexual and other traumata may become translated into later physiological arousal towards children.

(2) Psychodynamic explanations of sexual behaviour were for many years, constrained by adherence to Freud's theories of childhood sexuality which suggested that accounts of sexual victimization by adult survivors of sexual abuse were the result of fantasies of desired sexual contact with adult figures. Freud himself stated, 'I was obliged to recognize that these scenes of seduction had never taken place, and that they were only fantasies which my patients had made up' (1925).

Psychodynamic opinion, diverse on this issue as on many others, has formed into different schools of thought which have recently been reviewed (Vizard 1995b). However, there is a shared view that sexual violence is one consequence of a pathological resolution of early childhood development, in particular at the stage of separation from mother. For example, Cassity (1927) believed that the aggressive pedophile was denied maternal warmth as a child, where as the tender type of pedophile was supposed to have had an excessively satisfying relationship with the mother, resulting in over identification with her. Robert Stoller in his 1986 work *Perversion* termed sexual violence, together with other aberrant sexual acts 'The erotic form of hatred'.

In the United Kingdom the Portman Clinic (Glasser 1994) and others have explored ways in which inadequacies in the parenting of very young children may result in damage to the child's (and later to the adult's) ability to appropriately contain or give expression to emotions, including sexual and angry feelings which are subsequently acted out (Glasser 1994).

More recent work from a psycholanalytical perspective (Scharff and Scharff 1994) has attempted to integrate the conceptual frameworks of early British object relations theorists such as Fairbairn, Klein and Winnicott as well as covering the relevant research in relation to human development, trauma theory, sexual abuse and feminism. The Scharffs also discuss the dynamic origins of PTSD (Post traumatic Stress Disorder) and MPD (Multiple Personality Disorder) in a way which makes real links between traditional analytic thought and current clinical practice.

(3) The effect of trauma on the individual also has many repercussions. Traumatic sexualization (Finkelhor and Browne 1986), is one of the 'Traumagenic Dynamics' which results from childhood sexual abuse. These theorists believe that the adult abuser, often grooming the child to believe that what he or she was doing was 'normal', would have been able to develop a conditioned sexual arousal response in the child. In the long term, this would translate for the child into intense sexual preoccupation and promiscuity, thereby re-enacting the role of the abuser. In their identification with the aggressor, sexual orientation towards children is easily achieved and could eventually lead to child sex abusing (Finkelhor 1984).

The trauma model can also easily be fit into level 2 due to its heavy overlap with family models, and indeed, into level 4 due to its consideration of societal influences. Bentovim and Kinston (1990) regard traumatic events as the prime origin of 'disturbance'. This traumatic event can in turn be observed at individual levels (i.e. the traumatized parent performs, is involved with, responds to and is aware/ unaware of abusive acts involving children in the family), family levels (where the traumatized parent develops inappropriate structures concerning affection, physical contact, and sexuality within the family), or societal levels (where the traumatized parent will react against societal norms, rights, attitudes and taboos regarding sexual roles and activities in the family) (Bentovim 1991).

(4) Behavioural theories pay less attention to the past history of an individual. Sexual violence is typified as learned behaviour, sustained by rewards of sexual gratification, enhanced self-esteem and a sense of power and control, which is reinforced by repetition and masturbatory rehearsal. For example, Berkowitz (1970) suggested that aggressive behaviour can function as a conditioned response to situational stimuli, particularly when environmental cues combine with states of internal excitation to produce impulsive aggressive reactions. Langevin (1983) classified deviant sexual preferences as per their stimulus and response characteristics only. Able et al. (1978) proposed a behavioural treatment model for sexually deviant behaviours which assumed the behaviour itself as the disorder (rather then a deeper underlying problem which was causing a symptom that presented as the deviant behaviour).

(5) Cognitive theorists have provided an understanding of how distorted impressions of sexual attitudes and behaviour were learned and how

those distortions could lead to confused, inappropriate and violent sexual behaviour in individual children. Cognitive distortions are seen as based on information gathered from the environment which contributes to one's overall life 'schema'. This 'translates' into a metacognitive distortion that he will repeat or 'say' in his mind while carrying out sexual abuse. Laws and Marshall (1990), for example, believe that not all sex offenders necessarily have deviant sexual preferences, but that rather they acquire and then maintain sexual deviancy. Wolf (1985) utilized a multifactorial model which can also be broadly labelled as 'cognitive'. The three main concepts of Wolf's model include; (i) disturbed developmental history including potentiators for later deviant 'cognitions' and behaviours; (ii) situational contributors which disinhibit the person to 'normal' social controls against sexual deviance; (iii) deviant sexual cognitions in the aspect of fantasy which reinforces the positive thoughts about deviant sexual behaviours and desensitizes the person's inhibitions.

Level 2: Family based explanations

Family systems theories, often psychodynamic in nature, have also contributed to understanding hypothetical etiologies of child molestation, mostly in terms of child abuse within the family. These theories (Meiselman 1978; Mrazek and Kempe 1981; Sgroi 1982), focusing on the interplay of family dynamics, often view the father as a man who either has a personality disorder or belongs to a subculture that is accepting of incest. The mother, allegedly, has withdrawn from her role as sex partner to the husband and has taken the position in the family as a passive, masochistic, and dependent woman. The daughter is eventually groomed to take the role of mother's sexual role.

Some family based theories have developed from the observation of biological systems in plants and other life forms to produce an analogous objective analysis of the systemic negotiations and transactions between family members. The best known proponents of this explanation are the Milan based group of family therapists who have influenced practice development in both America and the United Kingdom (Palazzoli, Boscolo, Cecchini and Trata 1978).

The family systems perspective throws valuable light on the ability of a family to respond appropriately to the sexual violence of a young person within it. Recent work from a systemic perspective (Bentovim 1992), describes the nature of dysfunctional, abusive families as being 'trauma organized' as well as recognizing that there is a wider social construction of family violence. Assessment of the degree to which adults in particular are able to recognize such behaviour as problematic, to seek help for the vulnerable children, will influence prognosis for future treatment.

Level 3: Peer group

Influences outside the individual and family become somewhat more difficult to identify and evaluate. Sociologists and psychologists have looked at the influence of small groups in encouraging and justifying sexual assault and other delinquent behaviours by young people. As children enter adolescence and move away from their primary families, criminal and other acts become more common. Approximately one third of all sexual offences committed in England and Wales are carried out by young people under the age of 21 years and the statistics suggest that the majority of those offences are committed by young males aged between 14 and 18 years (Home Office, 1990 Crime Statistics).

Some have gone as far as to say that peer influence is the most powerful impetus for sexual aggression outside of the home (Commission on Obscenity and Pornography 1986). Two studies indicated that in separate samples of adult men and adolescent boys, the strongest prediction for sexual violence was involvement with delinquent peers and having sexually aggressive friends (Ageton 1983; Alder 1985).

Level 4: Formal societal structure

The formal structure of the society can greatly influence the manner in which child sex offenders are viewed by outsiders. In this fourth level we will briefly consider the feminist, historical, and anthropological models which have assisted in shedding light on this important issue.

(1) Feminist theorists initially described sexual violence as exclusively a male attribute which was an inevitable and intended consequence of male dominated, phallocentric, capitalist society. It has now widened to acknowledge the sexual victimization of male children and in some quarters to accept that sexual violence by women and girls, while a minuscule problem in comparison to male violence, does take place. Feminists point to the education and socialization of male children as significant factors in influencing subsequent behaviour. The impact of feminist thought in challenging stereotyped perceptions of male and female sexual roles and in particular their assertion that child sexual abuse was a real event and not the product of childhood fantasy, has completely changed our understanding of the experience of child and adult survivors (Russell 1984).

(2) Some theorists have considered the issue in a society wide context, looking at the implications of sexually violent behaviour rather than the characteristics of individual acts of sexual violence or the characteristics of perpetrators. Michel Foucault (1978) in a number of publications examined the emergence of sexual orthodoxy during

the past three hundred years and characterized the demonizing of any deviant sexual activity as one means by which the dominant heterosexual power group maintains control.

(3) Different cultures and societies have been known to have beliefs that sexual abuse against children may be overall profitable for many of the parties involved. For example, proponents of Pedophilia (O'Carroll 1980) have argued that sexual relationships between adults and children should be regarded as normal and beneficial to the sexual development of children. In addition, the Lepcha of India believe that girls cannot be mature without sexual intercourse and, consequently, it is socially acceptable for older men to have sexual intercourse with girls as young as eight years old (Gallagher 1987).

Incest, a practice which is taboo in most cultures, has equally had its share of acceptance in different societies. For example, inbreeding was a common practice of all classes in ancient Egypt, where inheritances were matrilineal and, in that way, ensured the preservation of family wealth. This was especially noted among the Pharaohs who often married their sisters and infant daughters (Middleton 1962).The lack of incest regulations has also been observed in old Iran (Slotkin 1947).

Level 5: Wider perspectives
The influence of such factors as pornography, the media, the behaviour of politicians and other public figures have variously been blamed in the search for an explanation of the behaviour of children who commit sexually violent acts (Sears, Poplau, Freedman and Taylor 1988; Johnson 1972).

With regard to pornography, many feminists agree that to view its effect on sex offending one must first separate out 'acceptable erotica' from violent or coercive pornography that degrades women and encourages sexual violence (Diamond 1980; Lederer 1980; Steinem 1980). Indeed, research has indicated that violent pornography produces a higher rate of sexual aggression then non-violent pornography does (Donnerstein 1980; Donnerstein and Berkowitz 1981; Malamuth and Donnerstein 1982).

At the time of the trial of two boys who at the age of ten had murdered two-year-old James Bulger in Liverpool, the opinion was expressed in some quarters that they had carried out the killing in imitation of a scene in a horror video owned by the parents of one of the boys although there was no evidence that either boy had seen the film. The desire for a simple explanation, which attributes blame in an acceptable way is sometimes hard to resist.

The YAP Integrated Perspectives Model

During the 1950s and 60s there was an optimistic drive on the part of social scientists to produce a predictive model which would identify at an early stage those individuals, or groups of children who would subsequently go on to carry out what were then termed delinquent acts. In America, Sheldon and Eleonor Glueck were at the forefront in examining the behaviour and characteristics which distinguished delinquent children from their law abiding peers. In the later 1960s and 1970s social work practice and penal policy which followed this approach was heavily criticized for establishing a self fulfilling prophecy which stigmatized or labelled children who were then diverted from normal developmental paths into delinquent careers. At present our understanding of the roots of sexual violence faces a similar dilemma. There is now considerable information available about the behaviour and backgrounds of adults who perpetrate sexual violence, based on statistical information about their offences and from self-report studies carried out by Abel *et al.* in 1987, which provide persuasive evidence that sexually violent behaviour begins to become an established trait before the onset of adolescence. Such studies suggest that both adult rapists and adult perpetrators of sexual abuse begin to carry out sexual assaults before they reach ten years of age.

It would be an important step forward if such information could be used to pinpoint those young people who pose a risk of significant harm from sexual assault to other children and vulnerable adults. However, it would be entirely wrong to attribute stereotyped and damaging labels to preadolescents who share the circumstances and characteristics of those adults who have committed sexually violent offences but who have the capacity for significant developmental change and who would not have gone on to be sexually violent.

The theories which have been described above do not alone provide a reliable explanation for the causes of sexual violence in young people. However, they each give valuable insight into the problem. The Theoretical Classification Diagram if related to one person is able to provide a static impression of their experiences. It cannot effectively reflect the developmental progression which leads to sexual violence. The following *Integrated Perspectives Model* is a graphic interpretation based on clinical and research evidence of the cyclical pattern which generates and sustains sexually violent behaviour and transmits the problem across generations. The model allows this process to be examined from a variety of theoretical views thus providing a more complete picture which aids diagnostic assessment and informs treatment.

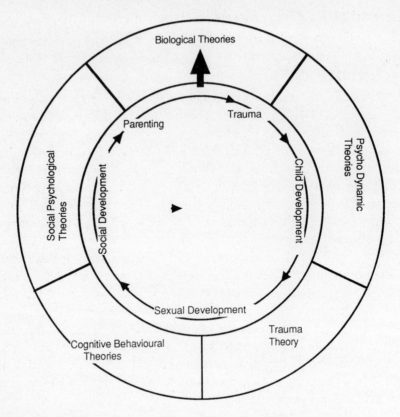

Figure 6.2: The Young Abusers Project Integrated Perspectives Model

The Inner Hub

(1) Trauma

The inner hub of the model can be seen as a clock face which charts events as they accumulate chronologically to create and maintain sexually violent behaviours. This process is a continuing one, but is most helpfully thought of as beginning with trauma. At the YAP almost all of the cases referred to us come with a recorded history of abuse (where n=29; 91% have suffered abuse).

These experiences are linked with Post Traumatic Stress Disorder, Conduct Disorder, and Academic Disorders which contribute to low self-esteem and emphasize the perception held by sexually violent young people that they are less well treated than other children.

Steven, a 17-year-old boy described in assessment how he watched 7- and 8-year-old children playing happily from his bedroom window. He explained that the abuse he had suffered from his father and his reception in to the care system had prevented him from enjoying this simple pleasure. Steven said that as he watched he felt filled with envy and anger at what had happened to him and planned how he could sexually abuse the children.

(2) Child development

The global effect of trauma on child development is shown on the next part of the inner hub. Difficulties in relationships with adults and peers and a preoccupation with intrusive and sometimes sexually arousing post traumatic mental images, can cause isolation (Fagan and Wexler 1988) and compound academic problems with the result that some children may be inappropriately classified as suffering from learning disability. For the traumatized young person the response of families and professionals to the problems which they manifest may be perceived as a further confirmation of their low self-esteem and feelings of being different.

For example, the following case clearly displays what anguish abused children experience towards the 'loss' of a 'normal childhood'. Peter, a cherubic-faced 10-year-old, explained that he had not had a childhood like others of his age because of the cruel bullying that he had received from his elder siblings in the chaos which ensued when his father left home and his mother began to abuse alcohol. Peter said he did not feel angry or envious towards other children but he began to torment and bully others, eventually, with another boy, abducting and killing a two-year-old child in a prolonged assault with a clear sexual element to it.

(3) Sexual development

The inner hub then moves on to reflect the incidence of problems in sexual development reported about sexually violent children. The traumatic history of sexual assault on a child can often result in sexually violent behaviours on the part of the individual, both to children and to adults. For example, Mary, a 9-year-old who had suffered anal and vaginal abuse, exposed herself to teachers and her peers and caused fear and distress in fellow pupils by punching and kicking their genitals.

With the onset of adolescence, young people who have experienced sexual trauma often display problems in participating in the normal process of experimentation which will eventually lead to adult sexual orientation. A frequent subject for anxious discussions in a treatment group for adolescent males, who had sexually assaulted young children, was the impact of their own victimization and the assaults which they had carried out, on their choices of future sexual partners. David, aged 17, with convictions for rape and indecent assault, asked, 'How do I know if the sexual feelings I have about men are there because I am homosexual, or are there because a man sexually abused me?'

However, those who have not specifically suffered sexual assault, but have experienced other abusive trauma, may find in adolescence a satisfying conjunction between physical violence and sexual assault. Richard, a 15-year-old with no known history of sexual victimization and without a background of inappropriate or over sexualized behaviour, abducted a 10-year-old boy, bound and gagged him before anally abusing him and carrying out other humiliating sexual acts. Richard described both the sexual pleasure and the sense of power and achievement which his assault gave him.

A significant proportion of those referred to YAP were diagnosed as suffering from other Paraphilias indicative of problems in their sexual development (Pyromania, 19%, Sexual Sadism 22%, Zoophilia 9%).

(4) Social development

The inner hub next indicates the problems which sexually violent young people have in finding their place in society. They struggle to build relationships and tend to keep their sexual feelings secret. It is possible that as a consequence of isolation and depression (Becker, Kaplan, Tanke and Tartlin 1991), adolescents may begin to resort to alcohol or drugs as an escape from depression with consequent reduction in impulse control and increase in the risk of offending.

Although sexually violent adolescents may find some peer group support for sexually aggressive attitudes, the more characteristic image is one of individuals who are not well integrated socially and who by the end of adolescence have already developed dangerous sexual behaviours which have become habitual.

(5) Parenting

The concluding part of the cyclical pattern on the inner hub of the IPM shows how the accumulation of factors results in sexually violent adults with a limited ability to anticipate, recognize, or respond to the needs of children. This consequence is particularly relevant when sexually violent or abusive individuals become parents. When this happens the potential for such behaviour to be transmitted across generations is clearly established.

The inner hub is therefore an image of the totality of experiences which contribute to sexually violent behaviour. It also displays the constituent elements which contribute to that total image. The outer ring of the diagram is divided into sectors representing theoretical perspectives from which both totality and constituent elements can be perceived. For purposes of clarity we suggest the inner hub is seen as moving independently of the outer ring and able to turn to allow the pointer to indicate from which theoretical perspective the inner hub is being examined.

For instance, in the figure of the model above, the pointer on the inner hub indicates biological theory. From this perspective information about brain damage (Moir and Jessel 1995) would be seen as significant. Richard, a 16-year-old boy subject to probation supervision for a number of indecent assaults on girls aged between 7 and 10 years at his local swimming pool, had suffered damage to the frontal lobe after a serious fall when he was 10 years of age.

From the same perspective evidence of genetic make-up might explain why the extended family of a sexually violent young person had a history of criminal convictions for physical and sexual assaults and public order offences. According to this model past experiences and family influences are not significant factors – children are drawn to repeat those experiences which satisfy and reinforce genetic dispositions.. However, other research describes the complex interplay between genetics and behaviour and allows an important role for external events as stressors within what Perry (1994) has called the diathesis-stress model of mental illness. This explanation argues that genetic factors will cause some individuals to lose control over sexual urges in adolescence without a necessary history of victimization or of earlier disturbed behaviour. Although nearly one quarter of the YAP population had not suffered CSA (Child Sexual Abuse) it seems that all boys referred had shown signs of long standing disturbed behaviour. However, this may be a referral bias, given the very specialized nature of the YAP and a comparison with other groups of young sexual abusers would be helpful.

If the pointer is then moved to indicate psychodynamic theories the entire developmental cycle and its elements are open to psychodynamic interpretation. An example from assessment is the significance given to verbal and non-verbal communication made to male and female therapists, who from this perspective may be seen as representing mother and father. One adolescent scratched on the arm of his chair the message that the female therapist was 'a slag'. Another boy, explaining why he found it so difficult to talk to the male worker said, 'I don't want to, whatever I say he just buggers you up'. Interpretations of those comments from psychodynamic perspective allowed the construction of a hypotheses about earlier experiences and informed the formulation of questions which anticipated difficulties in relationships and in the inner world of the child.

If the indicator is moved to trauma theory, sexual violence in young people is seen as an acting out of sexually aroused responses to earlier experiences of abuse. This model which is primarily derived from work done with child sexual abusers takes into account the way in which skilled adult abusers, family attitudes and societal influences normalize the sexually violent behaviour of a young person. When John, a nine-year-old boy who had experienced chronic neglect, physical abuse, and suspected sexual abuse in his earlier years sexually assaulted a three-year-old girl, his mother and her partner (a man with a conviction for sexually assaulting John's sister and a history of sexually assaulting his own sister) said, that this was no more then any boy of his age would do when a girl offered 'sex on a plate'.

The cognitive/behavioural view of sexual violence has proved to be of particular value in the design of treatment programmes for young people. The ability of this perspective to break down the detail of events, actions, thoughts and feelings which trigger and accompany sexual violence is essential in helping therapists and those in treatment to develop strategies to avoid risky situations and to take responsibility for and divert from sexually violent fantasies.

The model is one which can be adapted to the needs of young children and those of limited intellectual capacity as well as those more able. In a treatment group for adolescent males, Mark, age 17 years, with mild learning disability was eventually able to describe how sadistic sexual thoughts about children were triggered by a variety of stimuli, including proximity to children and arguments with adults. Mark recognized that he found it difficult to stop the progression of thoughts in his mind but took increasing pride in his ability to seek help from staff in his residential school as soon as he became aware of the onset of sexually violent thoughts.

If the dial is then turned to the perspective of social psychology, influences on socialization, such as the impact of media coverage of current sexual assaults would be considered. One 16-year-old male with convictions for rape disclosed that he became sexually aroused when he saw television or newspaper accounts of the rape of adult women. He would masturbate to these reports changing his mental image from a woman to a child in order to enable him to ejaculate. The frequency of reports and the graphic detail of offences gave him a contact source of arousing material. He found a collusive confirmation of his view that rapacious behaviour was available from peers and older males. The blurred distinction between coverage of real crimes and the presentation of fictional accounts of sexual assaults is thus interpreted by sexually violent young people in a distorted way which must be challenged in treatment.

The IPM is therefore a flexible model which can incorporate new information about the development of sexually violent young people and allows the examination of their increasingly comprehensive picture from a range of theoretical perspectives.

It is hoped that the cross referencing, complex nature of the IPM reduces the risk of premature labelling of sexual behaviour as pathological by acting as a check on the imposition of unilateral explanations which do not take into account the multi-faceted nature of sexual violence.

An examination of the attitudes held by professionals within the different agencies referring sexually violent young people to the Project has revealed a similar pattern of confusion, denial, and uncertainty. Understanding of the systemic issues involved has helped to structure professional consultations and has influenced the design of a support group for professional carers which accompanies group treatment for young people.

Summary and closing comments

This chapter has reviewed the major theories present which address the aetiology and maintenance of child sexual abuse, many of which were based on research and work with adult sex offenders and families in which there has been sexual abuse. From this literature review and from direct clinical work with abusive young people, the Integrated Perspectives Model has been developed. To date, there has been a certain amount of American research but little British research (Vizard 1995) based on work with juvenile sexual abusers. There are, however, certain important issues arising from existing research which need to be integrated into any thinking about the aetiology of abusing behaviour.

First, the recent research (Perry 1994: Le Doux 1994) into trauma, brain chemistry, memory and neurological pathways has originated in work with trauma victims, although other research (Moir 1995) has linked brain dysfunction with sexual violence. To date, no research has been undertaken with traumatized, aroused abusers to discern whether and how the lasting effects on the brain of sexual and other traumata may become translated into later physiological arousal towards children. In addition, the persistence of emotional memories through fear conditioning (Le Doux 1994) ties in closely with our clinical experience with young sexual abusers who suffer not only from the PTSD related symptoms of the 'hyperactive' sympathetic nervous system (SNS) but also suffer from 'recurrent and intrusive distressing recollections of the (abuse) event' (APA 1994). These flashbacks to earlier trauma also seem to correspond to the fearful 'emotional memories' described by Le Doux (1994) as being 'relatively permanent'.

The relationship, if any, between such recurrent fearful memories, the high levels of general arousal as a result of PTSD, the development of sexually arousing memories and the later (or concurrent) development of sexual fantasies about other children is one which would be of very great clinical and research interest. The links between victim and abuser are often discussed in work with child sexual abuse but to date it has not been possible to clarify any possible physiological–traumatic–behavioural paradigm which could give a biosocial basis for understanding the transition. Further research in these areas would be of great value in designing appropriate treatment interventions.

Second, the issues arising from the preliminary findings of the Young Abusers Project suggest that any physiological basis for the persistence of traumatic aftereffects needs to be put into the context of continuing traumata occurring in the external worlds of our client group. These young people have been repeatedly abused and emotionally deprived as well as suffering from many broken attachments during their contact with the care system. It does need to be acknowledged, therefore that the young people seen in the YAP are particularly disturbed and disadvantaged and that it is not possible to generalize widely from this group to other populations of young abusers or to the normal population without further comparative research.

In terms of object relations theory (Scharff 1994) the typical young sexual abuser seen in the YAP would have very few secure internal objects with which to relate or to refer to in times of stress hence adding to the difficulty in processing external experience and making good judgments. Clinical experience suggests that these young people have been very insecurely or even avoidantly attached to any past or present caretakers. Such experiences mean that it is difficult or impossible for these young abusers to develop trusting relationships with others or to have much of a sense of empathy for their victims, without psychotherapeutic help.

A Theoretical Classifications Diagram has been presented to provide the reader with a framework in which to view current theories. The YAP Integrated Perspectives Model (IPM) was presented as a method with which to view the developmental sequence of events leading to sexual offending by young people. This model, based on our research at the Young Abusers Project, views the core aetiology of youth sex offending as a cycle which begins with an abusively traumatic experience which leads to maladaptive child development. This in turn results in distorted sexual and social development, finally resulting in poor (and very possibly abusive) parenting practices, which encourage the cycle to begin once again with the next generation. Once viewing this inner hub as a static dial, one can then go on to view this development in terms of the many valuable models which currently exist, roughly categorized as medical, psychodynamic, trauma, cognitive/ behavioural, social psychology, and family systems models. Hence, the model can easily be seen as a way in which different perspectives can be integrated in order to develop a thorough way to view each child presenting with worrying sexual behaviours.

It was our hope that in developing the *YAP Integrated Perspectives Model* this would assist fellow practitioners with a much needed tool for diagnosis and the development of treatment strategies. As indicated earlier in the chapter, the lack of diagnostic categories for children who sexually abuse is puzzling and unhelpful. We propose that a new diagnostic category 'Sexual Arousal Disorder of Childhood' should be developed to further assist these children by 'naming' the issue and thereby giving credence to it. We hope that the data which we have collected will contribute to defining the developmental criteria required for such a diagnosis. However, clearly before such an important step in the field of youth sex offending is taken, there is a pressing need for further research.

CHAPTER 7

Violence in Adolescence

Arthur Hyatt Williams

Violence in adolescents hitherto meant violence in male adolescents, but this has changed in the past two generations and now, violence is in mixed groups of adolescents and in wholly female adolescent gangs, and it is appearing more. Some of it is associated with an upsurge of female group solidarity, and some in connection with the obtaining and partaking of drugs. There are solitary violent adolescents and delinquent violent groups (gangs). When a group becomes a gang and, in a recovery phase, when does a gang become a group again, has been studied.

Adolescent violence may arise as an explosive result of personal failure or personal confrontation with disturbing issues such as life-threatening illness in the family, breakdown of the parents or that of the marriage of the parents. It can also be the result of permanent failure of personal confrontation. Any change experienced as a catastrophe may turn out to be psychically indigestible to an adolescent and fracture the psychic framework which holds him or her together. If there happens to be a powerful endowment with instinctual – especially aggressive – drives and a flimsily structured framework which holds the adolescent together as a person, trouble is almost bound to arise.

When violence does occur, it may be a once-off shocking event which shocks its perpetuator and the law-keepers, whether they be family, teachers or police. The peer group usually experiences both shock, disapproval and an excited admiration with an element of approval.

I can recollect an incident which occurred in quieter days in my own schoolboy experience. A schoolmaster, not regarded as savage, struck a class-mate of mine who was not usually a trouble-maker, a very nasty blow. It was backhanded and across the face, and the blow was humiliating, and the general sympathy was with our classmates. He stood up and punched the master on the nose, making it bleed. The very considerable humiliation now rested in the master. I felt sorry for him and rather sadly against the classmate's savagery, but definitely excited by the whole dramatic interaction. Some fifty years later, I met the friend who sat next to me in the class and asked him, recalling the incident, what he felt about it at the time. He then stated what was virtually the same as I have just written, and only then was I able to suppose that that was what most of the rest of the class would have felt. How we digested this disturbing spectacle probably varied. For a while, I stayed out late and incurred parental reproaches – no blows! The friend had a violent clash with his highly religious father during which the self-righteous father knocked my friend flat, allegedly all for his own good!

What I would like to describe is the way in which psychically indigestible experience may be acted out repeatedly, or wholly or partly digested and not used to trigger off a sequence of violent episodes. Also, how often the main figures involved in the 'duel' pass on some of their problems to those who happen to witness the violence. Before elaborating this theme, I must mention that the master and pupil got together later the same day and shared apologies, not to mention some tears, and subsequently had no further trouble with each other.

Melanie Klein described how there were two kinds of anxiety: persecutory, where the experience of being 'got at' malevolently – the ultimate fear being that of annihilation – pervaded. The reaction is to fight or escape and in early infancy, to scream for help. About the end of the second quarter of the first year of life, the infant has developed sufficiently to recognize that mother or her surrogate is a whole person and that the person with whom he or she has been angry and is frightened of, is the same person as the one who has been the giver of all good things. Holding this concept with fortitude is one of the tasks which confronts all of us at this stage of life. Success is never final and absolute. Nevertheless, we can progress a long way. If later, the child and later still, the adolescent, has experienced a dearth of good, loving objects and experiences and a plenitude of bad ones, and has, him or herself, introjected these bad objects and identified with them, he or she is handicapped from the start, and it is easy to see that a likely sequel will be an easily detonated reservoir of violence. In practical terms, the expectancy is of being ill-treated, misunderstood and deprived. Sometimes, there is a defiant provocation in that response and a brutalization process at the core of which is a general disbelief in the expectation of good intention and a distrust of those who appear to be trying to give it. This extends to the caring and remedial services who offer something good. The process of debrutalization takes a long time in the more severely brutalized individuals. They tend to agglomerate into adolescent groups, more correctly labelled gangs, and in that setting, tend to become more alienated from ordinary citizenship and this sequence tends to go on and on. There are things which can reverse the process. The process is made more sinister if the group tends to become dependent upon drugs. There develops an overall majestic instancy in obtaining drugs and/or money with which to purchase them. The feeling shared, 'If I do not get what I want and what I need, I shall die' adds to the urgency and the ruthlessness with which those needs are satisfied.

The group expresses the will of its members, but there are, as Bion said, basically two kinds of group leader. In a democratically organized group, the leader tends to be the person who can best express and help to achieve the will of the group. But in a regressive or brutalizing process, authoritarian leaders tend to gain ascendancy and assert their leadership. Authoritarian leaders (like that kind of political leader) tend to impose their will and aims upon the group. Brutalization goes on apace and protesters or dissidents are subjected to punishment or banishment. If thought to be a danger to the survival of the group, they can be liquidated, i.e. killed, for example in the Mafia. At some stage of the process of brutalization, the truth becomes a victim and at first tends to be mutilated, but later abandoned altogether or reversed, as in the Faustian or Macbethian 'badness, be thou my good' – a reversal of values. Group rank and file tend to develop dependency upon the kind of leader who 'runs the group'. There is not much danger in a democratically organized and led group, as misfits are free to leave it without savage reprisals being inflicted. More important, however, is the fact that democratic groups tend to evolve:

From Gang   ⎯⎯⎯⎯⎯⎯⟶   To Group

and then follows debrutalization, and the de-escalation of violence, whereas authoritarian organizations and leadership go the opposite way, the way of brutalization, which is

Group   ⎯⎯⎯⎯⎯⎯⟶   Gang

and there is an escalation of violence and an attitude which develops and fosters brutalization.

So far, we have dealt with the macroscopic parts of the problem of adolescent violence and some of the interpersonal aspects. If we now turn to where violence and the proclivity to act out violence is situated within the individual, we may be able to get a more three dimensional view on the problem. Violence may be somewhere in the constitution or fostered during very early nurture (see Piontelli's (1992) work on ultrasound videos taken of a series babies in utero during the second half of intra-uterine life). Also, of course, there is the rare genetic phenomenon of the child endowed with, for instance, a triple Y chromosome, a supercharge of masculinity carrying considerable muscular power, size and a tendency towards aggressiveness. This is quite rare. The personality which reveals itself as development goes on shows that there are weak and flimsy controls over aggressive impulses; much of this is due to or made worse by later nurture, but there is a probability that the child who cannot tolerate frustration also cannot control impulses arising from within.

What happens to a person in infancy and childhood is likely to influence whether that child grows up with a predominate of good objects inside his or her psyche, or a preponderance of bad objects. Of course, there are varying degrees of good and bad objects and the balance is never totally one way or the other. The outcome of a violent episode such as the one I described between the schoolmaster and the schoolboy (the schoolboy, incidentally, was fully grown) varies considerably in accordance with what has gone on before in the life of the younger person and as to what stage the older aggressor has reached within himself. In the incident where the master hit the boy unwisely, it looked as though the whole thing was going to escalate anti-developmentally, but it did not do so because both master and pupil were almost immediately sorry and depressed about what they had done to each other. They then were able to not give way to excessive pride and resentment; they met, talked about it and forgave each other. They moved from the paranoid-schizoid position based upon a feeling of aggrievedness and a wish for revenge, to the depressive position which is dominated by a feeling of having done wrong oneself and concern about how amends can be made.

If there been an avoidance of regret, it may there have led to an explosive, almost murderous reaction, expelling the boy or getting the master dismissed from his job. In the family, of course, such a conflict between a parent and an adolescent boy may be satisfactory resolved, or the adolescent may disappear from home. This is a common way. In other words, there has been no working through, review and mutual forgiveness upon which the future depends.

By 'objects', of course, I mean mental images, experiences and intrapsychic representations of people and/or events. As far as internalized persons are concerned, these images are modifications of actual persons according to the experiences of the person in whom their images reside. Bad experiences not associated with people so much as catastrophes, such as earthquakes, floods, war, etc., may be linked in the mind of the child, adolescent or adult with people in their lives. In other words, those people are blamed for the disaster, maybe because they were unable to handle the distress which resulted from it.

The question of how a stress situation is handled, or as Bion said, 'managed', is most relevant to the problem of digesting and, it is to be hoped, metabolizing such situations so that there is recovery without any dangerous escalation of violence in external behaviour, and without resulting in a dangerous build up of violent tension within an individual or group. Some of the working through of a disturbed inner world may be accessible to individual adolescent sufferers and/or their families, or their peer groups or workers in the caring or legal services. A number of years ago I was asked to advise over a serious case in which there was a dramatic intensification of the threat of violence of a sixteen-year-old youth whose phantasy was of severe violence, together with powerful impulses driving him towards action. The story was as follows. The elder brother of a sixteen-year-old boy had been executed for his part in a gang mugging of a man which went wrong. The executed young man had not taken part in the murder, but a gang member, wit the disagreement of the executed brother, did kill the young man and both himself and the brother of the sixteen-year-old were executed. The other two members of the gang were below age and were detained during Her Majesty's pleasure. The surviving non-gang member was filled with anger and resentment and threatened to kill a policeman. Instead, he committed a minor crime of a very obvious shop theft, I think as a plea for help, as it was so obvious and he was certain he would get caught. He was given help. He felt very threatened by his impulses and therapy with a gifted probation officer in the forensic mental health field was provided.

After about two or three years, the situation had been transformed. He had recovered from all delinquent and violent impulses, was in regular work and was clearly established in late adolescent development. The impulse to kill had been digested psychically without action and the crisis of distress involving the threat of action to avenge the execution of his brother had passed harmlessly. The help given to him had been of good quality, was given when it was needed and the result was satisfactory.

Until this crisis of psychic digestion and metabolism, though not educationally gifted, there had been no previous personality problems in that particular adolescent. In those adolescents who do have character and behaviour problems, however, adequate and timely professional help is necessary and often the results are not as good as those just described.

Individual explosiveness and violence can be mitigated or potentiated by participation in a group. If a number of people are functioning in an articulated way, what takes place? When a number of people (usually male, but not exclusively so now) get together with the aim of terrorism, robbery, drug taking or acquiring or any other criminal activity, they resort to gang activities. If the aim is non-delinquent and the activities are educational, recreational and a sharing of common interests, the appropriate label is a 'group'. The structure of the two kinds of group is different. The gang tends to have an autocratic leader, as mentioned before, there develops a pecking/hierarchical order, the leader is usually the person who can most effectively impose his will upon the rest of the gang. Dissidents are very roughly treated and voluntary abduction from the group is punished. When the group tends to be democratic, the leader is selected and usually chosen as the person best able to facilitate and pursue the aims of the group and to achieve them. Bion stated the essence of the group activity more or less in terms of this paragraph, and has described the difference between military groups from democratic cultures and authoritarian groups from non-democratic cultures. Gianna Williams (1990) has described the transformation of youth gangs to groups and the regression of groups to gangs in some West European and American societies.

The implications of group/gang behaviour are first, whatever they do as a group/gang tends to become intensified. Dependency upon the shared aims of those gathered together intensifies whatever the aims are, whether it be in culture and sophistication and creativity, or in destructive behaviour, often violent and brutalized activities. These two tend to be intensified and get worse and worse. The intensification of violent and destructive activities of the gang are greatly facilitated by the process of brutalization, which makes brutal behaviour not seem to matter. The responsibility is divided by the members of the group, whereas the brutality is multiplied by the number of members of the group. I will give a brief account of what happened when a fairly harmless build up occurred in a gang formed within the curtilege of a custodial training institution for young offenders. There was a considerable problem posed by frequent escapes. A new headmaster was appointed who tried to find out the factors which fuelled the epidemics of escapes. He found that there was an identification with war-time prisoner-of-war camps and that to be a member of a prestigious escape club at the custodial institution, a youth had to escape at least once and, upon recapture, be punished by being beaten publically by the headmaster. At the next outbreak of escapes, this headmaster had the escapees paraded in front of him when they were recaptured, and he just left them standing in front of him until one of them said, 'When are you going to punish us, sir?' He said, 'I am not'. Then they went on for another half hour in front of him. With this kind of handling, the escape club collapsed. There were few escapes after that and those which occurred were to do with troubles at home, illness of members of the family and other urgent reasons. The drama had gone. The prestige aspect of the defiant acting-out had gone.

In violent action in a gang, there is a tendency for the gang members to vie with each other by getting more and more violent. This intensifies the brutalization process. It consists of a worsening violence with callousness and lack of compassion. There is little or no quarter given and no identification with the victim. The Mafia and its parallel societies are vivid examples of group intensified violence in the pursuit of aims which consist mainly of material gains and power. Perhaps power is more important even than the gain.

As far as adolescents are concerned, William Golding's book, *Lord of the Flies* gives a vivid account of the establishment of a brutal youth organization, a gang, which took power in the absence of adults. It was significant that the choir which became powerful and cruel, was the part of the organization which had preceded and existed before the catastrophic air crash as a result of which all the young boys were marooned on a tropical island.

It will have been noticed that there is a difference between violence used as a policy which includes, of course, personal or group power and gain, and violence which stems from a high aggressive tension in the individual or collection of individuals. This violence may be purposeful in that it includes such solitary or group phenomena as break-ins or break-outs. It tends to be impulsive and relatively uncontrolled.

Violence in pursuit of drugs or money with which to buy drugs is a new and important kind of violence which has developed in the last generation. It is organized and coldly purposeful on the part of the drug pushers, while for the drug-taking habituees, it is urgent, violent and ruthless, dynamized by urgent needs by persons with drug modified states of mind. Much serious violence, even amounting to murder, takes place in this area.

In addition, there is group violence associated with sexual perversions and sexual abuse of the victims of abnormal sexuality is harmful, cruel and responsible for some long-term psychic damage. Of course, in adolescence the sexual abuse tends to be carried out by individuals rather than by groups and it is more in an adult person suffering from some kind of sexual deviation that the group phenomenon occurs (mostly).

Individual violence is quite common in adolescence when the controls do not develop to a degree which matches and is adequate to modify and mellow actions. Outbursts can be over any controversial issue. Insult, humiliation, purposeful provocation all figure in triggering off violent responses. The response may be self-limiting, like the wave of a sea which runs up a sandy beach, losing force, stopping and then receding. On the other hand, it may have the characteristics of a tidal wave which gathers power at each of its escalations. These do become very dangerous.

A group-shared form of these two kinds of violence is that which occurs among spectators at football and other games, but mainly football. As is expected, violence at such concentrations of spectators, though shared by relatively small proportions in numbers, tends to be fuelled by group processes and to get out of hand, sometimes leading to numbers of dead and also many injured people. In some way, some people seek opportunities for violent action. This is a distorted caricature of the ordered conflict between the opposing teams. One violent football fan told me that he and his friends went to the match to enjoy 'a good punch-up' with spectators of the opposing side. In football violence, there is the use of partisanship to camouflage really serious aggressive violence and destructiveness.

There is a difference between encapsulated violence and its possessor from whom it erupts when the old experiences which put it into its sufferer, who was able to encapsulate it but not digest or metabolize it, so that this particular kind of violence is reactivated from a position in the psyche out of some kind of limbo. Group, or gang violence, as it is more correctly termed, seems to be similar to Bismarck's statement that 'war is merely an extension of diplomacy' and violence is used as the diplomacy of war or force. This kind of violence differs from the person who explodes when his psychic Achilles Heel is touched upon painfully, and who therefore then breaks out into an extreme degree of violence which can escalate to murder, or can diminish and even result in apology.

CHAPTER 8

A Violent Child and his Family

Richard Davies

I am going to discuss an act of violence committed by an adolescent boy against his best friend. In a mode of 'forensic enquiry' I will attempt to offer some explanation as to the purpose of this act and its meaning to the perpetrator. The violence which had been considered by the police, the newspapers and the court as senseless and mystifying, had also seriously perplexed the boy himself. What I hope to illustrate is that from the perspective of this boy's internal world it would not have been puzzling and would certainly have had to make sense in order for him to have committed the act. Through some understanding of the family gained both from interviews with them and through the initial psychotherapy assessment of the boy I will explore what might have been the conscious and unconscious elements contained in the act. Through a more comprehensible understanding of the act I will discuss what the perpetrator may have been attempting to resolve through the act.

Theoretical Background

First it would be useful to introduce some of the ideas on which I have based my discussion. Generally I would consider any anti-social, delinquent or violent act as being something which has outwitted thought. It may have translated directly from an impulse or feeling into an action, or if it has been subjected to thought, this has failed in terms of an effective solution which would not be able to exclude action against the person or property of another. In relation to the violent act, Glasser (1982, pp.1–2) reminds us that we all have aggression 'built into us by biology' and we thus 'all have the potential for violence'. In the presence of danger the body will prepare us for 'fight' or 'flight'. Violence if it is invoked has, as he states, the 'purpose of...negation of the danger'. This is the obvious purpose of war or the act of self-defence or escape if attacked in the street. Glasser uses the term 'self preservative violence' which he does not limit to refer to an action which has been provoked by a 'threat to physical survival', but which he extends to include a response to a threat to 'psychological integrity'. When for example somebody feels threatened through an insult or some humiliating blow to the self-esteem, whether or not this was intended by the other, violence may appear to an individual to provide the only possible solution to negate the source of danger. The 'mugger', who hits the policeman who has arrested him, is acting through self-preservative violence if in doing so he is attempting to get away.

The second major category of violence to which Glasser refers is 'malicious violence' (*op.cit.*). This is distinct from 'self preservative violence' in which once danger has been negated, the experience or emotional reaction of the recipient is of no consequence to the person who was provoked. In malicious violence 'the emotional reaction of the victim is crucial: the specific aim is to cause the victim to suffer physically or mentally, crudely or subtly'. For example, the kidnapper who tortures his captive and gains sadistic pleasure and excitement from doing so is using 'malicious violence'. Glasser goes on to point out that some acts of violence do not fit easily into a single category and may contain mixtures of the two. A topical example is 'road rage' where extraordinary acts of dangerous driving and vicious assault have arisen through somebody being 'overtaken' by another. One act of 'road rage' may principally be that of self-preservative violence to preserve 'psychological integrity'. In such a case the aggressor will lose interest in his victim following the violence. Another scenario may develop into an act of malicious violence where the aggressor pursues his victim relentlessly, even deviating from his route, in order to inflict suffering on the 'offender'. In both these cases we can imagine how in a single incident, one form of violence may be displaced by the other.

During very early development a child could expect to receive help from his parents to tolerate his aggressive impulses and to acquire ways to manage them in a positive and creative way. Winnicott (1956, p.306) while referring to the 'The Anti Social Tendency' and not specifically to aggressive impulses, is helpful in thinking about this subject when he talks about the child '…looking for something, somewhere and failing to find it seeks it elsewhere, when hopeful.' He goes on to say that '…the child is seeking that amount of environmental stability which will stand the strain resulting from impulsive behaviour'. If both parents have problems with their own aggression then they will be ill equipped to 'stand the strain' of the child's repeated and 'hopeful' attempts to gain help with his aggressive impulses. The parents can provide neither a useful model for the child to emulate nor can they be in sympathy with the necessity to help the child to find his own ways to respond to difficult situations and encounters. The child will be inhibited in his attempts to acquire positive and fruitful outlets for his aggression such as assertion and creativity. More centrally, such a child will encounter difficulties in his future attempts to form relationships. The child's developing view of the world will be further complicated if both parents' difficulties with their own aggression leave them with little option but to persist in violence between them, usually by father against mother. While the child may be frightened and disturbed by father's violence he may wonder why mother continues to be willing to suffer the violence. Rather than acquiring an uncomplicated perception of a powerful male perpetrator and a helpless female victim, the child may thus feel and think that his mother in some way enjoys the suffering and that his father enjoys inflicting the pain. At times he may also witness his father's guilt and shame after a violent episode and his mother's relief or even pleasure at father's attempts at reparation. Father may sometimes appear humiliated and mother may appear to enjoy these moments of triumph.

As the cycle continues, far from having a clear picture of a separate perpetrator and victim, the child will become muddled about 'who' is doing 'what' to 'whom'. This 'sado-masochistic' way of relating, with the parents locked together, each parent alternately the 'attacker' and the 'victim', may be internalized by the child and become part of his expectations and repertoire. Dependent on the degree of sado-masochistic behaviour that he 'witnesses', compared to other healthier modes of relating which may also be present, the internalized experience of sado-masochism may form part of the basis for his future relationships. He may then in his own future life repeat his parent's relationship by finding 'willing' partners who will fall into this pattern with him. Such relationships may involve the use of violence and suffering or may be more subtle in the use of a reciprocal style of mental cruelty. He may also gradually come to the point where he treats people as if they are 'willing', whether they are or not. Generally, 'unwilling' partners without a similar internalized experience of sado-masochism will quickly object to the treatment they are receiving and will then quit.

The example of a violent act which follows is, in my view, predominantly one of 'self preservative violence' although it is not obvious that this is the case. Elements of 'malicious violence' are also present and in the later discussion I have attempted to delineate how both forms of violence might have been present in the same act.

The violent act

Nik was sixteen when he stabbed his best friend Joe three times with a knife on the way home from school. He describes having finally 'snapped' after being taunted and humiliated by Joe over a number of weeks. From the observations of teachers and family they had seemed to be best friends. They spent a lot of time together both at school and at weekends. In fact they were far from being 'best friends'. What was not seen from a distance was a relationship in which Nik was being constantly teased, baited and humiliated by Joe. For reasons which I will discuss below, Nik seemed unable to withdraw from the relationship and equally Joe seemed never to tire of his subject.

On the days preceding the attack Nik had been constantly persecuted by Joe to settle a debt which he did not feel he owed. Joe had bought a computer game on holiday abroad which was the wrong version for his machine. He somehow talked Nik into an arrangement whereby Joe would buy the correct version from a local shop but, if it did not work, Nik would either pay him for it or obtain a refund from the shop. Joe subsequently reported that he had failed to make the game operate and put pressure on Nik to keep his part of the bargain. Nik was eventually persuaded to go to the shop to attempt to obtain a refund but he was refused. In fact Joe had given him the imported version to return which of course the shop had recognized was not an item they had sold. It is unclear whether Nik was aware that he was participating in the attempted deception although it seems likely that he knew. Whatever the truth he had felt unable to resist Joe's demands. In accordance with their arrangement Nik was now pressed to pay Joe the money himself. He had thus placed himself in a position where he was being forced to purchase the useless import from Joe while, now, if not before, fully aware that the new working version would be retained by Joe. In other words although the arrangement had been clearly perverted and he was 'knowingly being deceived', Nik had felt himself powerless to stand up to Joe's relentless demands and instead paid him an instalment while somehow having to pretend to himself that the arrangement was still valid. Joe then pursued him relentlessly to pay the balance and on the day in question Nik had attempted to evade Joe on the way home from school. A knife appeared, probably owned by one of them but purportedly found and picked up by Joe. In a complex atmosphere between them of joking and taunting, Joe poked at Nik with the knife in a simulated attack and in doing so he deliberately cut through the strap of Nik's bag. Nik then asked Joe, as if in joke, to tell him where you would stab somebody if you wanted to kill them. Joe suggested the heart, the stomach and the back. Nik took the knife as if to continue the 'game' and then proceeded to stab Joe in chest, the abdomen and, as Joe fell, stabbed him again in the back. Fortunately help arrived and Joe subsequently made a full recovery.

After the event, Nik could not explain what made him do it. He had not wanted Joe dead and was horrified by what he had done. He experienced nightmares and flashbacks for some time afterwards.

The court

There had been a distinct possibility that Nik would receive a long prison sentence but fortunately the judge had been curious as to what had prompted the violence and was advised to ask for a psychodynamic assessment. He had also been made aware of Nik's obvious remorse. It was heard that Nik had never done anything like this before and in fact was described as a model pupil at school. He was apparently well liked, conscientious and viewed as fairly sensible. Following the assessment Nik was allowed his liberty and encouraged to undertake psychotherapy.

Family and personal history

In order to begin to try to make some sense of the violent event it is important to know some salient background details.

The family, which is of Greek origin, has strong, extended family and cultural ties, particularly on father's side of the family. Nik has a brother four years older. A year after the birth of this first child, mother became pregnant again and suffered a miscarriage at eight months. She became seriously ill as a consequence and the family reports that she was not expected to live. Although she recovered well she was advised not to consider any further pregnancies as she would endanger her life.

Mother explained to me that she had not intended to risk a further pregnancy after her previous experience but that father had been placed under considerable extended family pressure to have more children. Mother stated that when father had felt unable to resist further the demands of his own family, she then reluctantly agreed to another child. When she became pregnant with Nik she experienced a very difficult pregnancy and delivery but nevertheless survived and made a full recovery. Perhaps because of the traumatic loss of the previous child and the high anxiety that she experienced throughout her pregnancy with Nik, mother went on to develop an engulfing attachment to this 'special' child to the exclusion of the father. In her mind, through father's pressure on her to have another child, he had endangered her life and thus remained a threat to her baby, a part of her self. In her protective shell with her baby she would allow little contact by father with either of them and the marital situation deteriorated.

It emerged that the marriage had been poor for some time following the birth of the first child. Father drank heavily and was frequently violent towards his wife. After Nik was born, father's drinking and violence became more pronounced. By the time Nik was two his parents had separated, the children remaining with mother. Mother and father subsequently remained in touch on fairly amicable terms for the sake of the children. From time to time they attempted to reunite, only to separate again after further violence. Mother's endurance of her husband's violence for many years indicated her difficulty with her own aggressive feelings as well as indicating the more obvious difficulties of father in his lack of capacity to manage his aggression.

Nik was over indulged by mother. As a toddler, when his aggressive impulses naturally began to emerge in an obvious way, his mother's inability to cope with her own aggressive feelings limited her capacity to help her son cope with his. Instead she tolerated his noise, mess and rage without being able to respond appropriately, perhaps through some fear that she might harm him. A year or so after the marital separation, mother became unable to cope with her children and looked to her extended family for help. Subsequently, when Nik was three, he went to live with an aunt and uncle who assumed responsibility for his care on a permanent basis. Nik's brother, who was then seven, remained with mother as she felt more able to manage him, an older child, and because she felt at that age he would also be able to help her in some ways.

When Nik was seven his uncle began to sexually abuse him. This continued for four years until Nik was eleven. Because the abusive relationship had extended unchallenged for so many years, Nik had gradually adopted a position of 'enjoying' it. Also through his desperate need for a father figure Nik would have formed an attachment to his uncle in the absence of any other available (non abusing) parental figures. When the abuse was finally discovered Nik was returned to mother. The uncle was prosecuted and sent to prison. While in prison, over a period of years the uncle regularly phoned Nik at home to say that he was looking forward to his release so that they could continue their relationship. Nik not only felt powerless to resist speaking with his uncle on the telephone, but, through the attachment, responded compliantly as though the perverse relationship had never been interrupted. It transpired that mother, who spoke little English, always allowed Nik to answer the phone in order to translate for her if it was required. She was apparently aware of the uncle's phone calls, as was father, but neither took any steps to prevent them. The explanation that Nik offered for his parents' apparent lack of concern was that a complaint might lengthen the uncle's prison sentence and thus delay the return to his aunt. The aunt, mother's sister, was reported to have been highly distressed and unable to cope in her husband's absence. In some way, perhaps through Nik's eventual disclosure of the abuse, his mother had felt responsible for the fact that her sister was separated from her husband.

Nik's violent attack on Joe occurred at a point where he knew his uncle was due to be released from prison six months later.

Assessment

Initially I found Nik to be over polite with an ingratiating smile and anxious to please. He displayed the typical characteristic of the compliant superficial cooperation of a child who has been persistently sexually abused. This defence relaxed a little and he revealed his horror at what he had done. He was grateful that his family believed as he did that the stabbing had been an accident. Equally he was puzzled and worried by his action and wanted to understand it. His ambivalence was obvious and to some extent he could recognize this. It was quite clear that he had not meant to hurt Joe and yet at the same time he had also quite clearly wanted to kill him. He had felt tied to Joe in some way but had felt unable to change the situation. Later, in therapy he continued to feel aggravated by and angry towards Joe for some time. He complained that Joe was going about telling lies about him and it was clear that he could not let Joe go from his mind. It emerged that, a year after the event, they were both keeping close track of each other's movements.

Nik had been portrayed as a model pupil with no record of violence, but told me that he had often had angry outbursts at home when he thought about what his uncle had done to him and had sometimes smashed furniture. As had been the case when he was a child, his rage had been simply tolerated without intervention by his mother. Undoubtedly his mother would have understood correctly his anger towards the uncle. However, as well as being inhibited by her own difficulties with aggression, mother may also have been reluctant to intervene through feelings of guilt at what she had unintentionally 'allowed' to occur with the uncle. Thus, an environment that could understand and help him make sense of his feelings continued to be lacking.

Discussion

I should make clear that some of the ideas expressed below are speculative but based on the assessment and the history, they attempt to offer some under-standing of this boy's internal development which led to his violent act.

In his early development Nik was a precious 'replacement' child who was over protected by mother and to whom there was little access by a father who might have been able to help him to deal with his natural aggressive feelings. As the 'product' of his father's weakness (his father's inability to stand up to his own parents) and with an overwhelming mother who had excluded the 'weak' father, Nik's male identification would have been impeded. Later, as a toddler, when his parents separated, it was at the stage in his development when he would have especially needed a father to help him separate and individuate from a pre-Oedipal tie to the mother. It is possible, then or later, that he might have felt responsible for father's departure. The circumstances of Nik's birth and the subsequent rapid deterioration in the marital situation offers some support to this notion.

With the loss of a father, who himself had been unable to manage his own aggression, Nik was left with a mother who also had difficulty in tolerating her own aggressive feelings and who was inhibited in her capacity to help her son in this respect. With depleted external resources to contain and help him, Nik's attempt to develop an internal capacity to manage his frustration and utilize his aggression creatively and productively would have been impaired. When his mother finally became unable to manage him and handed him over to relatives, he may have experienced this as a confirmation that his aggression could not be understood or tolerated. The feeling of utter helplessness that he would have experienced when he was placed with others who had felt free to abuse him, must have produced in him the conviction that there was no external or internal resource available to help him.

Nik's only available means of adaptation to the constant frustration caused him by his aggressive feelings was to turn them inwards: that is, he became passive in the way he related to the world with occasional frightening (to him) outbursts which only served to confirm his need to repress his aggression. This passivity, accompanied by a developing veneer of pseudo coping and functioning, would have become well established in later years in order for him to have maintained the credible presentation of the 'well behaved model pupil'.

Through his own internalized experience of his parents' sado-masochistic relationship and with the absence of a satisfactory means to deal with his aggressive feelings, Nik developed an identification with the 'helpless victim' represented by mother. This 'helpless victim' moreover would also have been perceived in father, both in relation to his father's lack of capacity to contain his own aggression as well as in the way he demonstrated that he could not stand up to his own parents.

It might be considered that when Nik was 'handed over' to the extended family which then later abused him that he was 'ready made' for the compliant role of helpless victim. We see a generational pattern in the way he had identified with the father who could not stand up for himself, and with similar lack of resources neither could he. Furthermore, with the internalized experience of his parents' sado-masochistic way of relating, the aggression beneath Nik's passivity may have gradually been utilized, not just to comply with, but to promote the abusive engagement with uncle as the only apparent means of coping with his aggression. In other words his aggression became sexualized. As I have mentioned above, Nik would at the same time have formed an attachment to his uncle and for this reason he would also have wished to maintain the relationship. This same need for an attachment, and the wish to maintain it, was echoed in his relationship with Joe; someone who had also shown an 'interest' in him.

Nik's prolonged abuse by his uncle, which for four years had continued unobserved by parents, teachers and peers, could only have served to compound his internal world constellation of sado-masochism in which he was largely the helpless victim of his own aggression being made to 'enjoy' suffering, while healthy self-preservative aggressive impulses appeared to have no status.

Interestingly, the only occasion when he became angry during the assessment was at my suggestion that he might have wanted his mother to intervene to prevent the uncle's telephone calls from prison. I understood his anger to relate more to a wish to 'preserve' the attachment with uncle rather than a 'self preservative' wish for his mother to have severed the 'connection' with uncle. In ostensibly defending mother, Nik was in fact perpetuating the sado-masochistic relationship with uncle.

A more comprehensive picture emerges of Nik's relationship with Joe in the way he would seem to have had no choice about the way he allowed himself to comply with a 'bad deal'. He actually felt he *had to* pay Joe the money but at the same time he *knew* that it did not make sense for him to be in this position. In some ways this reflected the early situation of the unsatisfactory arrangement or 'bad deal' between his parents which had culminated in Nik's birth. Perhaps as more of a family script than an identification, Nik had re-enacted the way his parents had felt constrained to have another child while at the same time knowing that this would be unwise.

In the way Nik allowed the matter to continue with Joe over many months, trapped and frustrated by a situation from which he had no internal resources to extricate himself, we can observe a parallel with three interconnected situations in his life. The first was as a baby trapped with warring parents with no means (internal or external) of liberating himself from an overwhelming mother or of freeing himself from the frustration of his aggressive feelings. The second was when he was 'trapped' in his uncle's sexual perversion for many years and then in the absence of anybody else showing an 'interest', forming an attachment. The third was when even after the authorities had intervened and imprisoned the uncle, Nik's willingness to talk to him on the telephone revealed that he was unable to be free of his uncle, internally or externally. That situation was also reinforced by the 'sadistic' side of mother who effectively aided and abetted the uncle by not preventing the phone calls. In this respect Nik could be thought of as having an internal 'sadistic' mother who had not allowed his mind to 'disconnect' from his preoccupation with Joe's movements a year after the violent event.

One striking aspect which emerges from the story is the complete absence in Nik of any sense that anything had been unfair in his life. As the object of his parents' strife he had no complaint. As the child handed to his uncle to be treated as a receptacle for sexual abuse there was no complaint except through the later occasional outbursts of rage which he did not properly understand. The unfairness of the deal made with Joe only marginally impinged on his consciousness initially, largely hindered by his wish to preserve the attachment.

It was only in the days leading up to the attack that Nik's mounting frustration began to allow some feeling of injustice to permeate his mind. When he finally 'snapped' and stabbed Joe, I think he was trying to extricate himself from an intolerable situation (internal and external) in which he felt endangered. His need for his attachment to Joe weakened as his sado-masochistic defence no longer protected him from an increasing sense that he was being both taken over and humiliated by Joe. Nik had tried increasingly to evade Joe and his failure to achieve this might have left him feeling that his entire sense of self was under threat; that he was being *invaded*. Nik's 'psychological integrity' was under strain and to negate the danger he employed violence which was self-preservative. He needed to be rid of this oppressor who had pursued him relentlessly for months causing him to feel controlled and humiliated.

For a long time Nik had managed his anxieties about his aggression and attachment through the sado-masochistic relationship in which he had been entrenched with Joe. In making the deal, which he need not have made, Nik had felt powerless and could do nothing except comply in the same way as he had with his uncle. More important, he had been powerless even to be able to *think* that he had an alternative to complying. However, as I have discussed above, Nik's passivity was maintained by his inwardly directed aggression. His suffering at the hands of his uncle's sexualized aggression was utilized by him to reinforce his repression of his own aggression. Although there was no sexualization in his relationship with Joe, Nik had effectively placed himself in a similar position with Joe. At the point that he 'snapped', his sado-masochistic defence temporarily broke down unleashing self-preservative violence to 'free' himself.

The internalization of a masochistic 'world' must also require the internalization of a 'sadistic' world in order for an individual to self-perpetuate such relationships. Nik was not equipped with the usual adolescent capacity to reciprocate normal teasing and goading to fend off others until the banter inevitably subsides. He would have appeared as a passive recipient of such activity which would only provoke others to continue with the intent of obtaining a response. When Nik could stand no more of Joe's baiting, he momentarily snapped in much the same manner as he might have witnessed his father behaving. At that moment he 'identified with the aggressor': his violent father, his abusing uncle and Joe, who had persecuted him.

Although I have discussed how Nik's violence was predominantly self-preservative, I think that through his identifications with violent and sadistic 'aggressors' that there would also have been a wish to 'repay' the humiliation and suffering which had resonated throughout his attachment to Joe. When he stabbed Joe, finally, in the back, when he could see Joe was already in considerable pain, there was probably an intention to make him suffer. In more concrete terms I am therefore suggesting that while the violent act was initiated by the wish to rid himself of his oppressor, the final stab may have been motivated by a wish for emotional gratification from Joe's suffering. On the one hand Nik wanted to kill Joe efficiently and on the other he wanted Joe to suffer so that he could 'enjoy' it. From Nik's description of the event, the wish for gratification would not have been prolonged and in fact his immediate horror at what he had done suggests that his sadistic aim was short lived before it became displaced by the more familiar repression of his, now, clearly experienced dangerous aggressive feelings.

The sado-masochistic defence, temporarily disrupted, reasserted itself and this was revealed through his continuing acceptance of his uncle's telephone calls over six months later. His wish to rid himself of his 'oppressor' was also diminished, revealed by his preoccupation with Joe over a year later even though Joe kept had kept a safe distance from Nik.

Conclusion

There were certain hopeful indications that Nik may benefit from psychotherapy. His violence had been accompanied by severe guilt and shame and also a wish to make some reparation; another identification with father. It will be evident that Nik had replicated with Joe, something of his earlier experience of relationships. As a target for the attack Joe would have represented to Nik more of a symbol or composite figure of all his past and more seriously abusive attachment figures. It was perhaps some recognition of this that allowed Nik to be genuinely concerned and perplexed at how he could commit such an act.

In looking at Nik's violent act in terms of what it was trying to resolve, it may be regarded as an attempt to retrieve the 'lost' father who could help him with his aggression. The resolution in representational terms would have been for father to 'rescue' (the child) Nik from mother and then for the parents to function together in a way which could contain and manage their own aggression and by implication that of their children.

By the time Nik was about to appear in court, father had resolved to give up drinking and he and his wife began to discuss a reconciliation. A few days before Nik went to court his father suffered a heart attack. He recovered and subsequently began to take a greater interest in Nik. On his release from prison, the uncle continued to telephone Nik and again Nik was 'powerless' to resist. This time father took steps to deter the uncle but without going so far as to report him to the police.

It was interesting and hopeful that the violent act had had such an impact on father. Such a shift in the family dynamic might be considered a partial resolution when thinking in terms of the 'intention' *behind* the violent act. Although his father's active interest was important and even hopeful for Nik, it came much too late in his development for immediate resolution of his conflicts.

It is to be hoped that Nik will pursue psychotherapy, which over many years may help him to obviate sexualization of his aggression and to avoid repeating his uncle's behaviour. Even more hopefully he may be able to form satisfying relationships through discovery of new and creative means of utilizing his aggressive feelings.

In this chapter I have attempted to illustrate the importance of understanding the meaning of the violent act. Through what I have called a mode of 'forensic enquiry' into the perpetrator's internal and external worlds, clues can be discovered which will have direct implications for constructive treatment and management.

CHAPTER 9

Racial Violence and Young People

Surya Bhate and Soni Bhate

There has been a substantial increase in disturbance exhibited by young people in the last four decades in nearly all developed countries. The documentary evidence is lacking in Third World countries; however, explanations may lie in the lack of adequate reporting of crime and disturbance in those countries. There has been a substantial increase in the rates of serious assault (apart from motor vehicle crimes and breaking and entering) in the UK and other countries. It is therefore not surprising that we are witnessing an increase in reporting of incidents viewed as racial violence and 'tit for tat' attacks between gangs of youths of various communities.

The UK is a multiracial and multicultural nation. Approximately five per cent of the population in the UK is from the Third World (non white) countries, most living in urban areas around London, Birmingham, Leicester, Manchester and Leeds. Concentration of ethnic communities in urban areas is linked to availability of employment opportunities and housing during the 1950s and 1960s, boom years of immigration of workforce from Third World countries to take jobs that indigenous communities did not want. The second and third generation of these immigrants have continued to reside in the urban areas with small, if any, numbers moving to rural communities.

In our attempt to understand inter-racial violence we need to reflect on the background and cultural beliefs of these immigrants, and also the effect of migration, racial discrimination, housing and educational problems encountered by the immigrants. Why are second and third generation migrants behaving differently then from the first generation? First, the second and third generation (immigrants) do see themselves as 'British' with the same rights and responsibilities as everyone else – yet encounter different treatment from the host community.

Historical factors

Immigrants to the UK from the Third World have largely come from the Asian subcontinent and the West Indies. These two groups are distinct and have brought with them different sets of value systems, religious beliefs and experiences. Nevertheless, they have encountered similar obstacles upon arrival. There has been a popular belief that Indian immigrants by and large are non aggressive and non violent in their approach to oppression. Up to a point this has to do with non violent struggle launched by Gandhi and his followers to achieve independence from their colonial British masters. To expect that that same stance will be adopted by descendants who are in the UK is to misunderstand the history and differing response at different times by groups of people. Dumont (1961) has written eloquently about factors which are of great importance to consideration of social honour centring on descent, lineage, and race. Hindus, of course, have a caste system which is both rigid and elaborate and based on birth and descent with historical association between caste and occupation. These are breaking down in modern India.

West Indian immigrants on the other hand have a heritage of slavery which in many ways has affected the 'family norm' (mother, father and child) and have developed the matrifocal family where the strongest bond exists between child, mother and grandmother. If the conventional wisdom of developmental psychology that a child needs both parent figures (male and female) is true, then the Caribbean parent and her children do experience deprivation in the absence of extended support system available in the West Indies.

Both these groups (Asian and West Indians) have experienced inequality prior to coming to the UK on the basis of inheritance of caste and colour. It is even more evident in the sphere of race relations as within the UK racial distinction continues to be a basis of social inequality. Race riots have been a feature of life in the USA, France, Germany and the UK. Recent convictions of arsonists in Germany, who burned a house of refugees, brought about a great deal of soul searching in Germany.

Racial violence and politicization of black immigration

Solomos (1992) has written about ritualization of the post World War II immigration of blacks and Asians – but not those from Europe and Ireland. The need to 'control' black immigration turned on the themes that too many coloured immigrants caused problems in relation to housing, education, employment, social habits and crime. The race riots in Nottingham and Notting Hill in 1958 spurred racialized politics. The supposed reasons for resentment against immigrants were said to be lack of work, dependency on State assistance and taking housing while white residents go without. It was also rumoured that blacks were likely to indulge in all kinds of misbehaviour, especially sexual (*The*

Times, 3 September 1958). Enoch Powell's famous 'rivers of blood' speech in Birmingham in April 1968 further popularized the common prejudice against black and Asian immigrants. Apart from successively restrictive legislations brought in to halt immigration, repatriation as an option became a part of political debate.

During the weekend of 10th–12th April 1981 major disorder and scenes of violence erupted in Brixton which led to the Scarman Inquiry and Report by Lord Scarman (1981). The Summary of Findings is still as relevant today. The report identified a marked incidence of social problems, severity of discrimination (on the basis of race and colour) levels of unemployment (higher for blacks) and problems in education and housing experienced by black people. (By now we do not have the first generation immigrants who were willing to accept the harsh realities of discrimination, but second and third generations who are born and brought up here.) The current black and Asian population also comprises second and third generation immigrants who are not as willing to accept the harsh realities of discrimination as first generation immigrants may have been.

Newspapers periodically report escalation of gang violence between both sides of the ethnic divide (colour divide). Richard Everitt was stabbed to death (*The Observer*, Sunday 21st August 1994) in an argument with a group of Asian youths on a London estate allegedly as a revenge for an attack on Bengali boys beaten a fortnight earlier. The recent killing of a young man (white) by other white youths (allegedly) (*The Times*, January 5th 1996) when he went to the aid of his father in a genteel town is a brutal reminder to us all of the extent of racial divide. The family had suffered months of racial abuse from a hardcore of youths because their mother was born in Malta.

The number of reported racial incidents (there is general acceptance that only a proportion of incidents are reported) is rising. Of the 5060 racial incidents reported in London in 1993 (*The Observer*, 21st August 1994) over 78 per cent were suffered by blacks, but 22 per cent, a significant proportion, were suffered by whites.

What has changed?

The young people are beginning to talk about defending their communities and vigilante groups such as the Drumond Street Posse are emerging. Is it possible that children and young people (of immigrants) who are growing up in Britain are learning the anti-social racist skills of those who attacked their parents and them? What are the possible explanations?

The problem of race relations has acquired considerable political significance across the World. Race riots in the USA, South Africa and Malaysia (between the Chinese and Malay) Sudan and India are endemic. The violence and conflict cannot be fully understood in political terms only. Social inequality and deprivation, apart from cultural roots contribute to the spectrum of difficulty encountered. Differences in colour and physique are socially evaluated. Skin colour, because of its visibility easily becomes the basis of social discrimination though names (e.g. Ahmed as opposed to Smith), different religion and clothing, identify individuals as different. The latter can be adapted, but not one's skin colour.

Aggression and violence

The universality of man as an aggressive creature has been commented upon by many writers. However what is true of a man may not be true of women. This is possibly explained by different social training and innate biological factors. There is however a problem in defining violence. For example, violence in a declared war is seen as legitimate. It need not even be declared, as violent struggle in Ireland is justified by IRA and Provisionals as 'legitimate'. Similar acts were justified in the Hindu-Muslim riots the world witnessed at the time of partition in India (when the British left) and even today. What about violence carried out by resistance movements during World War II – very few will regard it as unjustified even today. This confusion, in turn, is often used as a justification by a minority of young people to rationalize their behaviour.

There are many possible explanations. Freud (1930) wrote 'tendency to aggression is innate,…culture has to call up every possible reinforcement in order to erect barriers against aggressive instinct'. Aggression need not always be socially destructive. Society mandates aggression as a means of preventing greater aggression in the form of self-defence – there is evidence from experimental studies that aggression is greater and much more resistant to being switched off when the victim is seen as malicious or not the same as us (human). Perhaps Blake put it succinctly when he wrote

> I was angry with my friend:
> I told my wrath, my wrath did end.
> I was angry with my foe:
> I told it not, my wrath did grow

> (*A Poison Tree*)

The psychological theories about aggression have been summarized by Berkowitz (1989). The frustration hypothesis summarized contains the following points:

(1) Frustration leads to negative feelings.

(2) Negative feelings are associated with anger, thoughts and feelings.

(3) Anger does not necessarily cause aggression but may be accompanied by it.

Equally appropriate to consider may be the theory of displacement, in which an individual who has been abused by others displaces his violence on people who he can abuse. Groups of young people (black) many of whom themselves were victims of violence in the past may interact in this way. It is almost like a chain effect.

Social learning can influence or inhibit aggressive behaviour. We live in the age of the group. This is particularly so during adolescence. Harrington (1976) has written perceptively about the pitfalls in following simplistic explanations of group violence. There are, however, important facets of groups we need to understand.

Group dynamics

If the group cohesion is to be maintained then the aggression needs to be contained within the limits. The individuals conform to a mode of group opinion and behaviour that makes them follow group consensus. However, in certain groups the leader may make the decision, hence this type of group is at greatest risk to instigate or inhibit aggression. The group identity in these situations assumes primacy over individual feelings. The group may tend to scapegoat someone outside by a mechanism of displacement. Violence may help the group to bolster its reputation and once this is achieved the group may seek the opportunity to reinforce it. It may indeed be as a result of or attempt to compensate for feelings of weakness or inadequacy (Adler 1965).

Social determinants

Group violence is deeply embedded in political thinking and behaviour. The mass media may amplify and enhance the perpetration of it. The media attention gives social importance and attention, resulting in unwitting reinforcement of these behaviours.

Cultural determinants

The family plays a vital role in the patterning of behaviour and is the primary group in most societies. Children who are brought up in violent families and disciplined in a capricious manner are likely to be more aggressive than non-abused children. However, most studies are based on retrospective accounts in which abuse has not been independently verified and may be subject to the victim's biased recall. Temperament also plays an important part. Attitudes of communities to deal with differences also plays a part. A proportion of immigrants from the Asian subcontinent, for example Gujeratis, are known for their business acumen, strong support of education and non confrontational and non aggressive methods of solving disputes. Having migrated to the UK these communities have prospered in businesses. Bengalis are also not seen as a non aggressive group (in the context of the Indian subcontinent) but have not prospered in the UK (broadly speaking) and have had to endure considerable hardship, discrimination and unemployment in the UK (personal observation). Second and third generation Bengalis, not having family businesses to join, unlike Gujeratis, are beginning to express anger and frustration and are joining gangs to protect themselves. (example – the maze of estates around Camden) much to the dismay of community elders. The aggressive gangs often give status to the leaders, have their own value systems emphasizing strength, fighting ability and risk taking. The gangs often operate within territories and incursion by others leads to inter group violence.

The group begins to operate on the principle of 'them' and 'us'. This pseudo separation (whilst being part of the larger society) reduces the obligation to wider society and justifies violence.

Case study

I first met Tony (assumed name) when he was 11 years old. He was referred by the school and social services simultaneously in view of the serious difficulties encountered within the school and in the community. At school he was failing to learn, not co-operative in the classroom and often was disruptive and hostile to peers and teachers alike. He was excluded from class on several occasions. There were times also when he truanted from school and instigated others to join him. The mother in desperation had sought the help of the local authority social worker as Tony stole from home, challenged her authority and at times was destructive of the meagre family belongings when in a temper.

The second referral was at the age of 15 in a local authority assessment centre where he was remanded by Magistrates. The charge on this occasion was robbery. Tony candidly shared with me a number of other anti social activities he had been involved in since the age of eight. These included breaking in and stealing from cars, shoplifting, burglaries, etc. He had been suspended from his previous two schools, but was in the process of being rehabilitated back once again. He found the educational tasks within the grasp of his intellectual ability but did not find them interesting and often truanted by himself and at other times instigated other children. By now he had acquired the reputation in school for being 'tough' and Tony boasted about how he had intimidated some of the teachers in the previous school. He was proud of being the second best fighter in his gang.

His early childhood history was suggestive of deprivation, rejection and the break up of his parents' relationship. He was received into local authority care and had multiple short-term fostering. He claimed to have a close relationship with his mother but had found her weak and hence his unwillingness to accept her authority. He had occasional contact with his father but did not appear to have developed any relationship with him.

During in-depth interviews to assess various aspects of his life, including offending patterns it became evident that apart from the identified charges for which he appeared before the Court Tony was also involved in skirmishes and occasional violence between two gangs. He was proud of his Britishness and talked about ethnic minorities who also lived on the same estate (predominantly Bengali and Pakistani) and how he tormented those families and indulged in 'Paki bashing'. It was during this session that he suddenly became aware of my ethnicity and said 'You are all right, but they should be sent back home'.

Summary

I have seen Tony on numerous occasions since his first referral. It is evident that he suffered many disadvantages and is clearly posing problems to his family and the community in view of the anti social behavioural patterns he is presenting. He is a bright and able young man who in the process of his development appears to have picked up scapegoats including the minorities who live on the same estate. He perceives his anti social behaviours being challenged by his mother and society, but does not regard his 'Paki bashing' as particularly wrong, as until he met me no-one had specifically raised this aspect with him. So far he has escaped the charge of violent behaviour on the basis of racist behaviour. In my work with him he has become aware of the rights of others, including those of ethnic minority young people, but I am unsure how far the insight developed in the work with him will be sustained by him in the context of the gang ideology and the morality.

Summary and suggestions

Tackling racial disadvantage:

(1) The Race Relation Act 1976 placed upon local authorities for the first time a statutory duty to take steps to eliminate racial discrimination and disadvantage. The current situation, in spite of efforts, however, is that of confusion and acrimony. Pursuit of race equality issues have proved brief as a result of perceived heavier electoral costs. We appear to have reached a critical point if we are to meet the challenges of a multiracial society even though more blatant forms of racism have been tempered.

(2) There are certain inequalities common to members of all societies due to uneven distribution of power and wealth. Problems of unemployment are faced by all members of the ethnic divide.

However, members of ethnic minorities are over represented amongst the unemployed. Racial discrimination in employment is now well recognized and proven. As Lord Scarman points out in his Report on the Brixton Riots – high unemployment, bad housing, lack of amenities, social problems including family breakdown were a potent mixture present in contributing to social unrest. Politicizing and blaming members of ethnic minorities for the social ills of society merely exacerbates the frustration felt by the young on both sides of the political and ethnic divide.

(3) Asian culture attaches great importance to family values, tradition and religion. The African continent has an equally strong tradition of family. West Indian immigrants to the UK are descendants of enslaved Africans who were brought forcibly to the Caribbean as slaves by Western Europeans. The slavery interrupted and changed the pattern of relationships. The forced change led to evolution of matrifocal families where the strong bond is obvious through females. These two groups (broadly speaking) brought with them different cultures to be surrounded by the culture of the host community. In this context culture includes knowledge, belief, art, morals, law and custom. Arrival in a new country with a different cultural value system contributes to ethnocentric attitudes. In other words – one's own culture is the best. This in turn is challenged by the next generation of immigrants who are exposed to the influence of the host community. This evolution of culture is to be expected and ought to be a positive development but for the antagonism and perceived hostility of a proportion of the host community. Therein lies the potential for conflict.

The psychosocial disorders tend to increase during adolescence which is a period of multiple transitions – including separation and distancing from parents. Young people who are born and brought up here do not readily accept the inequities prevalent and are beginning to take the law into their own hands. This worrying development has roots in inequalities and the perceived unwillingness of the authorities to act in protecting the rights of minorities.

(4) The role of teachers and education in helping children to develop a sense of morality and understanding the difference between right and wrong has recently been commented on by Tate (*The Sunday Times*, 14th January 1996) who laments the pervasive hedonism of

our society. Parents and educators need to work together to find practical ways of tackling morality, spirituality and universal human values, apart from dealing with the educational underachievement by a significant proportion of all school leavers.

CHAPTER 10

Television and the Well-Being of Children and Young People

Richard Sparks

Introduction

The sight of children watching television, whether in silent and solitary communion or in a chatty group or in any of a number of other attitudes, is a mundane feature of contemporary domestic experience. Yet for all its familiarity, the image is also routinely attended by certain anxieties. That television is so intimately involved in the rhythm of daily life is testimony to its pervasiveness; that it pervades daily life is in large measure why we sometimes look upon it with misgivings and suspicion.

Our view of the medium, and more particularly of its place in the lives of children, is thus commonly characterized by a degree of ambivalence. We are well aware that television can captivate children, that it can excite and stimulate them. We know, by extension, that it can bring to their awareness an extraordinarily wide and richly sensuous array of sight and sound – stories, information, games; images of animals and sometimes of their endangerment; images of people in other places and cultures, and so on. And we know from experience that the sights and sounds of the television of our own childhoods (for an English person born, like myself, around 1960 these would include, to name only those that spring to mind first; the music to *The Magic Roundabout, Blue Peter, Robinson Crusoe, The Flashing Blade* – I probably need not go on) can evoke an extraordinary nostalgia. Their mere recollection can unite relative strangers in the shared intimacy of being members of the same birth cohort. The principal children's television shows of a given decade are surely, for a late twentieth century person, integral to their vision of 'the national culture', if anything is. They 'date' us as surely as the now unfashionable tastes in popular music that we went on to acquire in our teens; but in so doing they also situate us – they are amongst the fragments that we use to impose a sense of coherence and continuity on the narratives of our lives and identities. Yet is seems to me questionable whether this positive sense of television as a medium of discovery and a source of consolation is our dominant one. At any rate is has historically co-existed with a much more negative set of associations, of which most of us (I submit) carry at least the traces. This inheritance encourages a view of television variously as an insidious form of thought control; as inducing an unnatural passivity; as the enemy of reading and other more constructive pursuits; as interrupting interaction and the formation of relationships and, most alarmingly of all, as bringing on a truculent and surly aggressiveness that sometimes ends in criminal violence.

The latter group of dismal images are not perhaps as influential as they once were. Neither have they gone away, however, and, as I shall go on to suggest, they are prone to return to prominence at certain times and in conjunction with certain events. The starting point for discussion must simply be that we live with competing notions of what role television plays in the lives of our children; that these are sometimes articulated for us with some vehemence by the proponents of particular interests or political positions; and that this state of affairs seems unlikely to go away. Parents and other custodians of children are thus faced, in this respect as in so many others, with having to make decisions about the welfare of children on the basis of inherently imperfect knowledge and with the noise of debate ringing about their heads. An adult making these decisions is always in the wrong from one point of view or another; how much television should I allow the children to watch?; how far (and on what grounds) shall I resist their will when they want to watch and I want them to do something else?; would their time be better occupied in other ways?; what if anything shall I censor and how is this decision affected by their ages?; how far are my own decisions to be conditioned by what I know or suspect happens in other households?

This chapter does not presume to answer, or even really to advise on, any of these questions, but it is stimulated in part by the fact that I as its author, and much more important as a parent of small children, also live with them daily. It is thus in part personal reflection and in part scholarly overview of some relevant issues. Its premise is that if I continually favour decisions of a certain kind about the use of television on behalf of my children (on the basis of my beliefs about their best interests, or because I am under some form of social pressure or because I am sometimes too busy or too lazy to intervene) I cannot responsibly retreat under the cover of academic agnosticism and pretend that I have no view on the matter. On the other hand, I also know that I muddle through these decisions in very much the same way as everybody else. Therefore, to lay claim to definitive knowledge would likewise, in a parallel way, be in bad faith, and I am in any case doubtful that the available evidence gives grounds for certainty or clear guidance. The aim of social scientists when confronted with issues of this kind need not be to make either of these escape attempts. Rather than claiming detachment, it may be more fruitful to reflect upon the conditions under which one lives out an intrinsic involvement. What this chapter attempts is the limited ambition of offering some sense of context and perspective for understanding some of the more insistent concerns. One reason for preferring this modest (but not I hope evasive) tack is precisely the same pervasiveness of television to which we have already alluded. In that television is an integral, even emblematic, feature of the way we live now, and a mundane presence in the lives of most of our children, it is a matter too important for attitudinizing and triteness (so, unsurprisingly, these vices are endemic almost wherever it is discussed).

The outline of the chapter is as follows. I will argue that those aspects of children's experience of television that have received the most attention, principally the long-standing dispute over the imitative 'effects' of 'violence', have not been *ipso facto* the most interesting or consequential, though the extent of the interest in them is itself sociologically eloquent. I very briefly review some aspects of the 'violence' debate. I propose that, although not in any sense a trivial matter, the issue has seldom been discussed in the most helpful or theoretically open-minded way. One reason for this is surely the sheer intensity of the political passions that are implicated in an issue that folds together some of our tenderest and most fretful concerns. The debate on children and television has thus always been conducted in more than one register. It has deployed the vocabulary and methods of 'hard' science, but it has also spoken a less limpid and more impassioned language because its topics – childhood, violence, technology, the family – are felt to be so powerfully emblematic of the troubled present and dangerous future of our kind of society. I sketch one or two ways in which I think the question of children and 'violence' on television is beginning to be more fruitfully and sensitively explored,[1] principally with regard to the displays of rugged masculinity and physical prowess which the moments of 'violence' seem designed to accomplish.

The interesting question then becomes not so much 'how much violence do our children see on television and does it harm them?' as 'what should we infer from the tendency of our culture to present us from an early age with heroic stories of masculine force and virtue?'. Finally, I suggest that there are in any case other issues that might bear upon the well-being of children and young people in a more fundamental way but which have received rather less attention than the supposed 'violence' equation. Principal among these are the questions of anxiety and insecurity, and I draw on some sources in current social theory

---

1   I lean fairly heavily on the work of the Australian cultural theorists Bob Hodge and David Tripp whose book *Children and Television* (1986) seems to me to have introduced some particularly helpful revisions in the prevailing ways of conceptualizing the relevant issues.

(in particular the work of Anthony Giddens (1984, 1990)) in raising the questions (1) do we have reason to see any relationship between children's media use and their experience of anxiety or vulnerability?; and (2) what consequences may follow from children's (or their parent's) anxieties about violence for the quality of their daily lives?

The violence debate revisited

The 'effects' of television violence, especially on the growing child, have long been a much-researched topic. At least from the time that the networks achieved 'saturation' of the geographical territory of the United States (which is to say the late 1950s) there have been numerous, recurrent – though not continual – voicings of concern about the malign effects of the medium on youth. At least two strands have been evident in the history of this enterprise, but they have intertwined in all manner of confusing and engrossing ways.

(1) The cultural context

The first motor of debate, and in political terms perhaps the leading partner, is provided by a voice of moral concern (sometimes shading into outrage). It is primarily a conservative voice, at least in the sense that its worries have included that television (and other technologies of popular entertainment and youth culture) displaces community, erodes respect for parents and for authority, spreads secular hedonism, and so on. It is a concern that has both popular (associated in Britain especially but not exclusively with the campaigning activities from 1964 onwards of Mary Whitehouse) and 'elite' versions (in Britain especially the literary critical stances of T S Eliot and F R Leavis and their successors). Many differences subsist between the versions of this story of change and decay, and it is even now a territory which is inadequately mapped (but see Newburn 1993; Sparks 1992, ch.3). In the analyses of some critics there is simply a recurrent tendency for the most popular medium at any given time to attract special opprobrium: so television assumed (in spades) the mantles formerly claimed successively by fairs, music halls, movies, radio, and horror comics (see Barker 1984; Hirsch 1976). In another modulation, societies are seen as prone to a myth of the 'Golden Age', always located fleetingly some thirty years or so in the past, when we ourselves were children and things were done differently (Pearson 1983).

It is clear that the debate on 'TV violence' and its 'effects' has been overlain, indeed often driven, by cultural concerns and fears of this kind. The changes that have overtaken western societies during the lifespan of the medium have been astounding indeed. The spread of television, and its evident capacity to restructure the nature of domestic leisure, has itself been one of the more palpable of those changes. And, moreover, it has become a primary channel through which we gain awareness of those same unsettling social changes. *And*, furthermore, it has itself changed almost out of recognition in the last quarter of a century: it has diversified, proliferated, extended, intruded, and (at least from the point of view of those cultural conservatives who see contemporary society as being in the process of realizing their worst fears) fragmented. None of this is to say (and here I part company with some of the tone of condescension that has at times characterized the responses of liberal academics and other cultural elites to this debate) that the concerns that animate the discussion are themselves trivial. It is not a bit surprising that the heating up of technological and social change is not universally welcome: for every brave new world that is sighted on the horizon there really is a world that is lost. More particularly, whatever difficulties surround the quantification of crime (and as we shall see these are profound enough to raise some difficulty for much television 'effects' research) the six-fold increase in recorded crime in Britain since 1945 is no mere statistical artifact. It is the fact that these two symptoms of change – the rise in crime and the rise of television – really have both been so startlingly evident that has led so many commentators to over-argue (and over-simplify) the connection between them.

In both the United States and Britain interest in and funding for research into television effects have proceeded spasmodically, albeit at times in great quantity. The commissioning of research, its resources and its reception have in large measure been vulnerable to the prevailing conditions in the larger arena of public debate at a given moment: and the extent and intensity of that discussion has risen and fallen for reasons largely extrinsic to anything that the research itself reports. For example, in the United States the conclusion by Joseph Klapper (1962) that no behavioural effects of television viewing could be identified with confidence was for some time the academic orthodoxy. The subsequent resurgence of interest in the topic was in the first instance political in origin even if it then gave rise to a really very large programme of research (see Rowland 1983; Sparks 1992, pp.19–21). What had been regarded as a rather peripheral matter became, during the late 1960s and 1970s, perhaps the most intensively researched topic in the behavioural sciences (see Pearl, Bouthilet and Lazar 1982). On a more local scale, there was a significant re-politicization of the issue in Britain during 1993 (and since) in the wake of the murder of James Bulger and – although little new research was forthcoming – the contested results of the research tradition were again brought into focus (House of Commons 1994; Newson 1994).

There are a number of reasons why it is necessary to rehearse aspects of this history. The first is that it complicates to a high degree our attempts to get straight what if anything the research 'proves'. Untangling the intellectual quality of the work and its claims from the surrounding contention is an intricate, and perhaps impossible, task. But it is also important to accept that the history of debate and rhetorical assertion is more than just 'noise' that intrudes upon the quiet work of scholarly research: it is the condition of existence of that research in the first place. Seen from one point of view this just makes the topic impossibly messy and best avoided; or it prompts researchers to try to impose special controls (rigorous experimental conditions and so on) in an attempt to insulate inquiry from all that babble, and from the hurly-burly of daily life in which television viewing normally takes place. But from a third perspective, it is important to make some attempt to incorporate these layers of discourse that already surround the medium of television, and more especially its relation to the well-being of children, reflexively into one's apprehension of the issues. Otherwise one may never be able to answer the question: 'what is fundamentally at stake in this discussion?'. Similarly, without a sense of the historicity of the question, one would get nowhere in grasping why it is that some people (having read a good deal and in good faith) are able to assert with confidence that there is an extensive body of evidence in favour of the malign effects of television on children, whilst others (also having read a good deal and in good faith) insist that the matter is unproven. This is in part because people approach the research with *parti pris*. But it is also because the political character of the debate favours its periodic recurrence. In such a case the research itself often has a reiterative quality (indeed it often is the old research disinterred). Hence no-one is really required to shift their position. Either one sees the convincing corroboration of what was already known or one sees a stale rehash of familiar stuff.

(2) Rethinking 'TV violence'

Some of the main currents of research into effects of television violence are already very well known, and too widely reported elsewhere to need detailed treatment here. These include, for example, Bandura's 'Bobo Doll' experiments in the 1960s (in which, famously, children exposed to different kinds of television 'stimulus', were invited to wallop the stuffing out of the hapless dolls under the watchful eye of the experimenter) (Bandura, Ross and Ross 1963) or Berkowitz and Green's (1966) manipulations of responses to provocation. Such contributions have entered the folklore of social psychology (and its detractors). Later commentators (see Murray and Kippax 1979; Noble 1975 for good overviews) seem agreed that such laboratory work was suggestive but far from conclusive. It provided not so much 'proof' as a series of rather dramatic vignettes (the image of children whacking dolls is surely an evocative and unnerving one) that might stimulate further concern and enquiry. Moreover, whilst such early laboratory studies certainly had hypotheses (and whilst their practitioners often had pronounced theoretical preferences) they were commonly rather uninformative on what many have come to see as the McGuffin of the whole debate, namely, what was this 'violence' that made it happen? If visual/aural imagery exerted influences on children or adults what was it about what they saw and heard that did the influencing? And what processes of comprehension (or miscomprehension) intervened between what passed for the 'stimulus' and what was interpreted as the 'response'? In short, for all that it multiplied rather vigorously, the laboratory tradition of 'effects' research continued to be faced with certain basic difficulties: that it inherited the term 'violence' from ordinary language and consequently lumped many different forms and styles together (so that two experiments with ostensibly similar methods could not confidently be said to 'show' the same thing); that by extension, even where an 'effect' of some kind seemed plausible, the cognitive or affective dynamics through which it might act upon the viewer remained somewhat enigmatic; that the differences of context between experimental conditions and naturalistic settings of reception might be crucial, but in ways that could only be guessed at.

Over time many attempts have been made to evade or overcome these problems. The range of methods employed has extended to include surveys, longitudinal studies, 'natural experiments', and observation, as well as the traditional experiment (see by way of summary Comstock 1991). Whilst many such studies have retained a somewhat traditional outlook on the research enterprise (e.g. in their assumptions about the terms 'cause' and 'effect') there has also in the main been an increasing tolerance of complexity. The research has turned, as Comstock puts it, towards the identification of 'contingencies', or the conditions under which certain kinds of material might sometimes (amongst all the other influences that they receive) influence some children in some way. It is a less grand, but perhaps more intelligible, position either than was held by some investigators in the past or than has been advocated by moral entrepreneurs of various stripes down the years. This modest stance (what I think of as the 'weak-but-robust-traditional-effects' view) also has the advantage that it gels rather comfortably with the intuitions of many parents and legislators. Television, that is to say, is not all-powerful; but as a matter of prudence it would be unwise to expose children to whatever the free market in imagery chose to provide. There are therefore grounds for the regulation of that market as well as of children's own viewing preferences.

This only means that television is not exempt from the same kinds of concerns that the socialization of children ordinarily raises. There is no need to demonize the medium; but neither is it inert. In terms of policy, the regulation of television will probably take place within the same nexus between care and control as other children's issues, like schooling, and will raise the same dilemmas. So far, so good; and at the time of writing it may well be fair to say that, in Britain, one can detect the outlines of an emergent consensus around a view something like this (see for example the evidence submitted to the House of Commons Home Affairs Committee in its 1994 report), albeit that there are still proponents of agnosticism (such as Cumberatch and Howitt 1989). There is, however, still much more to be said, and space dictates that I shall only signal here what that might include.

First, it remains the case that there are many 'findings' but less theory; and adequately theorizing the audience/screen relation probably involves departing quite substantially from the familiar tramlines of 'effects' research. The objection that much research proceeds without an adequate account of either textual meaning or viewers' activity (of how the viewer imbues the screen's fleeting patterns of light with meaning) still has some force. If one wants to move away from a 'bucket theory' of television's effects ('violence' is like a bucketful of something nasty, someone comes along and dumps it over your head) then some account of these matters is needed. This would involve, to paraphrase Hodge and Tripp's helpful account, a move from 'pseudo-mechanical' to 'semiotic' causality (1986, p.201). 'Violence' (no more than any other social category) never appears in a pristine, context-free form. It is always something that occurs in a setting of some kind; in television its position in a narrative designedly holds certain significances; narratives make use of stylistic devices which conventionally mark their action as realistic or fantastical, serious or comedic or whatever; all of this is further interpreted by viewers in light of their own needs and desires, assumptions, skills, and so on. There is little work on television violence which attends to this level of analysis, and to do so is to complicate the story one tells about the nature of the medium's influences substantially (for suggestive contributions see Hall 1976; Schlesinger *et al.* 1992).

Second, therefore, in addition to refocusing attention on texts and their interpretation, we would seem to require some more substantial account of viewers (and especially of children as viewers) – their pleasures and aversions, identifications and repulsions. This is to stand at some remove from traditional quantitative concerns (how much violence is too much?) and to attend instead to some properly *social* questions about the character and setting of children's development, or as Hodge and Tripp put it 'the formation of structures of thought and feeling as they evolve over a lifetime' (1986, p.201). Seen from this point of view it is rather stunning how relatively little explicit discussion one finds of one of the more evident features of television 'violence' debates, namely that these have been much more about boys than girls. Once this is granted, the relevant questions have principally to do with boys' sense of their developing masculine identity and the images they receive of heroism, virtue, force, prowess and so on. Whether or not an image is 'violent' may be subordinate to the prior question of whether it is presented as conduct that is admirable in a man. In their short but constructive and thoughtful study *Young Offenders and the Media* (1994a) Ann Hagell and Tim Newburn asked young male offenders and their law-abiding peers to name their favourite film-stars. The two lists were barely distinguishable: Arnold Shwarzennegger and Jean-Claude van Damme were pre-eminent ahead of Bruce Willis, Sylvester Stallone, Mel Gibson and the rest. Whatever else may have differentiated the two groups it is not this: instead the iconography of heroic masculinity is part of the common culture of all young males. The more pointed question concerns the uses made of this gender patrimony: is it the case that some young men take too much to heart this mythology of the proud, undaunted rebel male? If so, in what familial, sub-cultural and economic contexts is this most likely?[2]

Third and, for now, finally, the tradition of 'effects' research has, historically, been conducted largely in a strange kind of isolation from other forms of social inquiry. Its concern has been primarily to identify an *independent* effect of television viewing (and to *prove* its disputed robustness) rather than to show how television connects with and informs other aspects of social being. In its more drastic versions (Schulman 1973) this leads to a tendency to attribute much or even most of the increase in post-war crime rates to the advent of mass television in a way that anyone who understands the dynamics of those trends (or even simply their collation as numbers) is likely to find unintelligible. It is sadly a somewhat forceful generalization that media scholars for the most part know almost nothing about criminology, and criminologists *vice versa*.

However, the more challenging possibility, and the one I want to pursue a little further, is that the predominant focus on the issue of violence (construed overwhelmingly in terms of its imitative or desensitizing or legitimating effects) has simply distracted attention from something more important and more consequential for the habitability of our everyday environments, namely fear.

Children, television and social anxiety

In recent years the related terms fear, anxiety and insecurity have brooked large in the work of students of crime and criminal justice. Indeed, the more protean and inclusive notion of 'risk' has become one of the central preoccupations of current social theory (see for example Douglas 1992; Giddens 1990).

An intemperate argument has raged about whether the fear of crime is a well-founded and 'rational' response to real threats (this is broadly the position of some feminists (Hanmer and Saunders 1984) and of 'left realist' criminolo-

---

2   In this regard the study of screen violence is continuous with, and has much to learn from, the study of men's uses of pornography. Studies of pornography have shown that one can combine a sophisticated awareness of the dynamics of representation (the *how* of image-creation) with a concern for long-term consequences for social action and social relations. Feminist students of pornography have had to confront the fact that whatever 'effects' ensue must have something to do with what is consumed as pleasurable, and physical pleasure is evoked through fantasy and visual iconography (see Itzin 1993: Kappeler 1986).

gists (Young 1987)) or whether is is at least in part an invention of media and political alarmism (a view ironically canvassed with the greatest verve by a journalist, Simon Jenkins of *The Times*). There have been a few attempts at mediation (e.g. Sparks 1991), and the debate has moved some distance beyond its former polarities.

A somewhat parallel argument has continued amongst students of television. Here Gerbner has entered the very strong claim that television, through its preoccupation in both news and fiction with stories of crime and violence, 'cultivates' in its viewers a 'mean world' outlook. Those who watch a lot of television (the ambiguously named 'heavy viewers') are said to develop a more television-dependent outlook than those who watch less. In response to survey questions about crime they are more likely to give the 'television answer', and this includes that they are more likely to hold punitive attitudes to offenders (Gerbner and Gross 1976; Gernber *et al.* 1984). To cut a long story short, this position is criticized by those who suggest *inter alia* that the 'mean world' finding is an artifact of place. The 'heavy viewers' and the scared viewers are the same people because those who are already scared stay in more and seek information about what concerns them (Doob and Macdonald 1979). Gunter (1987) provides a helpful overview.

Neither the criminological nor the media studies 'limb' of these debates has as yet seriously explored the implications of such issues for children. What might such an account look like, and what issues would it address? Here are some suggestions. They can only be conjectural because so little research exists; but they may help sketch some future lines of inquiry.

It is a commonplace observation that children's imaginative worlds are full of danger and overcoming. In his fantasies and play my four year old is often assailed by burglars, monsters, people-eating crocodiles and so on. He vanquishes them, usually with the help of his own impressive magical powers, but occasionally with some adult assistance. Traditionally, too, children's literature is replete with instances of children in extraordinary situations, overcoming great peril and returning to security. Children's stories are usually rather 'closed' narratives, and to that extent usually optimistic, even if the imagery itself (of the Queen of Hearts say, or goblins, wolves and witches) can be overwhelming for too small a child. But perhaps vanquishing fear is also important. Amongst the media memories I raised at the start, which British person of my vintage cannot remember the delicious apprehension of hiding behind the sofa during *Dr Who*? It seems plausible to suggest that children's intellectual and emotional growth intrinsically requires growing *away* – away from dependency and towards autonomy. The mastering of certain fears must be an important component in the development of a sense of oneself as a capable social actor.

The rhythms and routines and familiarities of domestic existence are presumably a key setting for the development of a sense of safety against which these imaginative dramas of fright and mastery take place. Television, which is *par excellence* a routine activity (its very scheduling of daily and weekly programming is an imposition of order on the use of time), may have an important role here in the confirmation of what Giddens nicely terms 'onto-logical security'. In Giddens' view such routinized activity makes possible the management of anxiety by the actor (1984, p.53) and provides for the development of 'trust' – the implicit confidence in the continuity and reliability of the physical and social environment (p.60). But all of this seems to presuppose that the impression of the world that the child gleans from such diurnal events is in essence comforting. Giddens' depiction of this basic stage of acquisition of social competence has an air of inevitability. Yet it must be a fallible process, or one realized often only in very partial and problematic form. One way in which the domestic setting provides little basis for ontological security is if the nature of familial social relations there are just too unreliable or unsettling or, at worst, flagrantly abusive. Another might be if the impression of the wider world that the child gained from watching television was more unnerving than consoling.

If then I were mounting some notional new research programme into children's experience of television I would make this kind of question central to it. And I would place the sort of reader-response analysis proposed by Hodge and Tripp close to its heart in order to query whether the kinds of images to which children are exposed, whether in designated childrens' programming (such as cartoons) or in others which they may see deliberately or otherwise (principally news bulletins) are things that they can comfortably assimilate or not. My own impression, for what it is worth, is that in Britain currently programming targetted at very young children (*Playdays*, *Postman Pat* and the rest) is a rather carefully protected space but that we are, collectively, rather less than clear on our ideas about appropriateness for children over the age of about six. What concerns about the meanness or otherwise of the world may children contract? How much may they have to steel themselves to watch things that we adults see as anodyne? I think we just don't know these things with any certainty.

Of course there is another sense in which we can say with some confidence that the diffusion of social anxiety about crime, stimulated in some considerable degree by the focus and style of media coverage, already does materially affect children's quality of life. Here I have in mind the fears of parents for their children's safety, especially with respect to the risk of violent abduction. It has long been clear that the fear of male violence has spoiled women's enjoyment of public (and indeed of private) spaces, and radically inhibited the freedom of movement of many women and girls. Increasingly it is also apparent that parents' fears of 'stranger danger' on behalf of children has a similarly limiting effect. Many parents would probably admit (with regret) that they do not allow their children the same liberty to roam – indeed commonly not even to walk to school – that they themselves enjoyed. Many practitioners in public health and sports education worry that this impinges directly on children's physical well-being. Whether the parents are being 'rational' in this regard I do not presume to say. The unanswered question is: does this encourage children to form an apprehension of the world as a basically hostile place? But I suspect that the impact of these parental fears on the privatization of domestic existence, on car-dependency, and on the outcasting of deviant or merely suspect others may be profound (perhaps in some of the ways that Mike Davis's chilling anatomization of life in the fortress-like middle-class enclaves of contemporary Los Angeles warns about (Davis 1990)).

Conclusion

My general conclusion is that the impact of television and other media on children's well-being (a topic of which I have discussed only a very few aspects) is probably far-reaching, though we should guard against a received tendency to discuss the matter in exclusively negative terms. Those 'effects' that are most profound, however, are not necessarily the most directly observable nor the most readily quantifiable. We should dispense with some earlier assumptions of directness in the discussion of media 'effects' on violence, and consider the issues more carefully in terms of attraction and gratification, the construction of social identities (especially in respect of aggressive masculinities) and the interpretation of texts. By these means we may gain some closer understanding of the infiltration of media imagery into the everyday culture of the young. But in this respect, as in many others, we should not think of young people principally as potential perpetrators of violence. The young are also, and more commonly, the victims and survivors of the hostility or indifference of the adult world – and this may be true both in terms of physical violence and of their subjection to imageries of violence. Ultimately this raises questions of the status and entitlements of young people that far exceed the scope of this discussion.

CHAPTER 11

Risk and Danger in Young People's Leisure

Ken Roberts

Introduction

This chapter is not about particularly violent young people. Other chapters explain how and why some children acquire violent predispositions and how these might be treated or otherwise controlled. The following passages consider ordinary young people, their contemporary situations, and the uses of leisure and youth cultures in which they are involved. Nearly all 'ordinary' young people are personally non-violent, in public situations at any rate. Nevertheless, it is argued that risk and danger are features of many of their regular leisure settings, and that these features add to rather than diminish the attractions for today's normal young people. They do not seek to inflict, and certainly do not wish to become victims of violence, yet they are drawn to milieux which also attract and are known to attract the potentially violent. Moreover, violent conduct is legitimized within the relevant sub-cultures.

Much of the evidence in this chapter is from the Economic and Social Research Council's 16–19 Initiative which was a set of longitudinal studies of representative samples of young people in four parts of Britain (Kirkcaldy, Liverpool, Sheffield and Swindon) where most of the fieldwork was conducted between 1987 and 1989 (see Banks *et al*. 1992). A more comprehensive account of the young people's leisure activities and companions is available elsewhere (Roberts and Parsell 1994), and likewise a full analysis of the extent and nature of the Liverpool sample's football support (Roberts 1994).

The chapter draws on evidence of the sample's leisure, and also on some conclusions from the broader research programme about recent trends in young people's family, educational and labour market situations. It thereby identifies features that distinguish current youth cultures from those of earlier generations and seeks to explain why these milieux have become more risky. What follows, however, is not a test using evidence collected to check a pre-formulated theory.

Rather, the argument should be treated essentially as an exercise in grounded theory construction.

Recent youth cultures

Virtually all young people follow popular music, albeit in different ways and to different extents. The ESRC enquiries found that almost everyone expressed an interest in some kind of popular music. Classical music, in contrast, was very much a minority taste. Very few played a musical instrument but nearly everyone was an interested listener to pop. The questions on their particular musical tastes were probably among the more interesting sections of the questionnaire to many respondents if not their investigators; the latter were more interested in the young people's education, jobs, training and unemployment.

Music is now a pervasive part of nearly all young people's lives. It is usually in the background whether they are in their own rooms, alone or with company, and in most places of entertainment. It is difficult for young people, and indeed adults, to avoid the sounds of pop in today's society. The majority of the young, however, see no need for avoidance strategies. The majority do not just like pop but can distinguish a variety of types and have definite preferences. They demonstrated this in completing the questionnaires in the ESRC study. A minority followed their preferred styles and performers 'fanatically' by purchasing cassettes and discs, attending the relevant concerts, and going to clubs where their favoured music was played. Some of the young people's musical tastes were a part of broader styles (see Hebdige 1979) which also governed their appearances – their choices of clothing and hairstyles for example – and the places to which they went on their nights out. Needless to say, none of this is particularly new. Nor are the violent and macabre tones and lyrics of some pop genres.

However, the 'rave scenes' where many young people have been congregating on their nights out in recent years are a post-1970s development (see Redhead 1993). These are events where music is played loudly throughout an evening, into the early hours of the mornings and sometimes all night. Some young people drink heavily on these occasions. Others dance continuously and may use their drugs of choice as additional intoxicants. Dance drugs have been recognized in recent research as a distinct though illegal type of consumer produce (Measham, Newcombe and Parker 1994). Such drugs had become such a common part of everyday teenage life that by 1995 schools were being advised by the Department for Education that it was unnecessary to suspend pupils who were caught in possession, or using the drugs on school premises.

Most of the young people who attend raves are just playing. This applied to the participants in the youth cultures of the 1950s and 60s (see Elkin and Westley 1955, 1967; Turner 1964), and it applies equally to the way-out cultures of the 1990s (see Eygendaal 1992). Their Saturday night personae are not their real selves. By Monday they are ordinary kids, back in their schools, training schemes and places of employment. Their core concerns are their education, jobs, and present and future families. But they still relish dressing up and becoming part of the night time society. They are attracted again and again to venues where some of those present become ill, where trouble is always likely outside if not inside the premises, where police attention is frequent and where 'heavies' are needed to protect the core clientele. In Liverpool two-thirds of the females in the ESRC study, and two-fifths of the males reported feeling unsafe in their city centre at night, but this was not preventing them going to city centre pubs and clubs. Rather than repellent, the risks seemed to be a part of the night life's attraction. This is a phenomenon that the generations who squealed at Sinatra and the Beatles, the grandparents and parents of today's teenagers, can find it hard to understand.

Throughout the 1970s and 1980s thousands of young football supporters exposed themselves to comparable risks week after week. During the 1990s all-seater stadia, inflated admission prices and restricted access for non-season ticket holders, especially at away matches, have helped to remove some of the former hooliganism from football along with much of the atmosphere formerly associated with the terraces. Needless to say, the hooligan problem has merely been displaced or marginalized rather than cured or completely excluded from the game. In the 1990s professional football in Britain may have been sanitized and packaged as an acceptable media commodity, but the puzzle remains as to how and why, through season after season in the 1970s and 1980s, Saturday violence became predictable outside if not inside football grounds. The answer lies in how football was adopted as a suitable arena for certain male youth cultures to parade their styles, and how these styles themselves changed during the 1970s and 1980s.

Liverpool youth's involvement in football is particularly interesting since one of the city's leading clubs has been involved in two of the main soccer tragedies of modern times – at the Heysel Stadium in Brussels in 1985 where 39 Italian supporters were killed and at Hillsborough in 1989, at or following which 96 Liverpool followers lost their lives. The latter tragedy arose from terrace congestion rather than hooliganism. Other football disasters have been caused by fire and crushing rather than fighting fans. But all these events highlight the risks to which football supporters have been exposed, and this exposure has been voluntary. Those attending matches have been aware of the risk and, indeed, have often been ambivalent if not flatly opposed to measures aimed at risk reduction.

In the late-1980s most young people in Liverpool had intense feelings about the Heysel and Hillsborough disasters. This was to be expected given the breadth and depth of football support on Merseyside. The ESRC enquiries found that 90 per cent of Liverpool youth, males and females, supported one or the other of the city's leading football clubs. A majority of the females, and the overwhelming majority of the males, had been to Anfield or Goodison Park at least once. Most of the males had been to Wembley. In 1988, when he managed Liverpool AFC, Kenny Dalglish was the number one choice of the young people as their city's best representative.

Liverpool is now world famous as the home of the Beatles and for its football, but probably less so for its startling economic decline, though in 1994 the city was given Objective One status by the European Union. Objective One is the elimination of poverty, and the status is reserved for Europe's poorest cities. Since the 1960s Liverpool has been among Britain's unemployment blackspots. The city's cultural vitality and sporting success have contrasted starkly with the surrounding commercial and industrial decline. Since the 1960s the success of the football teams has helped sustain the local population's pride in the city. Moreover, many young people have retained football support as a favoured leisure activity despite, in many cases, lacking employment and earned incomes. Saturday afternoons on the terraces, possibly followed by evenings in the city centre, have been highlights in some otherwise bleak lives. Trips to away grounds, especially into Europe, into alien and potentially hostile territory, have been occasions when excitement has reached fever pitch. This excitement, and the partisan feelings, have always been among the core attractions of live football. Fans have always taunted match officials, opposing players and supporters, and have endeavoured to win the battle of the terraces, but throughout most of the game's history these battles were fought without inflicting or risking real injury. Crowd disorder has occurred throughout the history of football but its character and significance have not remained constant (see also Pratt and Salter 1984).

There were changes in the 1960s and 1970s when the behaviour of many groups of young male supporters provoked or invited trouble. Needless to say, very few went to matches with violent intentions (see Marsh 1978 and Marsh and Rosser 1978). The 'real hooligans' were always a very small minority. The puzzle is not just that normal young people, though a declining number of adults, remained in attendance, but that they often opposed measures intented to isolate, expel and punish the perpetrators of violence. Robins and Hobbs (1990) found that young mainstream supporters viewed hooligans with a mixture of fear, admiration and acceptance. This was apparent in Liverpool in the late 1980s when, among the city's young people, there was as much opposition as support for the extradition to Belgium of suspects identified on video following the Heysel disaster. After Hillsborough there was similar antipathy towards the prospect of membership schemes and all-seater stadia. The closure of Liverpool's Kop was mourned rather than celebrated. Many young people were strongly attached to situations in which their personal safety was manifestly at risk. This has been a common denominator in certain football and pop music youth cultures in recent years, and an explanation can be found in the broader social situations of young people in present-day society.

It is worth noting that raves and following football are unlike the Outward Bound programmes in which young people have been impelled into new experiences and encouraged to push themselves to their limits so that they might discover the extent of their own capabilities and learn to trust them (Roberts, White and Parker 1974). Ordinary young people in recent years have attended pop occasions and football matches accompanied by their own good mates intent on avoiding trouble, and on sticking to their known capacities for beer, Ecstasy, confrontations with opposing fans, or whatever. But they have done so in the full knowledge that others in their vicinities will break such limits, and maybe themselves and others in the process. Too many young people have placed themselves in risky situations too regularly for their exposure to be considered accidental. What has impelled them?

They have been using long-standing forms of recreation in rather different ways than earlier generations. Attending football matches and following pop are not recent additions to Britain's youth scenes. But young people in the 1980s and 1990s have not really been acting in basically the same ways as their parents' generations. Of course, there have been continuities, but there are also important differences. The activities may be the same but in recent times they have been approached and experienced amid different social relationships on account of broader changes in young people's situations which have invested familiar leisure activities with a new significance.

Youth's new condition

(1) Prolonged

The life phase between childhood and adulthood has lengthened in so far as entry to the latter is signalled by an independent lifestyle including domestic arrangements backed by a job (or a partner's job) which provides the necessary earnings and security. Access to adulthood has been delayed by the economic restructuring which has eradicated many of the jobs which school-leavers formerly entered. For the remaining jobs young people have faced more intense competition from experienced adults who have been displaced from their own former occupations, and the adult women who have been re-entering the workforce in growing numbers. The result has been a persistent youth unemployment problem mitigated by a rise in enrolments in post-compulsory education. Many of Britain's new students have been discouraged workers who would have entered the labour market if they had given themselves reasonable chances of obtaining decent jobs (Raffe and Willms 1989). Other young people have entered the training schemes which have become the normal next step for statutory age school-leavers in many parts of Britain. By the late 1980s it was only at age 19 that the majority of a cohort were in full-time employment (Banks *et al.* 1992) whereas 25 years previously two-thirds of all young people left school at 15 and nearly all obtained jobs immediately.

Economic restructuring has been the recent trigger, but it has been super-imposed upon a longer-term trend in which each generation has tended to seek more education than its parents. A generation rachet effect has operated throughout the twentieth century. Virtually all parents want their children to do at least as well, and preferably better, than they themselves did in their own school careers. A desire for educational qualifications was once considered middle class but stratified diffusion has changed that. The working class has got the message that education is the key to subsequent life chances. So recent cohorts of 'ordinary kids' have wanted to become as well-qualified as possible in order to get on (Brown 1987). The pace at which young people have been staying longer in education and improving their qualifications has out-distanced the upgrading of the occupational structure (the decline in the proportion of manual jobs, and the increase in the proportion of higher level occupations). So all levels of qualifications have been devalued in the labour market. Young people have been discovering that A-levels are now demanded for entry to occupations for which the equivalents of GCSEs were once sufficient and that degrees are required for what were formerly A-level types of employment. Meanwhile, most of Britain's recent university graduates have been unable to enter the kinds of employment formerly considered suitable for degree holders. Up to now, rather than leading to disillusionment with education, the main effect of this devaluation has been to fuel the public's appetite for qualifications to still higher levels (Dore 1976).

Alongside the rise in the typical ages at which individuals obtain adult employment, there have been rises in the mean ages when they first marry and become parents. The effect has been to prolong the life stage between childhood and adulthood. Youth was once described as a brief flowering period. Flowering may or may not remain an appropriate adjective, but there is no question that the life phase today is not as brief as formerly. There has been no upward movement in the ages at which young people begin to escape from the restrictions of childhood and develop lives of their own, typically, in the first instance, in their leisure time and through leisure tastes and activities. Experience of full sexual intercourse is probably as sensitive as any single indicator of young people's independence, and the ages at which young people cross this threshold (typically 16 nowadays) have not been rising. From age 12 and sometimes earlier young people experience independent leisure, usually with the support rather than in defiance of their parents. The majority are consuming alcohol regularly in licensed premises by age 16, and by age 18, when the behaviour becomes legal, those concerned are deserting the fun pubs where many of the customers are mere kids. Most young people participate in youth scenes from age 14–15 or before, at which time there are still many more years before the majority can expect to be in adult employment and homes of their own. New social practices have been developed within this new life space, cohabitation being among the better known examples. Affluent teenage consumers may have been reduced in number but there has been a pronounced growth in the number of 20-somethings in the pre-parenting life phase. The English language still lacks an appropriate word for these individuals. Adolescents and youth, given their traditional teenage connotations, seem inappropriate. Post-adolescents and young adults are among the alternatives.

However they are described, the presence of the 20-somethings has transformed the young singles scene. These young adults are virtually immune to parental and other 'traditional' types of adult authority. Many have plenty of cash to indulge their tastes. Yet they are not anchored in the wider society through adult domestic responsibilities and long-term career commitments. They are available as role models, or otherwise as parts of the leisure environments, for younger teenagers who, in turn, can act as an appreciative audience by whom the 20-somethings are accorded a status that the wider society is hesitant if not completely unwilling to confer.

(2) Individualization

The use of this term postulates a trend towards every person acquiring a unique biography. A crude index is the number of associates known to any person who were reared in the same neighbourhood, attended the same schools, entered similar kinds of employment, and still know each other. Ask any group of present day adults how many such people they know and most will answer, 'Few if any'.

Individualization is not a new trend. It began with the birth of modern industrial society. Employment in these societies has always been of individuals, and in politics votes have always been cast by individual electors. However, in recent years the trend has taken a giant stride. There was never a time or place where absolutely every boy in the village went down the pit or every girl into the local textile mill. However, in many parts of Britain there were such normal careers. Of course, there were always some individuals who broke out but today this has become less possible because the once normal patterns have fragmented. This has occurred alongside the contraction of the major firms and industries that once dominated many local labour markets; the introduction of new and varied forms of post-compulsory education and training which result in young people experiencing spells in schools and colleges, on training schemes, in jobs, and episodes of unemployment in a bewildering variety of sequences; increased rates of geographical mobility; the weakening of extended families, neighbourhood and religious communities; and the sheer pace of economic change which has made it more difficult to experience a stable or progressive lifetime career. Entire cohorts of young people used to travel into and through adulthood as if in public transport vehicles whereas today they make their journeys in private motor cars. This analogy can be pushed further in so far as the cars have differently powered engines.

The subjective counterpart of objective individualization is that people tend to feel, not necessarily autonomous and in control of their own lives, but that their own prospects are independent of any broader social categories whether defined by place, gender, family or educational background. This has numerous implications. In politics it has become more difficult for parties to appeal to, and to rely on the support of any broad classes of electors. In leisure it makes it impossible for people to draw upon pre-formed groups where membership is simply given.

Individualization has undermined formerly effective kinds of youth research. For example, it used to be possible for ethnographers to make contact with groups of young people on the streets or elsewhere in particular neighbourhoods and to emerge with portraits of their typical backgrounds, current situations, lifestyles, future prospects and attitudes. This type of research no longer yields the same returns. The old neighbourhood communities have disappeared. Wherever today's young people congregate – for education, training or leisure – the participants tend to be from diverse backgrounds, and their relationships with one another are usually temporary because they proceed to many different future lives.

However, it is in leisure that young people are most likely to experience relatively stable group membership. Music, sport or any other activity can supply shared interests and enthusiasms which are the sole conditions for acceptance. Leisure has always been important for young people but some of the reasons for its importance have changed. There have been constants, of course. Leisure has always enabled young people to demonstrate independence from adults, to learn to feel adult by dealing with equals without surveillance by any authorities, and to learn to play sexualized gender roles thereby acquiring adult identities. These are the major developmental tasks that our society sets for its young people, and are therefore among the latter's focal concerns (see Hendry, Shucksmith, Love and Glendinning 1993). Leisure has sometimes enabled young people to express their membership of other social aggregates defined by region, neighbourhood, or family and educational background (key components of social class), for example. Nowadays, however, young people are less able to bring such pre-formed group memberships into their leisure. Leading football clubs draw support from throughout their base regions, sometimes from most parts of the country, not just from the districts, towns or cities after which they are named. The supporters of Liverpool AFC and Everton today have little else in common, and likewise the fans of particular pop groups and genres. Young people's leisure tastes and activities no longer clearly divide the main socio-economic classes (Roberts and Parsell 1994). Rather than expressing group membership, nowadays it is more likely to be through youth cultures that membership groups are defined (see Laermans 1994).

These youth cultures are typically sites for the formation of temporary communities or proto-communities (Willis 1990) which have been likened to *bunde* and tribes (Hetherington 1994; Maffesolli 1994). Such collectivities are defined essentially by their members' common tastes, appearances and places of recreation, and can give young people a sense of belonging which they are otherwise denied. This is not to say that participation in youth cultures becomes young people's main life concern. Their major concerns and commitments remain to their families, present and future, and to their educational and occupational careers. As always, for the majority youth cultures are simply arenas for play, but nowadays group creation rather than simply expressing and cementing membership of some pre-formed category is often a condition for full enjoyment.

(3) Risk

Another new feature of young people's condition is that their adult destinations are uncertain. There has been a change of era since the 1960s when many young people struggled against the predictable futures in dull bureaucracies and little family boxes towards which their society seemed to be ushering them. Rather than dropping out, the concern of young people in the 1990s is to get in. The transitional period between childhood and adulthood has been prolonged, the situations of those in transit have been individualized, and while in transit few individuals today can be sure of their eventual destinations. Of course, the future was never 100 per cent predictable for anyone, but in the past most young people had realistic expectations around which they were able to make firm plans. Indeed, by age 20 many knew not only their main lifetime occupations but also the individuals to whom they would be married for the rest of their lives and where they would live.

Uncertainty is partly a direct consequence of individualization. When all members of a social category have common futures it is relatively easy for people to foresee their own. They need only to look at what happened to their counterparts of a decade or so previously. Generation followed generation in a predictable life cycle. Individualization obscures future trajectories. Even when their prospects are objectively predictable from evidence that social research can assemble, individuals themselves are less able to look ahead. However, uncertainty is also a product of the pace of change, especially in the economy, which has made it impossible to be confident that any career will last for life. A central fact of young people's current predicaments is that the social roles that will be available during their adult lives are objectively unknowable. Uncertainty is also a product of the introduction of new training schemes and educational programmes which have no track records, and the growth in the numbers on longer established routes, in higher education for example, which means that students can no longer be confident of 'glittering prizes' or even any deferred gratifications.

Uncertain futures have added to the risks in all the career steps that young people can take. Opting for higher education may lead to a high rising management or professional career but today's university entrants know that they would be unwise to bank on this. Employer-based training may lead to a skilled occupation that can be practised until retirement but, once again, no-one can be sure. Yet young people must take career decisions. These are unavoidable. And in taking their decisions, whatever these are, they have to take risks. They invest their time and often money in acquiring qualifications and skills in the hope of achieving particular goals, but at the time they can only hope that their investments will pay off.

Uncertainty in economic life is paralleled by the state of the family. The overwhelming chances were once that marriage would last for life whereas today no-one can be sure. Embarking on a relationship with an opposite-sexed partner and becoming a parent may lead to lifetime domestic bliss or pain and despair. Today's young people realize this. They can be certain that the decisions that they take when young will affect their futures but they cannot be equally sure of what these effects will be. And in individualized societies it is individuals who are required to take the risks. The scope for sharing the decisions, the blame and any good fortune is narrow. This is the crucial sense in which today's young people stand on the threshold of risk societies.

An implication of their uncertain futures is that young people are unable to use the roles towards which they are heading as a base for social identities. Doing this would be a foolish risk. Those concerned would stand to lose too much. And they have alternatives, namely, to accept that their futures are uncertain and to base their social personae and self-concepts on a combination of ascribed statuses (family background, sex and ethnic group for instance), past and current achievements in education, training and the labour market, aug-mented, if they wish, by the tribes, *bunde* or proto-communities to which they become affiliated on the basis of their publicly displayed leisure tastes and activities. For many young people these are their most reliable anchors. Otherwise uncertain prospects intensify their need for the relatively secure group membership and identities, albeit usually temporary identities, that youth cultures can supply. These identities are secure because while individuals are able to relinquish them whenever they wish, they are unlikely to fail to meet the standards required for social recognition and acceptance in the roles and groups in question.

Bonding within the tribes

In all age groups there are numerous processes linking leisure to the rest of life. Interests, skills and relationships developed elsewhere may spill-over into leisure. The spill-over may be from families or work situations, and such processes occur among young people. Males and females transport masculine and feminine identities initially nurtured elsewhere into leisure settings. Spill-over is always most likely when individuals value and identify with the skills, interests and relationships in question, and this almost always applies to gender roles and identities.

It may be useful to stress at this point that the present chapter is not suggesting that this is how violence is normalized within contemporary youth cultures. The argument is not that young people who experience risks in other areas of their lives develop a liking for risk taking which then governs their spare time. Rather, young people, like adults, normally seek to minimize risks and look to leisure for security. Leisure may have a reputation for its freedom and scope for choice, but most people use their discretion to lead highly predictable and routine leisure lives.

Another type of connection between leisure and the rest of life is compensatory. Individuals can use leisure to express parts of their characters that are suppressed, and to obtain experiences that are not available elsewhere. Thus individuals with sedentary jobs may seek physically challenging recreation. Individuals whose working lives are subject to tight control by bosses or machines may use leisure to express their freedom ostentatiously. If other spheres of life fail to deliver experiences that people consider important or fail to meet basic biological, psychological or social needs, individuals are likely to seek to fill the gaps during leisure. Young people's needs for group membership and social identity fall into this category. These can be supplied by sport and pop music cultures. Young people's socio-psychological needs explain much of the attraction of these milieux, and why contexts of risk and danger can add to the attractions.

As recognized earlier, present-day young people have few leisure activities that appear unfamiliar to their parents. Sport and pop music are obvious examples but the continuities can be deceptive because in much of leisure the social relationships and milieux are at least as important as the activities themselves. This applies with family holidays, much television viewing, and with many young people's days out at sports events and nights at pop venues. So the changes in the kinds of social relationships in which young people are involved as a result of youth being prolonged, situations becoming individualized, and career choices risky, necessarily change the significance of what may appear to be enduring uses of leisure.

In the past youth cultures developed within broader social divisions. This made it possible to distinguish working and middle class youth cultures, and masculine and feminine roles within each (see Hall and Jefferson 1976; Mungham and Pearson 1976). Individuals tended to acquire their specific leisure tastes and interests as members of pre-formed groups. The football teams that males supported were typically family or neighbourhood choices, and likewise entire neighbourhoods or specific sections of them would go mod, punk, skinhead or whatever. Friends from neighbourhoods, schools and work-places – often exactly the same individuals in all these locations – would listen to and discuss pop music, and establish group evaluations of the sounds on offer. The young people's leisure was based on given social relationships and was only exceptionally required to create new social bonds. Groups went to places frequented by other groups similar to themselves, and the groups' general norms of social conduct, acquired from their broader social contexts, governed their behaviour in these places. Those who broke the rules were soon made unwelcome. Social identities needed only to be confirmed, employment and wages obtained, and sexual partners selected, for each cohort to conclude its flowering period and join the adult generations.

Today's young people have escaped from some of the constraints, but have simultaneously lost the security of their former situations. This does not lead the majority to behave in violent or otherwise completely unregulated and chaotic ways. The majority have internalized other norms of conduct. However, they need to search for inter-personal security outside their families within loosely organized crowds in which they can feel accepted because everyone shares common tastes, and apparently thinks and acts alike. Risk and danger within these milieux can enhance the attractions. They give the situations an edge. Most young people who enter, typically in the company of their own good friends, protect each other from the risks, and prevent each other transgressing the boundaries which keep their involvement in youth cultures as mere play and ensure that their longer-term commitments to normal family lives and occupational careers are not jeopardized. However, potentially violent young people are neither excluded from, nor entirely unwelcome in the new tribes. Rather they are accorded roles which, given the manner in which youth has been prolonged, they can occupy for long periods of time while they establish and enjoy reputations. The presence of potentially violent young people, and the risks that this creates, can generate excitement and strengthen the bonding among ordinary participants. Involvement in the relevant youth cultures both expresses, and simultaneously offers a solution to normal young people's feelings of being alone and having no certain futures in an otherwise uncaring and at times hostile society.

This chapter has not been proposing an alternative mono-causal explanation of either the rave culture or football hooliganism. A full explanation of current night time youth scenes would need to examine in detail the structure and development of the pop music industry, and the independent socio-historical trajectories of alcohol and drug use among young people. Similarly it has been acknowledged that crowd disorder at football and other sports events has a long history. In the case of football, rowdy conduct on the terraces has historical roots in 'rough' working class sub-cultures (Dunning, Murphy and Williams 1988; Williams, Dunning and Murphy 1984). Moreover, the excitement of being part of a partisan crowd, in the presence of opponents, not just witnessing but participating in a struggle for victory, has always been among the core attractions of the game. Violence, whether this occurs spontaneously on the streets or at state organized public executions, has always been able draw and stimulate crowds. The above analysis has taken all this as given. Youth's new condition, which has arisen independently, is the additional factor required to explain the normalization of violence, and the regularity with which young people from all social backgrounds, of both sexes, now participate in situations where their safety is at risk. The football rowdies who have been arrested in recent years have not all been deprived teenagers from rough working class homes. Teachers and members of other respected professions have also found the football mob a haven in an otherwise heartless world (Robins and Hobbs 1990). The extent to which risk and danger have been legitimized among the normal participants in the relevant sub-cultures was indicated by the widespread opposition among young people during 1993–94 to legislation empowering the police to control the organization of raves, and long before then by the expressions of crowd sympathy inside football grounds towards supporters in the process of being ejected by the police.

Youth's new condition can explain why violent or near violent situations have become normal contexts for normal young people's leisure. One can ask who the violent participants are and what makes them violent, but we also need to ask why ordinary young people repeatedly become part of these situations, and why they do not insist on the exclusion of the individuals, usually well-known in the places in question, who are regularly associated with trouble. This chapter has developed an explanation of this normal conduct of ordinary young people who are implicated in the production of much youth violence. It is their involvement, and their socio-psychological stakes in the processes, which make the control of violence, together with the identification, exclusion and treatment of the principal offenders, so difficult.

CHAPTER 12

Groupwork with Violent Children and Adolescents

Kedar Nath Dwivedi

Aggression and violence

Behaviours, whether desirable or undesirable, usually arise due to a convergence of inner and outer forces. Effective management of outer socio-political aspects is therefore as important as that of the inner intrapsychic ones. Some of the medical conditions such as brain disorders, epilepsy, intoxications or mental illnesses may also have a contributory role to play in violent outbursts. Retrospective studies of violent youngsters have identified at least three developmental etiological factors in their personal histories (Lewis 1983). These are: (i) neuro-psychiatric vulnerability in the form of insult to the central nervous system; (ii) history of witnessing extreme aggression; and (iii) experience of physical abuse.

In a therapy situation, where it is suspected that violence may emerge, it may be possible to make use of the available body of knowledge for dealing with aggressive and violent situations; for example, how to sense impending trouble, how to approach a potentially dangerous situation and what may be the right thing to do in different aggressive situations. Even very simple things, such as one's body posture, demeanour and looks can either aggravate or calm a potentially dangerous situation. For example, it may be less threatening to stand with feet apart, looking relaxed and at a distance from a potentially aggressive person, avoiding eye contact (by watching the chest or the hands of the person), being and appearing relaxed (by checking for any tension in one's fist and face in order to avoid looking angry or frightened and by relaxing one's breathing because shallow breathing in a state of arousal may lead to impaired thinking; shallow breathing can also produce a high pitched voice giving the impression of being frightened or angry). However, one has to remain ready for any action required such as by standing in such a way that the dominant foot remains behind, bearing the weight of the body and the other foot is in front with the knee bent. Similarly, before talking to the person, it may be useful to think of some ways of introducing humour or empathy into the conversation, and distracting the person's attention away from oneself (Moran 1984). One may also need, if necessary, to acquire skills in restraining an individual in a way that is effective but less dangerous, such as restraining from behind or by getting hold of clothing rather than limbs.

Incidents of violence are very distressing experiences and can be potentially psychologically damaging to all the parties concerned: victims, witness, protectors and perpetrators. Immediate interventions to comfort and contain the feelings and the situation can be extremely helpful, and can reduce a number of problems (such as Post Traumatic Stress Disorder) from emerging in future. The incidents of violence not only reflect the possibility of such incidents in the psychic experiences of the perpetrators but also the possibility of future violent behaviours in the victims and the witness. Appropriate help is therefore essential not only to alleviate the distress but also to prevent and treat the post traumatic stress disorder and to prevent the emergence of further violent disorders or the vulnerability to such traumatic experiences. Similarly, the perpetrators need help in making contact with the hurt and screaming child within so that the harmful ways of reaching out are replaced by kind, tender, caring and soothing ones.

As early as in 1920s, Aichhorn (1955) classified delinquents into three groups; first, those with 'harsh' superegos who commit punishment provoking acts to relieve their guilt; second, those with 'non-social' superegos identifying with faulty social values of their parents; and third, those with little evidence of superego functioning. These and other psychodynamic explanations (see below) led to psychotherapeutic help for the delinquent, conduct disordered and/or violent youngsters. However, there has been a tendency in the literature to quote the negative findings of the Cambridge-Somerville study (Powers and Witmer 1951), as evidence that psychotherapy has nothing to offer delinquents (Keith 1984). In fact the project did not provide psychotherapy but used 10 counsellors for 235 youngsters. Many were nurses or camp counsellors with little or no formal training in the mental health field, much less in how to do psychotherapy. They were instructed to do whatever they thought best for the youngsters. As each 'counsellor' had 35 boys, a boy, on an average, was seen only 5 times a year. Moreover, these contacts were mainly to make practical arrangements such as camping, physical examination and so on. Other studies, however, using psychotherapy have shown beneficial effects (Glover 1962/3; Shore and Massimo 1979).

Group work

Group work has gradually evolved, over several decades, as an important way of helping children and adolescents. In the early part of this century, Moreno, in his therapeutic groupwork with young children, used psychodrama techniques. In the USA, the Jewish Board of Guardians then started groupwork with latency age children (for 8- to 12-year-olds) in 1934 which later came to be known as Activity Group Therapy. The main aims of such therapeutic groups included: (i) offering opportunities for genuine interest in leisure time activities; (ii) improving their ego strength and self worth (so often crushed in children with difficulties); (iii) providing substitute love if they were unable to find this in their own homes; and (iv) rebuilding their distorted personalities.

> The members of the group work together: they quarrel, fight – and sometimes strike one another; they argue and haggle, but finally come to some working understanding with one another. Sometimes this process takes six months or more, but once it has been established it becomes a permanent attitude on the part of the individuals involved. We have evidence that these are carried over to the other group relationships in the home, at school and in play. (Slavson 1940, p.526)

Ginott (1961) also popularized therapeutic group work with children during the 1960s. Similarly, in the UK, Anthony (1965) and Skynner (1971) promoted therapeutic group work with children and adolescents. It was taken up by the Intermediate Treatment movement to help youngsters in trouble by utilizing leisure, outward bound sport, adventure and other activities to cultivate corrective group processes. It has been the essential ingredient of Youth Services (Adams 1993) and many schools too have now started utilizing group work principles for helping children in trouble or as a way of extending personal and social education (Coppock and Dwivedi 1993).

The child mental health services too have been utilizing group therapy, usually in conjunction with family therapy for a variety of mental health problems: post traumatic stress disorders (such as due to physical, sexual or emotional abuse), bereavement, encopresis, emotional disturbance, conduct disorders and so on (Dwivedi 1993a; Dwivedi and Bell 1993; Dwivedi, Brayne and Lovett 1992; Harrower 1993; Howard 1993; Smith and Pennells 1993). It has also proved as an important mode of working with youngsters in residential institutions such as children's homes (Evans and Cook 1993), therapeutic communities (Wright-Watson 1993) and adolescents in psychiatric in patient units (Evans 1965).

Group work has obvious advantages over other approaches (Dwivedi 1993b). For most children and adolescents this is a very attractive and natural setting. It can easily simulate the real world for them as it resembles the natural peer group. In contrast, the individual therapy sessions can generate inhibitions due to the huge disparity between the status of the adult therapist and the child. Similarly, in family therapy sessions, the habitual ways of relating to the family members along with the communication difficulties are brought into the sessions from the very beginning. Thus the feelings, perceptions, preoccupations, viewpoints and concerns of the children can sometimes remain hidden in such therapeutic modes. Group work, on the other hand, may provide an easy access to such materials for further working through. Even if a child is not too forthcoming in a group situation, the similarity of the issues being dealt with in the group in relation to other children, can still have an enormous therapeutic impact. It can quickly create an atmosphere that is conducive to getting in touch with relevant issues and feelings. It provides an opportunity for sharing these in a group of peers. It facilitates contributions by all, empathizing with each other's feelings, attempting to help each other and benefiting by identifying with each other. Jointly working on one person's problem can also influence every one else's in the group.

Groups provide opportunities for a variety of therapeutic group activities that may not be possible in any other setting. Group reinforcement, particularly peer reinforcement is usually much more effective than adult reinforcement. 'Offering positive feedback is a highly valued skill in our society; there is good reason to believe that as children learn to reinforce others, they are reciprocally reinforced by others and mutual liking also increases' (Rose and Edleson 1987, p.3). Thus effective group work can enhance one's ability for reality testing, social skills and self-esteem. It helps children learn how to give of themselves to others, master narcissistic impulses, delay gratification, cultivate creativity and inculcate the sense of interdependence.

However, it is important to keep in mind not only the potential for the unleashing of the healing power of the group bur also of the destructive power. The significance of training and skills in the group worker can not be emphasized enough. The issue of control and boundary setting can easily trigger counter transference responses in the group workers that may be equally unhelpful. There are numerous accounts of dangerous behaviours frequently encountered in group work with children and adolescents (Dwivedi 1993c). In group work with conduct disorders or violent individuals the situation can be extremely and constantly volatile.

There are a variety of approaches that can be used in group work with children and adolescents. One way of classifying these could be in terms of 'experiential' and 'psycho-educational' groups. In an **experiential group** an attempt is made skilfully to harness the therapeutic aspects of the situation created by each child in the group. Such experiential groups are usually unstructured but can include activities such as painting, cooking, playing, collage, drama, games and so on. The **psycho-educational** groups are usually structured and the workers tend to determine most of the agenda and activity by presenting exercises and by engineering discussions. The discussions can range from theoretical, experiential, to practical matters encompassing feelings, perceptions, coping strategies and skills.

Experiential groups

Experiential groups can provide a suitable setting for working in a psychody-namic manner. Some examples of making sense of violent behaviours from the psycho-dynamics point of view are briefly outlined below.

Distorted proximity seeking behaviour

From early infancy children begin to approach repeatedly certain stimulating objects. This leads to the development of bonding or attachment. At times of stress there is a particular need to seek such soothing attachment figures and to behave in a proximity seeking manner towards them. Even grown ups faced with disasters, loss or stress need to seek proximity with familiar persons or environments, even though that very person may be the cause of the stress. If the attachment figures are unavailable or rejecting, or the intensity of the stress is extremely distressing, this proximity seeking attachment behaviour can become disorganized and manifest as being hostile and even violent. This intense desire to 'reach out and touch someone' therefore could become disguised, confused, violent and even fatal (Mawson 1987).

Dreading the feeling

The skilful parents allow their babies and young children to experience plenty of emotions but, if the particular emotion begins to exceed the baby's tolerance in terms of its intensity or duration, the parents intervene to protect the baby from being overwhelmed. If the parents are unable to protect a child in this way, a sense of psychic trauma can develop, threatening to disrupt all psychic functions. Subsequently such emotions are perceived as particularly dangerous. This leads to a dread of being flooded with such feelings (e.g. abandonment, hurt). This dread then leads to the employment of defensive strategies (such as violent outbursts, induction of altered states of consciousness, substance abuse, soothing or distracting rituals) at the slightest possibility of the dreaded feeling emerging into one's consciousness (Dwivedi 1993d; Krystal 1988).

Law of the jungle

As a toddler becomes mobile, he or she runs, climbs and explores the environ-ment around. The various objects that are encountered can be very exciting on the one hand, but can also be frightening and dangerous on the other. These can produce sharp loud sounds, electricute, burn, bite, attack, cut, poison, slide and so on. The parents, therefore, have to keep a close enough eye to protect the adventurer from getting hurt in a 'jungle'-like environment full of fierce and dangerous objects. The child develops a positive, powerful love of the parents who are experienced as protectors. However, if the parents are unable to provide this protection or become hurtful, abusive or damaging themselves, the children are then left to rely upon their own primitive and aggressive instincts to defend themselves in such a dangerous world. Violence then becomes natural and habitual and the child grows with this. The child also continues to use the violent and risky behaviours as a desperate attempt to stimulate anxious concerns in the care-givers and others. The child (even when grown up) feels convinced that the parent figures are not going to watch out for the child's safety unless they are forced to. The majority of child's dangerous behaviours are, therefore, aimed at achieving this (Dwivedi 1993e; Willock 1983).

Dangerous play

Experience of separation anxiety, loss and hurt can arouse very distressing feelings and stress. From very early on children learn to cope with such feelings and develop a capacity to tolerate them as they mature. One of the ways of this kind of learning is through developmental play such as peek a boo, tossing objects and finding them, waving bye-bye, hide and seek and so forth. (Kleeman 1967, 1973). When such a line of development is distorted but the need for such an interactive play continues, it can take on more and more hurtful and dangerous forms even continuing later in life such as, running away or joy riding and being chased (Dwivedi 1993e; Willock 1990).

Identification with the aggressor

'Identification' is a psychological process through which one acquires the attitudes, views, feelings and behaviours belonging to some one else. This is a normal healthy process and takes place as a result of close, usually loving or admiring relationship. However, the same mechanisms may be involved in pathological situations. For example, a child who is tormented, attacked or tortured and is in a state of inescapable suffering, may end up identifying with the torturer. In this way it may be possible to detach emotionally and dissociate from the otherwise unavoidable pain. This process of 'identification with the aggressor' then leads (even when one is grown up) to behaviour outbursts originally belonging to the aggressor. These are usually triggered by the subtle reminders of the painful past experiences. This process of identification can be so subtle and pervasive that the person even 'looks', sounds, talks and attacks like the past perpetrator, as if 'possessed' or 'bewitched' by that person. Even the memory of the childhood abuse may be lost or if remembered the associated emotions are unavailable. The traumatic experiences from the preverbal period can perhaps only be communicated through action and not words (Fraiberg, Adelson and Shapiro 1980). However, there are many who had traumatic experiences in their childhood but do not inflict their pain upon others, particularly upon their children. They remember their own experiences and make sure that they would never let their children experience what they themselves had been through. For these parents the pain and suffering was not totally repressed and they found a way of coping with their emotions without pathological identification or dissociation (Dwivedi 1984). Some, however, end up at the other extreme of being so paralysed by this awareness that they can't exercise even the normal and healthy acts of assertive firmness, boundary setting or disciplining.

An experiential group work situation is ideal for exploring any or many of these mechanisms as they become manifest and apparent in the context of the group through multiple transferences. These can then be examined and made sense of in its safe and trusting atmosphere. For example, within the violent youngster there may be a screaming child feeling hurt. The job of the group therapist is to help this youngster to listen and make contact with the feelings of hurt within him, and to comfort him so that the need for dissociation and identification with the aggressor can gradually diminish. One may get in touch with the mechanism in oneself by seeing it in the other, a kind of mirroring. Various activities and play utilizing play-therapy and dramatherapy principles can further facilitate this. For example, various improvised versions of 'hide and seek', holding and trust games may be able to help compensate for the developmental games that an adolescent missed in his early childhood like peekaboo, chasing, dropping and games involving trust. The group also provides an experimental setting for trying out and practicing new and corrective behaviours.

One may also begin to see the interconnectedness of different mechanisms. There are opportunities for checking out one's fantasies about others in the group (learning the role of projection). One discovers how one makes others behave in certain ways (such as the mechanism of 'Projective Identification') and how to free oneself from its unhealthy aspects.

For a baby the experiences of being fussed over by the parent generates a rather pleasant feeling which contributes towards the formation of the central ego. Similarly the frustrating experiences lead to a feeling of distress and rage with an impulse to attack and destroy. However, the baby regards these impulses as located outside and attacks them. This is a naturally occurring protective device, in terms of object relations theory and is known as the mechanism of 'projection'. The parent, however, by being comforting instead, helps the baby to feel comfortable (a phenomenon of 'introjection'). Sometimes the parent can also be possessed (identified with) by the baby's feelings (a phenomenon of projective identification) which helps the parent better to appreciate the baby's needs, impossible to put into words by a baby. These fundamental processes help the child gradually to learn to cope with the intensity of feelings.

Emotional maturation leads to these processes being used only in moderation. However, in some children these processes continue in their primitive form even when the child grows up. The individual goes on seeking suitable figures in the outer world to coerce them into the role of inner objects. These figures are made to feel guilty as if they are rejecting, destroying and damaging the individual. Understandably, they find it difficult to tolerate this. The individual, therefore, makes them behave in accordance with the projections leading to projective identification. According to Ogden (1979), this process takes place in three steps: (i) fantasy of projecting a part of one's self into another person; (ii) an inter-personal pressure on this person to think, feel and behave in a manner congruent with the projection; and (iii) because of such a pressure the person may act in congruence with the projection or may be able to tolerate and modify these dumped feelings and hand them back to the projector for reinternalization.

Thus by means of projective identification an individual can continue to exert pressure on others until they are possessed by the projected qualities such as a harsh punitive response. The effectiveness of treatment depends upon the setting that can deal with this pull of projective identification in a therapeutic manner. In this way, an experiential group helps the youngsters to look at the ongoing relationships and events in the group to discover the underlying forces in terms of their past experiences on the one hand and also in terms of the interpersonal transactions, on the other.

Michael

This young man was referred to our service because of his violent outbursts. He was growing up in a very unhappy situation. On the one hand, he was required to be a 'parent' to his emotionally deprived, anxious, inadequate and infantile mother, and on the other his own needs were treated as infantile and crushed with the help of the mother's boyfriend who was himself an immature violent man and for whom Michael had very little respect. The relationship between his mother and her boyfriend was also unstable, precarious and ambivalent. Thus, Michael's violent outbursts were actually used by his mother to plead with her boyfriend to stay in the relationship. The treatment consisted of helping his mother appreciate his situation and build up her confidence through effective parenting and also group therapy for Michael.

Within the group Michael gradually began to recreate his family circumstances and predicament by turning some of the group members into the caricatures of his family members. The therapeutic setting of the group, however, provided opportunities for such explorations by different group members and experimentation with alternative modes of relating. Similarly, other psychodynamic processes became manifest as he continued attending the group, such as the issue of insecure attachment, dread of abandonment, deprivation of normal developmental play, and parentification leading to his acting like a parent to his own parent. The trusting setting of the group and the experiential learnings from the various relationships that developed within the group helped Michael to make sense of his feelings and behaviours and begin to master them and mature.

Psycho-educational groups

1. Cognitive therapy approaches

In an aggressive situation, we rely upon our cognitive processes to help us determine as to what or who are the provokers and why (causal attributions or misattributions and of intent in the provoker), to decide how best to react, to anticipate the consequences of our aggressive actions, and to discriminate between the possible targets. But the state of our physiological arousal has a considerable influence over our cognitive processes (Zillman 1979; Dwivedi, Beaumont and Brandon 1984). These processes can be seriously impaired at a very low level of physiological arousal (e.g. drowsiness) or at a very high level of arousal (e.g. fear, anxiety, anger, rage and so on). In such situations of poor cognitive control there is an emergence of simple learnt aggressive responses which take over. Such a kind of reckless emotional outburst is often termed 'annoyance-motivated aggression' because it is an efficient means of alleviating annoyance with contingent positive reinforcement (Fehrenbach and Theler 1982).

There is an intricate relationship between the psycho-physiological processes and the cognitive processes. On the one hand, the psycho-physiological arousal influences the cognitive processes as outlined above and, on the other hand, the cognitive factors influence the psycho-physiological arousal. People differ in the way they habitually perceive things, the type of belief systems that they harbour and the kind of automatic thoughts or private speech they encounter in their consciousness. These have a strong influence on one's emotional responses. The incidents and situations that provoke anger may not do so if these are perceived or construed differently.

Various studies indicate that aggressive youngsters appear to have distorted cognitive processes (Lochman and Lenhart 1993). Their social goals operate as more enduring cognitive schema. Dominance and revenge play as major motivational factors guiding their behaviours. These schema are formed over the course of a person's development through the whole chain of experiences and influence the way the individual interprets subsequent interpersonal interactions. Thus, they have definable deficiencies and distortions at each of the cognitive processing steps such as encoding social cues, accurately and appropriately attributing and interpreting social events, generating a whole range of solutions to the perceived problem, deciding the best solution on the basis of the perceived consequence of hypothetically enacting each solution, and executing the chosen strategy.

There are ways of quantifying one's tendency to anger with the help of self-report inventories such as Anger Inventory (Novaco 1975; a 90 item inventory that presents hypothetical anger evoking situations with a 5-point Likert scale to indicate the degree of anger), Children's Anger Inventory (Finch, Saylor and Nelson 1983; a 71 item inventory designed to measure children's probable anger responses to hypothetical situations using 4-point pictorial Likert scale) and Anger Control Inventory (Hoshmand and Austin 1985; a 128-item inventory with 15 subscales and items in two sections: situations that engender anger reactions and individual responses to anger eliciting situations).

Aggressive youngsters tend to have a set of beliefs that maintain aggressive behaviour, demonstrate social problem solving deficiencies and exhibit an egocentric perspective taking style and hostile attributional biases (Short and Simeonson 1986; Dodge *et al.* 1990; Slaby and Guerra 1988). Thus, an individual's anger and resulting aggression are influenced by his or her cognitive structuring of the situation, such as meaning of the provocation for the individual, what is expected to happen and what the person says to oneself (self-statement). Negative self-statements (e.g. 'I can't let him get away with that') increase anger, while positive self-statements (e.g. 'I am not going to play the fool for him') can help control anger. Some of the common thoughts that might be conducive to producing anger may be: 'It is going to be dreadful', 'It is dreadful already', 'I can't let him get away with this', 'This is the story of my life', 'I am always rejected', 'They always end up humiliating me' and so on.

The cognitive therapy approach to anger management is best suited to be conducted in a group setting (Dwivedi 1993a). Such an approach utilizes the intricate relationships between cognitions and emotions for therapeutic pur-poses. The approach involves the following components.

(1) To identify various triggers that tend to stir up anger.

(2) To map out various habitual thoughts, feelings actions and consequences associated with those triggers and construct a plan to replace them with their useful counterparts.

(3) To keep an anger diary to learn how one is better managing the provocation situations by making a note of the situations that make one angry; the details of what happened, when and where; what exactly one felt; what thoughts went through one's mind; what

irritated one most; and what one actually did (e.g. not showing anger, being verbally angry, being physically aggressive, leaving the situation, and so on).

In this way, an attempt is, therefore, made to list all the mal-productive thoughts, such as the ones mentioned above, and then to explore the possibility of some helpful alternative thoughts, for example: 'I don't have to rise to the bait', 'I don't need to prove myself', 'There is no point in getting mad; they probably want me to but, I will surprise them', 'My muscles are getting tight; this is time for me to take a deep breath', 'My anger is a signal of what I have to do', 'The situation is getting difficult, but I do have a plan of how to handle this', 'Let me remember to stick to the issues and not take things personally', and so on.

Aggressive behaviours are often associated with a phenomenon of 'de-individuation', that is, an increase in the attention to environmental cues for behaviour direction and a decrease in private self-awareness (Prentice-Dunn and Rogers 1983). Such individuals need to be taught the art of private self-awareness so that they can also learn to recognize internal stimuli that precede aggressive outbursts, the skill of *cue identification* (Lee 1979). A parallel technique is used in the treatment of tics on the assumption that a tic is a movement that relieves an unpleasant sensation (Bullen and Hemsley 1983). Similarly, aggressive individuals can be trained to recognize the internal sensations which build up before the aggressive outburst, and having identified such sensations and their transient nature, it is possible to cope with them without resorting to an aggressive outburst.

Many aggressive adolescents have been brought up in an angry environment and have little experience of feelings other than that of anger. They do not have sound cognitive structures to appreciate other feelings and tend to mis-attribute anger to any aroused emotional state. Thus an excitement induced by watching a football match may be experienced as anger (Garrison and Stolberg 1983). Through **Affective Imagery Training** such adolescents can be helped to build up cognitive structures for different affective states, for example fear, anger, sadness and happiness. This can be achieved by structured fantasy exercises to evoke certain type of feelings within and to learn to recognize and label these correctly. The exercises are aimed at re-experiencing different affective situations with the help of stories, imageries and recollections of past emotional incidents in order to focus on the cognitive and internal physiological states.

We may sometimes wrongly experience our internal sensations or states of psychophysiological arousal as anger. This process of inner labelling takes place through our self-instruction or private speech. However, one can learn to change one's private speech and thus relabel the internal sensations more accurately, such as excitement rather than anger (Novaco 1979). In a group training situation these sensations can be experimentally produced through 'stress inoculation', and the private speech can be altered by self-instruction i.e. repeating certain phrases (as if chanting) in one's mind (e.g. 'I'm excited, not angry'). Stress Inoculation Training combines training in relaxation, stress inoculation (exposure to stress), systematic desensitization, cognitive corrections (through self-instructions, statements or private speech), modelling and reinforcements in a group setting along with social skills training.

As we can get annoyed very quickly in certain situations for reasons which may not be under our full control, our anger may be habitually triggered by certain accents, voice tones, gestures, demands of people of certain race, sex, age or occupation. Some *counter conditioning procedures* such as systematic desensitization can be used to reduce the likelihood of such an annoyance. This is done first by training in relaxation and then exposure to stressful stimuli in order to teach how to cope with these triggers without responding to them angrily. One may be able to incorporate humourous thoughts to cushion the effect of the stressors.

Using repeated role play exercises, individuals can also be trained to do something other (such as take a few deep breaths, withdraw for a moment and so on) than reflexively attack under provocation, and when they have learnt such *alternative responses* they can then be trained to practise relaxation to dissipate feelings of anger and also to use problem-solving approaches in a systematic manner.

Different components of effective *problem-solving* can be taught to youngsters in an experimental group setting by using stories with a dilemma and by role playing. These components include: (i) defining the situation; (ii) considering choices; (iii) selecting the best choice; (iv) implementing the selected course of action and verifying that the selected choice was the best one (Camp 1980). As they are trained in the art of solving hypothetical problems in a step by step logical manner, they begin to use these skills in their day-to-day life.

We all automatically, inherently and almost subconsciously talk to ourselves inside our heads to guide our problem-solving attempts. This process becomes overt only when problems become difficult. Therefore, these *verbal meditation skills* are usually already present in aggressive individuals, but they often fail to use these skills when needed – i.e. they have production deficits. The youngsters therefore need to be taught to overlearn these skills with the help of role-play and games which may include saying aloud, to begin with, phrases such as 'What is my problem?', 'How can I do it?', 'Am I following my plan?', 'How did I do?', and so on. It will then facilitate their using such verbal meditation skills in real life situations. In fact, overlearning can be used to combat production deficits in the whole range of skills. Rabiner, Lenhart and Lochman (1990) found that even aggressive youngsters are able to generate appropriate solutions if they can be engaged in a 'reflective' or deliberate reasoning process rather than operating in an 'automatic' processing mode.

Feindler and Ecton (1986) provide the details of a 12 session group training programme for adolescents in managing their anger using the cognitive therapy approach. Similarly Lochman *et al.* (1987) provide a step-by-step programme for group work in schools for the management of anger over 18 sessions. Feindler, Ecton, Kingsley and Dubey (1986) describe an eight-week group work training programme for psychiatric inpatient adolescents. These programmes utilize the components of perspective taking, managing physiological arousal, self-statements, problem solving and so on, with good results. Many violent youngsters also have a history of attention deficit hyperactivity disorder. Braswell and Bloomquist (1991) have provided a very detailed description of a group work approach using cognitive and behaviour therapy principles with the youngsters suffering from attention deficit hyperactivity disorder. McGuire and Priestley (1985; Harrower 1993) provide a manual for working effectively with offenders utilizing offence analysis as well.

2. Behaviour modification

At an intermediate level of physiological arousal the cognitive processes may not be impaired (in contrast to the low levels or high levels of arousal described earlier). The ability to control one's aggressive responses may also be effective, but aggression may still be used for certain gains. The type of aggressive behaviour in such situations may be called 'incentive-motivated aggression', i.e. attaining incentives at a relatively low cost (in one's subjective evaluation). The clinical approaches in the situations of 'incentive-motivated aggression' may include reinforcement procedures, and social skills training. These are based on the assumption that the problems are either due to the presence of maladaptive behaviours which have been learnt or due to the absence of adaptive behaviours which have not yet been learnt.

Reinforcement Approaches are based on the assumption that aggression and hostility are learned and maintained by positive and negative reinforcement. The role of modelling and reinforcement in learning behaviours is now well established. There are a number of techniques that can be used either in the setting of a contingency contracting programme, or in a comprehensive retraining programme. These techniques include Extinction, Time-Out and Response Costing. Extinction can be achieved by ignoring inappropriate behaviours. It is unfortunate that people often unwittingly reinforce inappropriate (e.g. aggressive) behaviours by trying to 'get to the bottom' of things. Time-out provides an opportunity for an appropriate behaviour to emerge so that it can be reinforced. It helps extinction by withdrawing positive reinforcement of inappropriate behaviours. Time-out is most effective when it is of short duration – up to five or ten minutes. Any longer use prevents the child from learning a more appropriate way of dealing with the difficult situation.

Response costing allows privileges to be earned by appropriate behaviours, for example token economy.

These principles can easily be utilized in a group work setting with violent youngsters incorporating reinforcement by the group members as well. Similarly, 'time-out' can be from the stimulating activities of the group.

Social Skills Training is based on the assumption that aggression continues because more acceptable ways of handling inter-personal demands have not yet been learned, and the person lacks specific skills in coping with provocations to aggressive responses. It is therefore possible systematically to train a person in assertiveness and other social skills to correct the deficit in his situation-specific skills.

Bach (1971) has described several 'Fair Fight Training' games that can be played in a group situation in such a way that the individuals get opportunities to practice expressing their feelings and thoughts without being hurtful. These are based on the assumption that conflict, frustration and aggression are inherent in any intimate face-to-face group of emotionally inter-dependent people. Aggression, therefore, has two functions; informative impact and hurtful hostility. An effective coaching in fair fighting (such as 'Haircut', 'Virginia Woolf' and 'Clearing House') can alter the ratio between informative impact and hurtful hostility and can thus improve the constructiveness of aggression. To play the game one has to request the partner to participate in it. The partner who receives the request ('May I give you a haircut?') has the right to set the time limit, as well as the right to refuse or postpone acceptance. If the 'haircut' is accepted the partner is obliged to listen to a tongue-lashing without defence, for the time contracted. The 'Virginia Woolf', is a two-way, simultaneous, verbal exchange (e.g. 'this is for spoiling my painting'), accompanied by non-hurtful hitting by a bataca (a plastic bat usually used by toddlers as a toy and if used to hit someone it doesn't hurt but sounds as if it does and can be very dramatic). The 'Clearing House' is an expression of grievances and frustrations that arose since the last Clearing House. It is important to keep to the time allotted to each round, respect the 'beltline', i.e. the taboos requested by the partner, and to check out the meaning of what the partner says. One is scored for the style of the fight and penalized for the fouls such as not keeping to the time as agreed before starting the game, hitting below the 'beltline', evading a fight or 'mind-raping' (that is, imposing one's interpretation of what the other one says without checking them out).

Laslett (1982) has described a way of dealing with day-to-day grievances of communal living by the institution of a formal *youngster's court*, such as in a school situation. The youngsters can elect two justices, a clerk and a court runner. A set of punishments (such as apologizing, keeping off the grass, doing certain jobs) are made available to the judges. Any complainer can tell the grievances to the Clerk, who should write complaints in the complaint book and then the defendants are given the opportunity to clarify their points of view. This will help the judges to reach a verdict. A machinery for appeal can also be evolved, and similarly, if staff find a youngster not complying with the punishment, the staff can pass this on to the judges for future action rather than get involved in a hostile interaction themselves.

A *therapeutic community*, through the structure of formal community meetings, can mobilize group processes for communication (i.e. sharing of tasks, responsibilities and rewards), democratic decision making, confrontation with one's actions, and permissiveness to explore and understand one's feelings. This allows the youngsters to learn to see themselves as objects from another's point of view, as aggressive youngsters usually have a deficiency of role playing ability (Whiteley 1975).

CHAPTER 13

The Police Relationship with Violent Children and Adolescents

Nigel Fielding

Introduction

The basic distinction in policing between two kinds of police work – law enforcement and order maintenance – fundamentally affects the police relationship with children and adolescents. Law enforcement embraces police work in respect of crime control and is conventionally accomplished using formal disposals such as arrest or caution. Order maintenance involves police work directed to the maintenance of conditions of calm and civility and is conventionally accomplished using informal disposals such as dispersing groups who are disturbing public order. These types of work require different police actions and give rise to different role relationships. The demands of dealing with violent children and adolescents in a particular incident may primarily relate to law enforcement, or to order maintenance, or may move from one to the other as an incident unfolds. In the case of children and adolescents the conduct of an incident is not only affected by police decisions about whether it is a law enforcement or order maintenance incident but by considerations to do with children's responsibilities in law.

Rights and Responsibilities of Children in Law

There have recently been several important developments relating to the responsibility of children in law. Some have been motivated by adjustments of the investigative and court process in respect of child protection, so that child witnesses enjoy new processual protections such as being permitted to give their evidence-in-chief using video technology. Other changes have come about as children, such as adopted and fostered children, are given new rights over their domestic arrangements; for example, 'divorcing' one's court-appointed caregivers. With these changes in the law's regard for children's *rights* has come new thinking on childrens' *responsibilities*. Public anxiety over serious crime committed by children has reinforced official interest in the idea that children may be maturing earlier and that, if this is so, perhaps they should shoulder responsibility for their actions at an earlier chronological age.

In law it is conclusively presumed that no child under ten can be guilty of an offence (Children and Young Persons Act 1969). Ten is the so-called 'age of criminal responsibility', although it has until recently been necessary to satisfy the court that a child aged from ten to fourteen knew that what he or she was doing was wrong. The 'rebuttable presumption' of the common law was that up to fourteen the child lacked such understanding. However, in 1994 the High Court abolished the rule, which had protected some children from prosecution for crimes including murder and dated from a time when children faced execution for relatively minor offences. The judges ruled that it was 'perverse' and 'outdated' to permit conviction of those between ten and fourteen only if it were proven that they knew what they were doing was 'seriously wrong' rather than 'merely naughty'. Lord Justice Mann noted that the rule meant that children from 'what used to be called good homes' did not benefit in the same way as those from poorer backgrounds. The children most likely to offend were most likely to go unpunished; it was precisely those whose understanding of right and wrong was fragile or non-existent who were most likely to offend. The rule had helped a child escape prosecution in at least one murder case, and in the 1993 James Bulger trial psychiatrists were required to interview the two ten-year-olds later convicted of the murder to see whether the test was satisfied.

A 'juvenile' is one who has attained the age of ten years and is under seventeen. In relation to criminal procedure, this is the age range which is subject mainly to the juvenile court, whose procedures differ from adult courts in the degree of formality. The power to remand juveniles in secure accommodation applies only to defendants aged fifteen or sixteen but the Home Office plans to allow courts to order twelve to fourteen year olds to be so placed awaiting trial or sentence. The power would only apply, as with fifteen and sixteen year olds, where the defendant is charged with or has been convicted of a violent or sexual offence, or one punishable in the case of an adult with imprisonment for fourteen years or more, or where the defendant has a recent history of absconding and is charged with or has been convicted of an imprisonable offence committed while on remand. Finally, a 'young person' is one who has attained the age of fourteen years and is under seventeen. This distinction is chiefly relevant in respect of the type of custodial disposal available on a determination of guilt.

Sentencing

In fact, the picture is less clear than even this profile of age and the law may suggest. There are provisions under old legislation (section 53 of the Children and Young Persons Act 1933) for the sentencing of young children for serious crime. The legislation was introduced to deal with the rare cases in which children commit grave offences such as homicide but there is evidence that it is increasingly applied to less serious offences. There is also a worrying anomaly, in that those over the age of responsibility who are convicted receive determinate sentences whereas a confederate under the age of responsibility receives an indeterminate sentence (being 'detained at HM pleasure') and usually will spend much longer in custody (see Godsland and Fielding 1985). Despite these concerns, the Home Office plans to extend section 53 to allow long terms of detention for a wider range of offences.

Moves to alter the legal position of children in respect of liability to criminal prosecution should be informed by the American experience. Some see in US juvenile corrections the slow rise of a 'just deserts' approach meant to make punishment fit the crime rather than proceeding from an assumed dimunition of responsibility. There has been a marked increase in waiver hearings that allow juveniles accused of serious crimes to be tried as adults. This seems to have little to do with the seriousness or characteristics of the case; analysis of waivers in four states revealed that only eleven per cent resulted in custodial sentences (Champion 1989). Waivers were more likely to be applied to repeat offenders than violent offenders. Champion concluded that waivers were a largely cosmetic response to public concern. New York's Juvenile Offender Law 1978 requires that juveniles accused of violent offences be tried in criminal court and provides penalties comparable to those for adults. Research on the impact of the law on violent juvenile crime rates show that it failed to reduce juvenile crime (Singer and McDowall 1988). New York's initiative was not unique and other state prisons are increasingly receiving young, violent offenders with lengthy sentences. A study of young inmates who committed their crimes before age 17 and those who committed their crimes between ages 17 and 21 indicates that younger offenders are more than twice as likely to be problem inmates and three times more likely to have to be held in the most restrictive grades of custody (McShane and Williams 1989). There is little solace for advocates of lowering the age of criminal responsibility in these studies. Treating juveniles as fully responsible in an adult sense is particularly unlikely to have a deterrent effect, since individual deterrence requires that news of harsh sentencing be quickly disseminated amongst potential offenders competent to assess potential gains against potential penalties rationally.

Cautioning procedures and charging policies

We have already noted that police contact with juveniles may move between the two categories of law enforcement and order maintenance. This transitivity is complicated by the ambiguity related to the diminution of responsibility associated with chronological age. In determining how 'responsible' or culpable a juvenile may be, officers have to estimate the level of maturity of the juvenile suspect. This is, of course, also a consideration in respect of adult suspects (who may be mentally ill, 'inadequate' or under the influence of intoxicants) but is more demanding in the case of juveniles, both because their behaviour may be inconsistent and because of the legal protections that young people enjoy. Thus, difficult judgements are required of police in their dealings with juveniles of all sorts, whether as victims or as suspected offenders and, in the case of the latter, whether suspected of violent offences or some other sort. Juveniles pose a challenge to the discretionary authority of the police and the law has sought to regulate more tightly the exercise of police discretion in respect of juveniles than with regard to adults; for instance, in the exercise of the caution. Consequently, instant cautioning procedures, charging policies and the need to photograph and fingerprint very young offenders are all points of routine tension. In one case three black children, aged nine, ten and eleven, who were caught stealing sweets, spent five hours in a police station and the two eldest were charged, photographed, fingerprinted and required to prepare signed statements, acquiring a criminal record which would last until age 17 (Thomas 1989). The nine-year-old being taken to the station (below the age of criminal responsibility), the acceptability of a social worker acting as 'appropriate adult' within the PCEA Codes of Practice, and a 'standing order' in the station that all juveniles were to be fingerprinted were all legally doubtful. Social workers wanted the children to be 'reported' and then permitted to go, but the police preferred the instant caution because it required no further police action. However, what it did do was to put their record on computer. At 10.30 at night an inspector cautioned them, including the nine-year-old who should not legally have been present but was clinging to his sister. Access to a solicitor was not considered. The case exposes some of the factors influencing police in their dealings with juveniles.

While the incident suggests that the tighter regulations applying to juveniles present police with problems which they sometimes handle badly, another characteristic of the cautioning process is its assignment to the police of a quasi-sentencing role. Certainly sentencing is a 'moral' process but the caution would seem to open the door more widely to the moral thinking of those who effectively administer the sentence. For a caution to proceed there has to be an admission of guilt on the part of the person detained, but whether this may be more freely given by children because they are less able to grasp the consequences of acquiring a record is something which makes cautioning a risky disposal. Further, granting the police the sentencing role concentrates power in the hands of the same group which has the problem of detecting and detaining the suspected culprit. The administration of the caution is itself deliberately designed to include an element of moral censure, particularly where the stern admonition by a uniformed, ranking officer may be expected to intimidate the younger or more naive offender. It is not hard to imagine how the enthusiastic exercise of the process could be unduly intimidating to a youngster who already felt remorseful.

Types of crime

If we were to speak simply in terms of statistics, the proportion of contacts which police have with juveniles is much higher in respect of problems of order maintenance than in respect of law enforcement. When we further subdivide the law enforcement category so that we are examining police relations with juveniles suspected of involvement in violent offences then we are looking at a relatively small, if troubling, proportion of contacts. Under ten per cent of young offenders are arrested more than three times in a year and violent crime is rare even in this group (Newburn 1994). Most re-offenders commit traffic offences, burglaries, autocrime and criminal damage. The study identified 531 re-offenders under 17 who had on average been arrested four or five times in 1992 and had committed seven known offences that year. These persistent offenders were at their most 'persistent' for only short periods, rarely over a year. They are quickly replaced by other young offenders, most of whose offending falls in the nuisance category rather than being violent. Before we focus on relations with the small group of violent juveniles, we should note that in volume terms and in terms of the challenge they pose to the normal functioning of civil society, youth in conflict with police over order maintenance matters exercise a more compelling demand and a greater preoccupation. This is particularly so on large estates and where the groups of juveniles are from an ethnic minority. Problems with unruly youths will have been encountered by every police officer while encounters with youths suspected of violent offences are less common. Unruly youths who challenge police, be it by 'sassiness' or by throwing objects at patrols from the safe obscurity of a tower block walkway, are dealt with by responses ranging from ignoring the action to issuing threats to the bringing of 'resource charges' such as obstruction.

'Subcultural' groups and gang behaviour

However, order maintenance problems can escalate and there has been sustained concern since at least the 1960s that order maintenance challenges to the police are being aggravated by the membership of juveniles in 'subcultural' groups explicitly organized around an adversarial relationship with the police. There is a longstanding debate in criminology as to the criminogenic character of subcultural membership. It is thought that the term 'subculture' may have too freely been assigned to gangs which were in fact relatively loose and impermanent aggregations of young males. Cohen's original 'general theory of subculture' (1965) characterized the gangs he studied as exhibiting behaviour which was malicious, nonutilitarian and negativistic. Apart from the rather obvious moral tinge of Cohen's characterization of the boys, and the dubious pseudopsychological mechanism of 'reaction formation' by which the boys purportedly 'inverted' middle class values so as to arrive at their own, there is much doubt about how readily Cohen's 'general theory' applies to gangs outside the American cities of the 1960s. This is not to deny the demonology often associated with youth groups, the way that such groups are represented by the mass media and criminal justice personnel as symbols of what our children should not become. Compare Cohen's formulation to a group organized in 1993 at Luton to promote 'rave' parties. The group used the money from running 'raves' to assist in housing homeless youths and operated as a collective. These are not characteristics of a 'nonutilitarian' subculture. However, the press depicted the group in traditional subcultural terms, as a threat to civilized values. In fact, the only complaints received by police were about late-night noise, but it is interesting to note that the press coverage of the group coincided with the Home Secretary's announcement of his intention to make 'raves' illegal. Not all youth groups should be regarded as fully-fledged subcultures (to qualify as a subculture the group must have distinctive values and argot, and mechanisms to transmit these to new members, thus showing some endurance over time as the result of socialization processes). Nor are all youth groups organized around deviance. Subcultural theorists argue that during the 1970s and 1980s youth groups became more concerned with issues such as AIDS, unemployment and environmental problems (Wooffitt 1994), so that the youth subculture about which Cohen worried may have been the result of a particular moment in American society associated with the 'age of affluence', the rise of the 'teenager' as a distinctive social category and the 'status offences' associated with middle class adolescents.

This is not to deny that youth give rise to public order problems, nor that many such problems arise from youths operating in groups which are relatively stable over time. One implication of subcultural theory is that there are social class differences in the type of deviant behaviour which is observed. It may be that, rather than socialization into subcultural values, delinquent youth are being socialized into values associated with the lower working class. A large sample of adolescent males aged 15 to 18 was studied with respect to the nature and extent of violent offending of gang-affiliated youths in comparison with non-gang controls (Friedman, Mann and Adelman 1976). The boys were selected from residential correctional facilities, community-based job training programmes and from an inner city secondary school in Philadelphia. All the youths had lower socio-economic backgrounds; some 61 per cent were black and 34 per cent white. Gang members generally claimed much higher rates of activities such as getting drunk, using weapons, disregarding school demands and causing trouble. While the coercive and violent aspects of street gang behaviour were thus revealed, it is worth noting that non-gang members living in areas where the gangs operated also tended to have higher percentages of these problematic behaviours. This implies both that the example set by the gangs may affect others living locally and that the gang behaviour may not differ from what is regarded as 'normal' in the immediate environment. Those studying violent youth must bear in mind that there are different categories of 'youth' and that social class and ethnicity may actually be the governing factors in the relationship to offending rather than 'violence' itself as a distinctive trait.

There is a further point to note about police relations with youth gangs of the sort studied by Friedman *et al.* (1976). This is that there are certain similarities between the characteristics of the police and those they police in such circumstances. There is a 'contest' element in the vocabulary of such confrontations and it is sometimes very explicit. The constables who patrol tough estates are likely to be young, vigorous, crime-oriented officers, who may well embrace macho values which are the subject of external criticism of the character of the 'canteen culture' but which are also similar in their valorization of physical prowess and 'hardness' to the values espoused by young gang members. Ryder (1991) draws parallels between the culture of young offenders and that of the police and argues that conformity to peer group values of machismo, not deviance, chiefly motivates teenage offending. 'To gain the respect of your peers you have to prove you are tough. This means doing dangerous things which in your heart of hearts you would rather not be doing, such as burglary or joyriding. By doing these things you prove to others and to yourself that you are *hard*. Tough is good' (Ryder 1991, p.12). Perhaps it is no coincidence that urban disorder has developed a strongly 'tit for tat' quality, with both sides depicting riots in a contest vocabulary. One young rioter in Coventry commented, "'I've been out there doing the damage with the other lads this week because the police are out of order. They come on here harassing people and dragging them off to jail for no reason. There'll be more aggro if they don't pull out of our turf'" (*The Guardian*, 15 May 1992). Recent riots have been marked by youths monitoring police messages, explicit admissions of tactics to tempt police onto estates so as to ambush them, and driving 'displays' where stolen cars were driven hard to 'entertain' bystanders and demonstrate the inadequacy of law enforcement. Stereotypical macho values include the physical resolution of direct, violent confrontations construed in highly personal terms and justified by Levitical notions of punishment, qualities apparent both among those who cause and those who control major public order disturbances.

Violent offending

Turning to violent offending *per se*, there is a deal of research from a number of disciplines seeking the causes of violent offending. Aetiological accounts have been offered in respect of biochemical and physiological factors, genetics, medical status, neurological, psychiatric and neuropsychological factors, while social science disciplines have offered accounts based on differential social organization, anomie and strain, differential association and other deficiencies of socialization, economic determinism, gender roles, and polygenetic accounts combining two or more of these. Perhaps fortunately for our present discussion, it matters as little for the police relationship with violent juveniles which if any of these accounts a particular officer may favour as it does what criminological analysis an officer prefers in the investigation of any other type of offence. It is 'fortunate' in the sense that each theory has its advocates and works of synthesis are few (although, within social science, some progress has been made in identifying factors with more robust explanatory power; in respect of juvenile delinquency, parental attachment and the nature of peer group bonds. See Johnson 1979). At any rate, police action in respect of juveniles is rather little informed by aetiological accounts. It is much more closely informed by practicalities to do with the detection and apprehension of suspects for investigation and thereafter with the proper conduct of charge and remand arrangements and efficient case-handling.

There is often a 'chicken-and-egg' quality to the findings of aetiological studies. For instance, a study which looked at the effects of various perinatal events and central nervous system trauma on juvenile delinquency did identify a higher incidence among young males who suffered central nervous system trauma in respect of violent crime, but was obliged to conclude that while central nervous system trauma might be a cause of delinquency it might also be that the type of behaviour pursued by youths likely to commit violent crime also exposed them more often to circumstances in which central nervous system trauma was likely (Rantakallio, Koiranen and Mottonen 1992). Similarly, psychologists who looked at skills in differentiating object relations by 55 adolescents who had committed homicide found that a subgroup who had killed in the course of committing another crime, such as burglary, manifested inferior object relation skills (poorer object differentiation and more victim responses) than those who killed in the course of a dispute with the victim (Greco and Cornell 1992), but this may be no more than an artefact of the circumstances in which the two types of assaultive crime occurred. Research does indicate that it is unsafe to assume that violent offenders are by definition mentally ill. For instance, a study of a New York court diversion project which offered violent youths intensive psychiatric services found that it achieved only a 50 per cent utilization rate due to the small numbers who met the admission criteria given their careful application and the use of comprehensive screening procedures. The authors suggest that 'the time has come for an end to the assumption that all violent juveniles are mentally ill and that psychiatric care can resolve the problem of violent behaviour' (Cocozza, Hartstone and Braff 1981).

All of this is not to say that research into aetiological matters is not worthwhile but rather to note that police practice is responsive to more immediate practical considerations and that the correlational studies that have been mentioned do not generally help police to narrow the suspect population (if only because a good deal of background information is required which is seldom available at the initial stage of an investigation). What, then, are the factors to which the police respond? To establish these it is necessary to remind ourselves of the sequence of stages through which police contacts proceed with any group. Let us say that word has been received of a commotion in an adjoining flat via a 999 call by a neighbour. The usual response is to send a car patrol to investigate; officers in the vicinity on foot may also attend. These will all be patrol officers from the 'reliefs' who carry a time-based responsibility for the division. In short, they are all generalist officers and who responds is essentially a question of availability. On attending, a man is on the floor of the flat, unconscious and bleeding. The door to the flat is open, showing signs of a hasty exit by the culprit. Where to look? In this first stage, detecting and apprehending a suspect for investigation, the age of the suspect matters little. Until the victim is conscious and information can be given, police will simply look for anyone 'acting suspiciously', perhaps running in alleys or disposing of clothes (which may be bloodstained). Now our victim is conscious in a hospital bed and admits that, in the course of selling a young man some heroin, the youth has grabbed the drug without paying and stabbed him as they struggled at the door. Where to look now? Police involvement shifts. Now detectives and drug squad officers join the patrols. The latter will continue to detain 'suspicious' people. This remains the extent of their involvement. Meanwhile the drug squad officers will feed the detectives (and the Collator, the route by which patrols should get their information about the case) information about known addicts locally, particularly those who are 'weapon carriers'. The officers know that they are dealing with a juvenile from the victim. This knowledge affects the search by guiding officers towards schools, colleges and training schemes. One of these contacts brings them to a training scheme where young men are taught to make leather goods. Knives are freely available and in a bin by a workbench a blood-stained rag is seen. The young man at the workbench is uneasy when asked about the rag. Police invite him to the station to discuss it. In the car they question the youth and establish he has only just joined the scheme. He continually rubs his arm and seems all the time to be chewing though nothing is in his mouth. There is a small foil wrap on his person when he is searched. He is charged with possession of heroin and interviewing begins about the assault.

So far in our story there will have been no difference in the way the suspect is dealt with according to his being an adult or juvenile. At interview he has the right to legal advice and there is no difference in this respect. However, PCEA requires that a parent or 'appropriate adult' should also be present. During interview, with his mother and a solicitor present, he admits that he stabbed the dealer. He is charged with assault occasioning grievous bodily harm. Bail is refused and he is sent to a juvenile remand centre awaiting trial. Conditions in the centre are barely any different than for an adult, but in any case our story is almost over, for police involvement now relates only to offering evidence on behalf of the prosecution. When this is given it is checked to ensure that the few special conditions applying to juvenile suspects have been adhered to. Thus, there are few distinctive respects in which the suspect's age affects our story. We could have added 'black' to our description of the young suspect and this may well have affected police procedure (leading them quickly to the 'usual suspects') but then we would be in the realm of police/ethnic minority relations, not police/violent juvenile relations. Nor does the tendency to investigate the 'usual suspects' bespeak an unusual measure of stereotyping. Victimization and offending go hand-in-hand; the best predictor of the likelihood of someone having a criminal record is whether they have been recorded as a victim (Smith and Gray 1983). Statistically, the people who commit most offences operate in a milieu and have a lifestyle in which they also have high chances of being victimized. Thus, by their own lights the police are only acting sensibly in returning to the 'usual suspects' when characteristic types of offence need to be solved. Police relations with violent youths in respect of law enforcement tend, then, to be recurrent relations with a restricted suspect population.

Thinking of the investigation/interview stage, as opposed to the apprehension stage, the age of the youth would no doubt be used to pressure our suspect. If an admission of guilt was not forthcoming this could be useful. There is concern that, where there is scope for oppressive interviewing techniques to be applied they may particularly be used against juveniles, or indeed, lower-level techniques may be perceived by such a suspect as more oppressive. The Royal Commission on Criminal Justice did pay attention to legal safeguards concerning the interview process as it applied to certain groups of suspect. Among them were young people, but the focus of concern was the mentally inadequate. This is not to say that there should not be concern over malpractice in the course of criminal investigation, but these are general concerns.

Key issues

Thus the real issues relating to the police relationship with violent juveniles are those thrown up by the problems of order maintenance rather than those of crime control. Here the police face certain insurmountable problems. We are used to the idea that young people go through a rebellious stage as they work out their own place in the world independent of their family. Social theorists argue that each generation must test the boundaries of normality and deviant behaviour, and that this is one of the factors which prompts change in community standards over time. In this sense the story of order maintenance is also that of eternal recurrence, since each new generation comes into conflict with established norms. For the police it is the same story too. The police are highly visible representatives of the established order, literally set apart by their uniform. If it is indeed true that each new generation will test the boundaries (sometimes leading to change) then each will also encounter resistance by the police, for their brief is to maintain order as defined by existing norms. In major public order incidents people commit acts in crowds which they would not commit alone; the effect has been much-studied in research on riots. Thus it may not be possible to determine from which particular young person one may expect a violent response. It is also worth noting that the conflictual incidents on housing estates discussed above were not in the main 'political' but rather territorial, often representing no more than the naive claim that police had been unfair or biased simply by seeking to enforce the law. It is difficult to imagine that this kind of confrontation will ever disappear.

What, then, are the research findings that could inform the police relationship with juveniles? In light of the limited effect of age on police relations with juveniles charged with offences of violence, and in light of the recurrent nature of order maintenance problems, one conclusion is that it makes sense to direct effort to the police response to the latter, it being an issue which can, after all, affect relations with authority in a much wider circle than those directly taking part. There is an important role here for community policing, where this is organized around the long-term assignment of officers to a single geographical beat. The opportunities for befriending, research suggests, are limited. Police efforts at 'outreach' work with youths are doomed by the official image of the police, although the organization of sporting events with local youths does at least mean that for a time one knows where a high proportion of potential offenders are. However, by their regular presence on the beat, and because they are known as individuals, community officers are in a good position to collect information about order maintenance problems involving youths, for example, when training scheme youths have been sacked and are looking to demonstrate their anger against authority. Further, community police are in a good position to regulate local order using informal means (that is, not by arrest). They are able to identify local youths as such, rather than outsiders, and because the youths know this it becomes more difficult for them to ignore the officer's controlling interventions. For instance, a youth whose name and address is known to the officer will be considerably less inclined to assault that officer in the course of a street stop.

Police practice in both investigation and in monitoring local suspect populations could also be informed by research indicating the persistence of violent traits in males who commit sexual assault as juveniles. For instance, when sexually assaultive and violent male juveniles are compared with violent juveniles, those who had committed sexual assault prove significantly more likely to commit such offences as adults (Rubinstein, Yeager, Goodstein and Lewis 1993). They also committed significantly more violent nonsexual offences. Thus, sexually assaultive delinquents are at particularly high risk for subsequent violence. The group plainly merits close monitoring by police. Interestingly, the study also found, as have others, that childhood sexual abuse is associated with adult sexual offenses. Research on aggressive behaviour by youths demonstrates that these youths are often victims of abuse. Aggressive behaviour is manifest in early childhood and persists into young adulthood (Davis and Boster 1992). It is worth recalling the aetiological significance of parental and peer attachment and commitment (as against status frustration and subcultural theories). The conclusion is consistent with research on the characteristics that differentiate homicidal adolescents from nonviolent but delinquent adolescents. In one study, 71 juveniles who had killed were compared with 71 nonviolent delinquents matched by age, race, sex and socioeconomic status (Busch *et al.* 1990). Four major characteristics differentiated the two groups: criminally-violent family members, participation in gangs, alcohol abuse, and severe educational difficulties. The conclusion is reminiscent of the major, longitudinal Cambridge delinquency study by West and Farrington (1973). It suggests that, as well as criminal deviance, boys having long-term trouble with the law also exhibit other deviant traits, including domestic assault, inability to form sustained relationships, poor employment records, substance abuse and driving infractions. We can thus identify which young people are likely to engage in delinquency. Within the violent category, subgroups can further be distinguished by the type of assault (interpersonal conflict or crime-related) and the youth's relationship to the victim (parent or other) (Cornell 1990). The sub-groups bear different risk factors and reflect different developmental pathways.

Since this picture has been becoming clear for some time, one may rightly ask what lessons have been learned from it. In common with other research, Sorrells' study of juveniles convicted of homicide found that a disproportionate number lived in communities with serious problems of poverty and high infant mortality, that the juveniles were from violent, chaotic families, that they lacked the capacity to identify with other people or killed as an expression of intense emotional conflict or that they killed as a result of overreacting to a genuinely threatening situation (Sorrells 1980). Sorrells suggests that high risk communities need to be identified by a range of agencies who can pool their efforts, that children coming into custody should be screened for emotional problems regardless of the offense for which they have been referred, that correctional and treatment programmes should focus on empathy, the resolution of emotional conflict, and personal security rather than simply emphasizing discipline and respect for authority, and that the families of potentially homicidal children should be evaluated, with children being removed from violent, chaotic families. In such an agenda the police would play their part in the multi-agency effort (chiefly by giving information) and take on a role in screening.

During the 1960s a new argument achieved currency in criminology, to the effect that accounts of aetiology based on individual or social pathology neglected the role of social reaction in the process. Social agencies created deviance through their daily efforts, identifying some individuals as deviant while ignoring others. Assigning the label 'deviant' to an individual could transform their social identity, aggravating any tendency to deviate set in train by other factors (these primary causes were regarded as 'polygenetic'). It is now accepted that the labelling approach is a means of examining the counterproductive effects of the criminal justice system and the role of public opinion and the media in aggravating crime problems. Phillips and Dinitz (1982) researched the applicability of labelling ideas to a sample of 1100 violent juveniles. They found that offence information predicted outcome only moderately well; it predicted extremely severe sentencing outcomes far better than outcomes of lesser severity. Something was at work other than the characteristics of the offence of violence. The court's previous responses to the youth played an important role in any subsequent disposition decisions. The finding provided support for the characterization of courts as 'vortices' in which a label is attached to an individual and thereafter bears powerful consequences. Thus, when we assess the relationship of young people to the police, we must beware the power of official labelling, particularly in light of evidence that youthful offending is episodic and persistent offending rare. Despite the reported comments of senior police officers and Home Office ministers, violent offending by children and young people is not merely a sign of 'evil' but of something wrong in the state of society. As society's frontline, it is important that the police appreciate that there are social and psychological reasons that young people do not bear full responsibility as well as reasons of legal doctrine.

References

Abel, G., Becker, J.V., Mittelman, M., Cunningham-Rathner, J., Rouleau, J. and Murphy, W. (1987) 'Self reported sex crimes of non-incarcerated paraphiliacs.' *Journal of Interpersonal Violence 2*, 3–25.

Able, G.G., Blanchard, E.B. and Becker, J.V. (1978) 'An integrated treatment programme for rapists.' In R.T. Rada (ed) *Clinical Aspects of the Rapist*. New York: Grune and Stratton.

Achenbach, T.M. (1978) 'The child behavior profile: I. Boys aged 6–11.' *Journal of Consulting and Clinical Psychology 4*, 478–488.

Adams, J. (1993) 'Group work in the youth service.' In K.N. Dwivedi (ed) *Group Work with Children and Adolescents*. London: Jessica Kingsley.

Adler, A. (1965) *Superiority and Social Interest*. London: Routledge and Kegan Paul.

Ageton, S.S. (1983) *Sexual Assault Among Adolescents*. Lexington, MA: Lexington Books.

Aichhorn, A. (1955) *Wayward Youth*. New York: Meridian.

Akhtar, N. and Bradley, E.J. (1991) 'Social information processing deficits of aggressive children: present findings and implications for social skills training.' *Clinical Psychology Review 11*, 621–644.

Alder, C. (1985) 'An exploration of self-reported sexually aggressive behaviour.' *Crime and Delinquency 31*, 306–331.

Allee, W.C., Collias, N. and Lutherman, C.Z. (1939) 'Modification of the social order among flocks of hens by injection of testosterone propionate.' *Physiological Zoology 12*, 412–420.

Anthony, E.J.(1965, 2nd edition) 'Group analytic psychotherapy with children and adolescents.' In S.H. Foulkes and E.J. Anthony (eds) *Group Psychotherapy: The Psychoanalytic Approach*. London: Maresfield Library.

American Psychiatric Association (1987) *Diagnostic and Statistical Manual* (DSM-111-R), 3rd edition (revised). Washington, D.C.: American Psychiatric Association.

American Psychiatric Association (1994) *Diagnostic and Statistical Manual of Mental Disorders, fourth edition*. Washington, DC: American Psychiatric Association.

Arbuthnot, J. and Gordon, D.A. (1986) 'Behavioral and cognitive effects of a moral reasoning development intervention for high-risk behavior-disordered adolescents.' *Journal of Consulting and Clinical Psychology 54*, 208–216.

Armstrong, L. (1978) *Kiss Daddy Goodnight: A Speak-out on Incest*. New York: Pocket Books.

Aulich, L. (1994) 'Fear and loathing; art therapy, sex offenders and gender.' In M. Liebmann (ed) *Art Therapy with Offenders*. London: Jessica Kingsley Publishers.

Azar, B. and Sleek, S. (1994) 'Do roots of violence grow from nature or nurture?' *American Psychological Association Monitor 31*, October.

Bach, G.R. (1971) 'Constructive aggression in growth groups.' In A. Jacobs and W.W. Spradlin (eds) *Group as Agent of Change*. Chicago: Aldine, Atherton.

Bailey, S. (1996 in Press) 'Adolescents who murder.' *Journal of Adolescence 19*, 19–39.

Bailey, S., Thornton, L. and Weaver, A. (1994) 'First 100 admissions to a secure unit.' *Journal of Adolescence 17*, 000–013.

Bandura, A. (1973) *Aggression: A Social Learning Analysis*. Englewood Cliffs: Prentice Hall.

Bandura, A., Ross, D. and Ross, S. (1963) 'Imitation of film-mediated aggressive models.' *Journal of Abnormal and Social Psychology*, 1–589–95.

Bank, L., Marlowe, J.H., Reid, J.B., Patterson, G.R. and Weinrott, M.R. (1991) 'A comparative evaluation of parent-training interventions for families of chronic delinquents.' *Journal of Abnormal Child Psychology 19*, 15–34.

Bank, L., Patterson, G.R. and Reid, J.B. (1987) 'Delinquency prevention through training parents in family management.' *The Behavior Analyst 10*, 75–82.

Banks, M., Bates, I., Breakwell, G., Bynner, J., Emler, N., Jamieson, L. and Roberts, K. (1992) *Careers and Identities.* Buckingham: Open University Press.

Bard, B. and Mountcastle, V.B. (1948) 'Some forebrain mechanisms involved in expression of rage with special reference to suppression of angry behaviour.' *Research Publication: Association of Research in Nervous Mental Disease 27*, 362–404.

Barker, M. (1984) *A Haunt of Fears.* London: Pluto.

Baum, C.G. and Forehand, R. (1981) 'Long-term follow-up assessment of parent training by use of multiple outcome measures.' *Behavior Therapy 12*, 643–652.

Beck, S., Forehand, R., Neeper, R. and Baskin, C. (1982) 'A comparison of two analogue strategies for assessing children's social skills.' *Journal of Consulting and Clinical Psychology 50*, 596–597.

Becker, J.V., Barham, J., Eron, L.D. and Chen, S.A. (1994) 'The present status and future directions for psychological research on youth violence.' In L.D. Eron, J.H. Gentry and P. Schlegel (eds) *Reason to Hope: A Psychosocial Perspective on Violence and Youth.* Washington: American Psychological Association.

Becker, J.V., Cunningham-Rathner, J., Kaplan, M.S. and Kavoussir, R. (1986) 'Adolescent sexual offenders, demographics, criminal and sexual histories and recommendations for reducing future offences. Special Issue: The prediction and control of violent behaviour.' *Journal of Interpersonal Violence 1*, 431–445.

Becker, J.V. and Kaplan, M.S. (1988) 'The assessment of adolescent sexual offenders.' *Advances in Behavioral Assessment of Children and Families 4*, 97–118.

Becker, J.V., Kaplan, M.S., Tanke, E. and Tartlin, A. (1991) 'The incidence of depressive symptomotology in juvenile sex offenders of abuse.' *Child Abuse and Neglect 15*, 531–536.

Bellack, A., Hersen, M. and Lamparski, P. (1979) 'Roleplay tests for assessing social skills: Are they valid? Are they useful?' *Journal of Consulting and Clinical Psychology 47*, 335–342.

Bender, L. and Curran, F.J. (1940) 'Children and adolescents who kill.' *Criminal Psychopathology,* 297–322

Bentovim, A. (1991) 'Clinical work with families in which sexual abuse has occurred.' In C.R. Hollin and K. Howells (eds) *Clinical Approaches to Sex Offenders and Their Victims.* New York: John Wiley and Sons.

Bentovim, A. (1992) *Trauma Organised Systems. Physical and Sexual Abuse in Families.* London: Karnac Books.

Bentovim, A. and Kinston, W. (1991) 'Focal family therapy – joining systems theory with psychodynamic understanding.' In A. Gurnam and D. Kniskern (eds) *A Handbook of Family Therapy.* New York: Basic Books.

Beres, D. (1961) 'Perception, imagination and reality.' *International Journal of Psychoanalysis 41*, 327–334.

Berkowitz, L. (1970) 'The contagion of violence: an S-R mediational analyses of some effects of observed aggression.' In W.J. Arnold and M.M. Page (eds) *Nebraska Symposium on Motivation.* Lincoln, NB: University of Nebraska Press.

Berkowitz, L. (1989) 'The frustration – aggression hypothesis: an examination and reformulation.' *Psychological Bulletin 106*, 59–73.

Berkowitz, L. (1993) *Aggression: Its Causes, Consequences, and Control.* New York: McGraw-Hill.

Berkowitz, L. and Green, R. (1966) 'Film violence and cue properties of available targets.' *Journal of Personality and Social Psychology 3*, 525–30.

Bierman, K.L., Miller, C.L. and Stabb, S.D. (1987) 'Improving the social behavior and peer acceptance of rejected boys: effect of social skill training with instructions and prohibitions.' *Journal of Consulting and Clinical Psychology 55*, 194–200.

Blackburn, R. (1993) *The Psychology of Criminal Conduct.* Chichester: Wiley.

Blakely, C.H. and Davidson, W.S. (1984) 'Behavioural approaches to delinquency: A review.' In P. Karoly and J.J. Steffen (eds) *Adolescent Behaviour Disorders: Foundations and Contemporary Concerns*. Lexington, MA: Lexington Books.

Blaske, D.M., Borduin, C.M., Henggeler, S.W. and Mann, B.J. (1989) 'Individual, family and peer characteristics of adolescent sex offenders and assaultive offenders.' *Developmental Psychology 25*, 846–855.

Blom-Cooper, L. (1985) *A Child in Trust: The Report of the Panel of Enquiry into the Circumstances Surrounding the Death of Jasmine Beckford*. London: London Borough of Brent.

Borduin, C.M. *et al.* (1995) 'Multisystemic treatment of serious juvenile offenders: long-term prevention of criminality and violence.' *Journal of Consulting and Clinical Psychology 63*, 569-578.

Boswell, G.R. (1991) *Waiting for Change: An Exploration of the Experiences and Needs of Section 53 Offenders*. London: The Prince's Trust.

Boswell, G.R. (1995) *Violent Victims: The Prevalence of Abuse and Loss in the Lives of Section 53 Offenders*. London: The Prince's Trust.

Bowlby, J. (1951) *Child Care and the Growth of Love*. Harmondsworth: Penguin Books Ltd.

Bowlby, J. (1953) 'Some pathological processes set in train by early mother child separation.' *Journal Ment 99*, 265–272.

Bowlby, J. (1969) *Attachment and Loss*, vol 1. London: Hogarth Press.

Bowlby, J. (1973) *Attachment and Loss*, vol 2. London: Hogarth Press.

Bowlby, J. (1980) *Attachment and Loss*, vol 3. London: Hogarth Press.

Braswell, L. and Bloomquist, M. (1991) *Cognitive Behavioural Therapy and ADHD Children*. New York: The Guildford Press.

Bremer, J.F. (1993) 'The treatment of children and adolescents with aberrant sexual behaviours.' In C.J. Hobbs and J.M. Wynne (eds) *Bailliere's Clinical Paediatrics: International Practice and Research. Child Abuse 1*, 1, 269–282.

Brown, P. (1987) *Schooling Ordinary Kids*. London: Tavistock.

Bullen, J.G. and Hemsley, D.R. (1983) 'Sensory experience as a trigger in Giles de la Tourette's syndrome.' *Journal of Behavioural Therapy and Experimental Psychiatry 14*, 3, 197–201.

Bullock, R., Little, M. and Millham, S. (1991) 'Young offenders, grave crimes and Section 53.' *The Magistrate 47*, 7, 143–150.

Burgess, A.W., Hartman, C. and Hawe, J.C.W. (1990) 'Accessing memories of juvenile murderers.' *Journal of Psychosocial Nursing 28*, 1, 26–35.

Busch, K.G., Zagar, R., Hughes, J.R., Arbut, J. and Bussell, R.E. (1990) 'Adolescents who kill.' *Journal of Clinical Psychology 46*, 472–84.

Calkins, S.D. and Fox, N.A. (1994) 'Individual differences in the biological aspects of temperament.' In J.E. Bates and T.D. Wachs (eds) *Temperament: Individual Differences at the Interface of Biology and Behavior*. Washington: American Psychological Association.

Camp, B.W. (1977) 'Verbal mediation in young aggressive boys.' *Journal of Abnormal Psychology 86*, 145–153.

Camp, B.W. (1980) 'Psychoeducational training with aggressive boys.' In R.M. Knights and D.J. Bakker (eds) *Treatment of Hyperactive and Learning Disordered Children: Current Research*. Baltimore, USA: University Park Press.

Camp, B.W., Blom, G.E., Herbert, F. and Doorninck, W.J. (1977) '"Think Aloud": A program for developing self-control in young aggressive boys.' *Journal of Abnormal Child Psychology 5*, 157–169.

Carmen, E., Rieker, P.P. and Mills, T. (1984) 'Victims of violence and psychiatric illness.' *American Journal of Psychiatry 141*, 378–383.

Cassity, J. (1927) 'Psychological considerations of pedophilia.' *Psychoanalytic Review 14*, 189–199.

Champion, D.J. (1989) 'Teenage felons and waiver hearings.' *Crime and Delinquency 35*, 4, 577–85.

Chandler, M.A. (1973) 'Egocentrism and anti-social behaviour: the assessment and training of social perspective-taking skills.' *Developmental Psychology 9*, 326–332.

Chess, S. and Thomas, A. (1990) 'Continuities and discontinuities in temperament.' In L. Robins and M. Rutter (eds) *Straight and Devious Pathways from Childhood to Adulthood.* Cambridge: Cambridge University Press.

Cocozza, J., Hartstone E. and Braff, J. (1981) 'Mental health treatment of violent juveniles: an assessment of need.' *Crime and Delinquency 27*, 4, 487–96.

Cohen, A. (1965) *Delinquent Boys.* Chicago: University of Chicago Press.

Conners, C.K. (1969) 'A teacher rating scale for use in drug studies with children.' *American Journal of Psychiatry 126*, 884–888.

Cornell, D. (1990) 'Prior adjustment of violent juvenile offenders.' *Law and Human Behaviour 14*, 6, 569–77.

Cornell, D.G., Benedek, E.P. and Benedek, B.A. (1987) 'Juvenile homicide: prior adjustment and a proposed typology.' *American Journal of Orthopsychiatry 57*, 383–93.

Coie, J.D., Lochman, J.E., Terry, R. and Hyman, C. (1992) 'Predicting early adolescent disorder from childhood aggression and peer rejection.' *Journal of Consulting and Clinical Psychology 60*, 783–792.

Comstock, G. (1991) *Television and the American Child.* New York: Academic Press.

Commission on Obscenity and Pornography (1986) *Report of the Commission on Obscenity and Pornography.* New York: Bantam.

Coppock, C. and Dwivedi, K.N. (1993) 'Group work in schools.' In K.N. Dwivedi (ed) *Group Work with Children and Adolescents.* London: Jessica Kingsley.

Court-Brown, W.M. (1967) *Human Population Cytogenetics.* New York: John Wiley.

Craine, L.S., Henson, C.E., Colliver, J.A. and MacLean, D.G. (1988) 'Prevalence of a history of sexual abuse among female psychiatric patients in a state hospital system.' *Hospital and Community Psychiatry 39*, 300–4.

Crepault, C. and Couture, M. (1980) 'Men's erotic fantasies.' *Archives of Sexual Behaviour 9*, 565–81. (1996).

Crick, N.R. and Dodge, K.A. (1994) 'A review and reformulation of social information-processing mechanisms in children's social adjustment.' *Psychological Bulletin 115*, 74–101.

Crittenden, P.M. (1988) 'Family and dynamic patterns of functioning in maltreating families.' In K. Browne, C. Davies and P. Straften (eds) *Early Prediction and Prevention of Child Abuse.* Chichester: Wiley.

Crittenden, P.M. (1988a) 'Relationships at risk.' In J. Belsky and T. Nezworski (eds) *Clinical Implications of Attachment.* Hillsdale, N.J.: Lawrence Erlbaum Associates.

Crittenden, P.M. (1992) 'Quality of attachment in the preschool years.' *Development and Psychopathology 4*, 209–241.

Cumberbatch, G. and Howitt, D. (1989) *A Measure of Uncertainty.* London: John Libby.

Dalton, K. (1964) *The Premenstrual Syndrome.* Springfield, IL: Charles C Thomas.

Dangel, R.F., Deschner, J.P. and Rasp, R.R. (1989) 'Anger control training for adolescents in residential treatment.' *Behavior Modification 13*, 447–458.

Davar, E. (1995) 'Containment surviving and living (the inner representation of the matter)' 1995 Paper given at the 'Free Associations' Conference London.

Davis, D. and Boster, L. (1992) 'Cognitive-behavioural-expressive interventions with aggressive and resistant youths.' *Child Welfare 71*, 6, 557–73.

Davis, G. and Leitenberg, H. (1987) 'Adolescent sex offenders.' *Psychological Bulletin 101*, 417–427.

Davies, M. (1990) *City of Quartz.* London: Verso.

Dawes, A. and Donald, D. (1994) *Childhood and Adversity: Psychological Perspectives from South African Research.* Cape Town and Johannesburg: David Philip.

Dawes, Tredoux, and Feinstein (1989) 'Political Violence in South Africa: The effects on children of the violent destruction of their community.' *International Journal of Mental Health 18 (2)*, 16–43.

Denicola, J. and Sandler, J. (1980) 'Training abusive parents in child management and self-control skills.' *Behavior Therapy 11*, 263–270.

Department of Health (1995) *Children and Young People on Child Protection Registers Year Ending 31st March 1994.* A/F 94/13 Government Statistical Service.

Diamond, I. (1980) 'Pornography and repression: a reconsideration.' *Signs: Journal of Women in Culture and Society 49*, 5–21.

Dicks, D., Myers, R.K. and Klings, A. (1969) 'Uncus and amygdala lesions: effects on social behaviour in the free-ranging rhesus monkey.' *Science 165*, 69–71.

Dienstbier, R.A., Hillman, D., Lehnhoff, J., Hillman, J. and Valkenaar, M.C. (1975) 'An emotion – attribution approach to moral behaviour: Interfacing cognitive and avoidance theories of moral development.' *Psychological Review 82*, 299–315.

Dockar-Drysdale, B. (1990) *The Provision of Primary Experience: Winnicottian Work with Children and Adolescents.* London: Free Association Books.

Dodge, K.A., Bates, J.E. and Pettit, G.S. (1990) 'Mechanisms in the cycle of violence.' *Science 250*, 1678–1683.

Dodge, K.A., Price, J.M., Bachorowski, J. and Newman, J.P. (1990) 'Hostile attributional biases in severely aggressive adolescents.' *Journal of Abnormal Psychology 99*, 385–392.

Dodge, K.A. and Somberg, D.R. (1987) 'Hostile attributional biases among aggressive boys are exacerbated under conditions of threats to the self.' *Child Development 58*, 213–224.

Dolan, M., Holloway, J. and Bailey, S. (1996 in press) 'Psychosocial characteristics of a series of 121 child and adolescent sex offenders.' *Medicine, Science and the Law.*

Donnerstein, E. (1980) 'Aggressive erotica and violence against women.' *Journal of Personality and Social Psychology 39*, 269–277.

Donnerstein, E. and Berkowitz, M. (1981) 'Victim reactions in aggressive erotic films as a factor in violence against women.' *Journal of Personality and Social Psychology 41*, 710–724.

Doob, A., and MacDonald, G., (1979) 'Television viewing and the fear of victimization: is the relationship causal?' *Journal of Personality and Social Psychology 37*, 170–9.

Dore, R. (1976) *The Diploma Disease.* London: Allen and Unwin.

Douglas, M. (1992) *Risk and Blame.* London: Routledge.

Dumont, L. (1961) 'Caste, racism and 'stratification': reflections of a social anthropologist.' In Andre Beteille (ed) (1969) *Social Inequality.* Harmondsworth: Penguin Books Ltd.

Durlak, J.A., Fuhrman, T. and Lampman, C. (1991) 'Effectiveness of cognitive-behavior therapy for maladapting children: A meta-analysis.' *Psychological Bulletin 110*, 204–214.

Dwivedi, K.N. (1984) 'Mother baby psychotherapy.' *Health Visitor 57*, 306–307.

Dwivedi, K.N. (1993a) 'Group work in child mental health services.' In K.N. Dwivedi (ed) *Group Work with Children and Adolescents.* London: Jessica Kingsley.

Dwivedi, K.N. (1993b) 'Introduction.' In K.N. Dwivedi (ed) *Group Work with Children and Adolescents.* London: Jessica Kingsley.

Dwivedi, K.N. (1993c) 'Conceptual Frameworks.' In K.N. Dwivedi (ed) *Group Work with Children and Adolescents.* London: Jessica Kingsley.

Dwivedi, K.N. (1993d) 'Emotional Development.' In K.N. Dwivedi (ed) *Group Work with Children and Adolescents.* London: Jessica Kingsley.

Dwivedi, K.N. (1993e) 'Use of interpretation.' In K.N. Dwivedi (ed) *Group Work with Children and Adolescents.* London: Jessica Kingsley.

Dwivedi, K.N., Beaumont, G. and Brandon, S. (1984) 'Electrophysiological responses in high and low young aggressive adolescent boys.' *Acta Paedopsychiatrica 50*, 179–190.

Dwivedi, K.N. and Bell, S. (1993) 'Encopresis.' In K.N. Dwivedi (ed) *Group Work with Children and Adolescents.* London: Jessica Kingsley.

Dwivedi, K.N., Brayne, E. and Lovett, S. (1992) 'Group work with sexually abused adolescent girls.' *Group Analysis 25*, 477–489.

D'Zurilla, T. and Goldfreid, M. (1971) 'Problem solving and behaviour modification.' *Journal of Abnormal Psychology 78*, 107–126.

Easson, M.B. and Steinhilber (1961) 'Murderous aggression by children and adolescents.' *Arch. Gen. Psychiatry 4*, 27–35.

Egger, M.D. and Flynn, J.P. (1963) 'Effect of electrical stimulation of the amygdala on hypothalamically elicited attack behaviour in cats.' *Journal of Neurophysiology 26*, 705–720.

Eggers, C. (1978) 'Course and prognosis of childhood schizophrenia.' *Journal of Autism and Childhood Schizophrenia 8*, 21–36.

Elbedour, S., Bensel, R. and Bastien D. (1993) 'Ecological integrated model of children of war, individual and social psychology.' *Child Abuse and Neglect 17*, 805–819.

Elder, J.P., Edelstein, B.A. and Narick, M.M. (1979) 'Adolescent psychiatric patients: Modifying aggressive behavior with social skills training.' *Behavior Modification 3*, 161–178.

Elkin, F. and Westley, W.A. (1955) 'The myth of the adolescent culture.' *American Sociological Review 20*, 680–684.

Elkin, F. and Westley, W.A. (1967) 'Protective environment and adolescent socialisation.' In E.W. Vaz (ed) *Middle Class Delinquency*. New York: Harper and Row.

El Sarray, E. (1996) Quoted in 'Therapy for society', Esther Hectit. *Jerusalem Post*, 26 July 1996.

Epps, K.J. (1990) 'Managing violence in institutions for disturbed adolescents.' Paper presented at the 20th European Congress on Behaviour Therapy, Paris.

Eron, L.D. (1986) 'The development of aggressive behavior from the perspective of a developing behaviorism.' *American Psychologist 42*, 435–442.

Eron, L.D., Huesmann, L.R. and Zelli, A. (1991) 'The role of parental variables in the learning of aggression.' In D.J. Pepler and K.H. Rubin (eds) *The Development and Treatment of Childhood Aggression*. Hillsdale, NJ: Lawrence Erlbaum.

Eygendaal, W. (1992) 'The black heart – a qualitative study of the death metal culture in The Netherlands.' Paper presented to conference on *Internationalisation and Leisure Research*, Tilburg.

Evans, B. and Cook, P. (1993) 'Group work in residential child care.' In K.N. Dwivedi (ed) *Group Work with Children and Adolescents*. London: Jessica Kingsley.

Evans, J. (1965) 'Inpatient analytic group therapy of neurotic and delinquent adolescents.' *Psychotherapy and Psychosomatics 13*, 265–270.

Fagan, J. and Wexler, S. (1988) 'Explanations of sexual assault among violent delinquents.' *Journal of Adolescent Research 3*, 365–385.

Fahlberg, V. (1994) *A Child's Journey through Placement*. London: British Agencies for Adoption and Fostering (BAAF).

Fanon, F. (1966) *Black Skin White Masks*. Harmondsworth: Penguin.

Farrington, D.P (1989) 'Early predictors of adolescent aggression and adult violence.' *Violence and Victims 4*, 79–100.

Farrington, D.P. (1994) 'Human development and criminal careers.' In M. Maguire, R. Morgan and R. Reiner (eds) *The Oxford Handbook of Criminology*. Oxford: Clarendon Press.

Farrington, D.P. (1995a) 'The development of offending and antisocial behaviour from childhood: Key findings from the Cambridge Study in Delinquent Development.' *Journal of Child Psychology and Psychiatry 36*, 929–964.

Farrington, D.P. (1995b) 'The challenge of teenage antisocial behaviour.' In M. Rutter (ed) *Psychosocial Disturbances in Young People: Challenges for Prevention*. Cambridge: Cambridge University Press.

Farrington, D.P. and West, D. (1993) 'Criminal, penal and life histories of chronic offenders: risk and protective factors and early identification.' *Criminal Behaviour and Mental Health 3*, 492–523.

Farrington, D.P., Loeber, R. and van Kammen, W.B. (1990) 'Long-term criminal outcomes of hyperactivity-impulsivity-attention deficit and conduct problems.' In L. Robins and M. Rutter (eds) *Straight and Devious Pathways from Childhood to Adulthood.* Cambridge: Cambridge University Press.

Fehrenbach, P.A., Smith, W., Monarsterky, C. and Deisher, R.W. (1986) 'Adolescent sex offenders. Offenders and offense characteristics.' *American Journal of Orthopsychiatry 56,* 2, 225–233.

Fehrenbach, P.A. and Theler, M.H. (1982) 'Behavioural approaches to the treatment of aggressive disorders.' *Behaviour modification 11,* 4, 465–497.

Feindler, E.L. and Ecton, R.B. (1986) *Adolescent Anger Control: Cognitive-behavioural Techniques.* Oxford: Pergamon.

Feindler, E.L. and Becker, J.V. (1994) 'Interventions in family violence involving children and adolescents.' In L.D. Eron, J.H. Gentry and P. Schlegel (eds) *Reason to Hope: A Psychosocial Perspective on Violence and Youth.* Washington: American Psychological Association.

Feindler, E.L., Ecton, R.B., Kingsley, D. and Dubey, D.R. (1986) 'Group Anger Control training for institutionalized psychiatric male adolescents.' *Behaviour Therapy 17,* 109–123.Feindler, E.L. and Ecton, R.B. (1986) *Adolescent Anger Control: Cognitive-behavioral Techniques.* New York: Pergamon Press.

Feindler, E.L. and Fremouw, W.J. (1983) 'Stress inoculation training for adolescent anger problems.' In D. Meichenbaum and M.E. Jaremko (eds) *Stress Reduction and Prevention.* New York: Plenum Press.

Feindler, E.L., Marriott, S.A. and Iwata, M. (1984) 'Group anger control training for junior high school delinquents.' *Cognitive Therapy and Research 8,* 299–311.

Felson, R.B. (1978) 'Aggression as impression management.' *Social Psychology 41,* 205–213.

Fields, R.N. (1973) *Society on the Run: A Psychology for Northern Ireland.* Harmondsworth: Penguin.

Finch, A.J. and Eastman, E.S. (1983) 'A multi-method approach to measuring anger in children.' *Journal of Psychology 115,* 55–60.

Finch, A.J., Saylor, C.F. and Nelson, W.M. (1983) 'The children's inventory of anger: a self report inventory.' Paper presented at the American Psychological Association, Anaheim, CA (quoted in Feindler and Ecton 1986).

Finklehor, D. (1984) *Child Sexual Abuse: New Theory and Research.* New York: Free Press.

Finklehor, D. (1987) 'The trauma of child sexual abuse.' *Journal of Interpersonal Violence 2,* 348–366.

Finklehor, D. and Browne, A. (1986) 'Sexual abuse: Initial and long-term effects: A conceptual framework.' In D. Finkelhor (ed) *A Sourcebook on Child Sexual Abuse.* Beverly Hills, CA: Sage.

Fleischman, M.J. and Szykula, S.A. (1981) 'A community setting replication of social learning treatment for aggressive children.' *Behavior Therapy 12,* 100–106.

Fonegy (1992) 'Theory and practice of resilience.' York Conference: Rapid Social Change – Vulnerability and Resilience. Emanuel Miller Lecture

Ford, M.E. and Linney, J.A. (1995) 'Comparative analysis of juvenile sex offenders, violent nonsexual offenders, and status offenders.' *Journal of Interpersonal Violence 10,* 56–70.

Foucault, M. (1978) *The History of Sexuality. Volume 1: An Introduction.* London: Penguin Books.

Fraiberg, S., Adelson, E. and Shapiro, V. (1980) 'Ghosts in the nursery.' In S. Fraiberg (ed) *Clinical Studies in Infant Mental Health.* London: Tavistock Publications.

Freud, A. and Burlingham, D.T. (1943) *War and Children.* New York: Ernest Willard.

Freud, A. (1966) *Normality and Pathology inChildhood.* London: Hogarth Press.

Freud, E. (1930) *Civilization and Discontents.* Translated by J. Riviere (1958) Garden City, NY: Doubleday.

Freud, S. (1925) *An autobiographical Study.* In Standard Edition, 20, (translator J. Strachey). London: Hogarth Press (1959).

Fraser, M. (1974) *Children in Conflict.* Harmondsworth: Penguin.

Friedman, C., Mann F. and Adelman, H. (1976) 'Juvenile street gangs: the victimization of youth.' *Adolescence 11,* 44, 527–33.

Funkenstein, D.H. (1955) 'The physiology of fear and anger.' *Science America 192,* 74–80.

Gallagher, B.J. (1987) *The Sociology of Mental Illness* (second edition). New Jersey: Prentice-Hall.

Garbarino, J. (1992) 'Developmental consequences of living in dangerous and unstable environments – the situation of refugee children.' Paper presented to the Refugee Studies Programme Seminar, The Mental Health of Refugee Children Exposed to Violent Environments, Oxford, January 1992.

Garbarino, J., Kostelny, K. and Dubrow, N. (1992) 'The psychological well being of refugee children: research, practice and policy issues.' M. McCatlin (ed) *International Catholic Child Bureau*.

Garrett, C.J. (1985) 'Effects of residential treatment on adjudicated delinquents: A meta-analysis.' *Journal of Research in Crime and Delinquency 22*, 287–308.

Garrison, S.R. and Stolberg, A.L. (1983) 'Modification of anger in children with affective imagery training.' *Journal of Abnormal Child Psychology 11*, 1, 115–130.

Gentry, M.R. and Ostapiuk, E.O. (1989) 'Violence in institutions for young offenders and disturbed adolescents.' In K. Howells, and C.R. Hollin (eds) *Clinical Approaches to Violence*. Chichester: Wiley.

Gerbner, G. and Gross, L. (1979) 'The scary world of TV's heavy viewer.' *Psychology Today*, April, 89–91.

Gerbner, G., Gross, L., Morgan, M. and Signorielli, M. (1984) 'Political correlates of television viewing.' *Public Opinion Quarterly 48*, 283–300.

Gibson, K. (1991) 'The indirect effect of political violence on children: does violence beget violence?' Unpublished paper, Project for the Study of Violence, Psychology Department University of Witwatersrand, Johannesburg.

Giddens, A. (1984) *The Constitution of Society*. Cambridge: Polity Press.

Giddens, A. (1990) *The Consequences of Modernity*. Cambridge: Polity Press.

Gilligan, C. (1982) *In a Difference Voice: Psychological Theory and Women's Development*. Cambridge, M.A.: Harvard University Press.

Ginott, H.G. (1961) *Group Psychotherapy with Children*. New York: McGraw-Hill.

Glasser, M. (1982) 'Working with violent patients at the Portman Clinic.' In *Harvest: Journal for Jungian Studies 28*, 1982.

Glasser, M. (1994) 'Violence: a psychoanalytical research project.' *Journal of Forensic Psychiatry 5*, 2, 311–320.

Glover, E. (1960) *The Roots of Crime*. New York: International Universities Press.

Glover, E. (1962/3) 'Psycho-analysis and "controlled" research on delinquency.' *British Journal of Criminology 3*, 63–71.

Glueck, S.E. (1952) *Delinquents in the Making*. London: Harper Row.

Goddard, C.R. and Stanley, J.R. (1994) 'Viewing the abusive parent and the abused child as captor and hostage: The application of hostage theory to the effects of child abuse.' *Journal of Interpersonal Violence 9*, 2, 258–269.

Godsland, J. and Fielding, N. (1985) 'Children convicted of grave crimes.' *Howard Journal of Criminal Justice 24*, 4, 282–97.

Gold, M. (1987) 'Social ecology.' In H.C. Quay (ed) *Handbook of Juvenile Delinquency*. New York: Wiley.

Goldstein, A.P. (1986) 'Psychological skill training and the aggressive adolescent.' In S.J. Apter and A.P. Goldstein (eds) *Youth Violence: Program and Prospects*. New York: Pergamon Press.

Goldstein, A.P. and Glick, B. (1987) *Aggression Replacement Training: A Comprehensive Intervention for Aggressive Youth*. Illinois: Research Press.

Goldstein, A.P., Glick, B., Carthan, W. and Blancero, D.A. (1994) *The Pro-Social Gang: Implementing Aggression Replacement Training*. Thousand Oaks: Sage Publications.

Goldstein, A.P., Glick, B., Irwin, M.J., Pask-McCartney, C. and Rubama, I. (1989) *Reducing Delinquency: Intervention in the Community*. Oxford: Pergamon Press.

Goldstein, A.P. and Keller, H. (1987) *Aggressive Behavior: Assessment and Intervention*. Oxford: Pergamon Press.

Goldstein, A.P. and Soriano, F.I. (1994) 'Juvenile gangs.' In L. D. Eron, J.H. Gentry and P. Schlegel (eds) *Reason to Hope: A Psychosocial Perspective on Violence and Youth*. Washington: American Psychological Association.

Goldstein, J., Freud, A., Solnit, A. and Goldstine, S. (1986) *In the Best Interests of the Child*. New York: The Free Press.

Gordon, D.A. and Arbuthnot, J. (1987) 'Individual, group, and family interventions.' In H.C. Quay (ed) *Handbook of Juvenile Delinquency*. New York: Wiley.

Gordon, D.A., Graves, K, and Arbuthnot, J. (1995) 'The effect of functional family therapy for delinquents on adult criminal behavior.' *Criminal Justice and Behavior 22*, 60–73.

Gottfredson, M.R. and Hirschi, T. (1990) *A General Theory of Crime*. Stanford: Stanford University Press.

Gottfredson, M.R. and Hirschi, T. (1993) 'A control theory interpretation of psychological research on aggression.' In R.B. Felson and J.T. Tedeschi (eds) *Aggression and Violence: Social Interactionist Perspectives*. Washington: American Psychological Association.

Greco, C.M. and Cornell, D.G. (1992) 'Rorschach object relations of adolescents who committed homicide.' *J. Personality Assessment 59*, 3, 574–83.

Guerra, N.G. and Slaby, R.G. (1990) 'Cognitive mediators of aggression in adolescent offenders: 2. Intervention.' *Developmental Psychology 26*, 269–277.

Guerra, N.G., Tolan, P.H. and Hammond, W.R. (1994) 'Prevention and treatment of adolescent violence.' In L.D. Eron, J.H. Gentry and P. Schlegel (eds) *Reason to Hope: A Psychosocial Perspective on Violence and Youth*. Washington: American Psychological Association.

Gulbenkian Foundation (1995) *Children and Violence*. London: Calouste Gulbenkian Foundation.

Gunter, B. (1987) *Television and the Fear of Crime*. London: John Libby.

Hall, S. and Jefferson, T. (eds) (1976) *Resistance Through Rituals*. London: Hutchinson.

Hagell, A. and Newburn, T. (1994) *Persistent Young Offenders*. London: Policy Studies Institute.

Hagell, A. and Newburn, T. (1994a) *Young Offenders and the Media*. London: Policy Studies Institute.

Hall, S. (1976) 'Violence in the media.' In N. Tutt (ed) *Violence*. London: HMSO.

Hains, A.A. (1989) 'An anger-control intervention with aggressive delinquent youths.' *Behavioral Residential Treatment 4*, 213–230.

Hambridge, J.A. (1990) 'The grief process in those admitted to regional secure units following homicide.' *Journal of Forensic Sciences 35*, 5, 1149–1154.

Hamburg, D.A. (1966) 'Effects of progesterone on behaviour.' In R. Levine (ed) *Endocrines and the Central Nervous System*. Baltimore, MD: Williams and Wilkins.

Hanmer, J., and Saunders, S. (1984) *Well-Founded Fear*. London: Hutchinson.

Harrington, J. (1976) 'Violence in groups.' In N. Tutt (ed) *Violence 1976*. London: HMSO.

Harris, D.P., Cole, J.E. and Vipond, E.M. (1987) 'Residential treatment of disturbed delinquents. Description of Centre and Identification of therapeutic factors.' *Canadian Journal of Psychiatry 32* 579–583.

Harrower, J. (1993) 'Group work with young offenders.' In K.N. Dwivedi (ed) *Group Work with Children and Adolescents*. London: Jessica Kingsley.

Hawkins, J.D., Catalano, R.F., Morrison, D.M., O'Donnell, J., Abbott, R.D. and Day, L.E. (1992) 'The Seattle Social Development Project: effects of the first four years on protective factors and problem behaviors.' In J. McCord and R. Tremblay (eds) *Preventing Antisocial Behavior: Interventions from Birth Through Adolescence*. New York: Guilford Press.

Hayes, J.R., Solway, K.S. and Schreiner, D. (1978) 'Intellectual characteristics of juvenile murderers versus status offenders.' *Psychol Rep 43*, 80–2.

Heath, L. (1986) 'Effects of media violence on children.' *Arch General Psychiatry 46*.

Hebdige, D. (1979) *Sub-Culture: the Meaning of Style*. London: Methuen.

Hellsten, P. and Katila, O. (1965) 'Murder and other homicide by children under fifteen in Finland.' *Psychiatr Q Suppl. 39*, 54–74.

Hendry, L.B., Shucksmith, J., Love, J.G. and Glendinning, A. (1993) *Young People's Leisure and Lifestyles.* London: Routledge.

Henggeler, S.W. (1989) *Delinquency in Adolescence.* London: Sage.

Hendrickson, W.J. and Holmes, D.J. (1960) 'Institutional psychotherapy of the delinquent.' In J. Masterson and J.L. Moreno (eds) *Progress in Psychotherapy 5.* New York: Grune and Stratton.

Herbert, M. (1987) *Conduct Disorders of Childhood and Adolescence: A Social Learning Perspective* (2nd ed). Chichester: Wiley.

Herman, J.L. (1992) *Trauma and Recovery.* New York: Basic Books.

Herrenkohl, R.C. and Herrenkohl, E.C. (1981) 'Some antecedents and developmental consequences of child maltreatment.' *New Directions for Child Development 11,* 57–76.

Herrenkohl, E.C., Herrenkohl, R.C. and Toedter, L. (1983) 'Perspectives on the intergenerational transmission of abuse.' In D. Finkelhor, R. Gelles, G. Hotaling and M. Straus (eds) *The Dark Side of Families: Current Family Violence Research.* London: Sage Publications.

Herzberge, S.D. (1983) 'Social cognition and the transmission of abuse.' In D. Finkelhor, R. Gelles, G. Hotaling and M. Straus (eds) *The Dark Side of Families: Current Family Violence Research.* London: Sage Publications.

Hetherington, K. (1994) 'The contemporary significance of Schmalenbach's concept of the Bund.' *Sociological Review 42,* 1–25.

Hirsch, P. (1976) 'The role of television and popular culture in contemporary society.' In H. Newcomb (ed) *Television; the Critical View.* Oxford: Oxford University Press.

Hirschi, T. and Hindelang, M.J. (1977) 'Intelligence and delinquency: A revisionist review.' *American Sociological Review 42,* 571–587.

Hodge, R. and Tripp, D. (1986) *Children and Television.* Cambridge: Polity Press.

Hodges, J. (1991) 'The use of story stems to assess attachments in children.' Presentation, London Institute of Child Health.

Hodges, J. (1992) 'Early experience and what we make of it.' Unpublished. Jack Tizard Lecture.

Hodges, J., Lanyado, M. and Andreou, C. (1994) 'Sexuality and violence: preliminary clinical hypotheses from psychotherapeutic assessment in a research programme on young sexual offenders.' *Journal of Child Psychiatry 20,* 3, 283–308.

Holland, T.R., Beckett, G.E. and Levi, M. (1981) 'Intelligence, personality, and criminal violence: A multivariate analysis.' *Journal of Consulting and Clinical Psychology 49,* 106–111.

Hollin, C.R. (1990) *Cognitive-behavioural Interventions with Young Offenders.* Oxford: Pergamon.

Hollin, C.R. (1993) 'Advances in the psychological treatment of delinquent behaviour.' *Criminal Behaviour and Mental Health 3,* 142–157.

Home Affairs Committee (1993) *Juvenile Offenders: Memoranda of Evidence.* London: Her Majesty's Stationery Office.

Home Office (1992). *Criminal Statistics for England and Wales.* London: HMSO.

Home Office, Department of Health, Department of Education and Science, Welsh Office (1991) *Working Together under the Children Act 1989. A Guide to Arrangements for Inter-agency Co-operation for the Protection of Children from Abuse.* London: HMSO.

House of Commons (1994) *Fourth Report of the Home Affairs Committee: Video Violence and Young Offenders.* London: HMSO.

Hoshmand, L.T. and Austin, G.W. (1985) 'Validation studies of a multi-factor cognitive behavioural anger control inventory.' Unpublished manuscript (quoted in Feindler and Ecton 1986).

Howard, A. (1993) 'Victims and perpetrators of abuse.' In K.N. Dwivedi (ed) *Group Work with Children and Adolescents.* London: Jessica Kingsley.

Hughes, J.N. (1988) *Cognitive Behavior Therapy with Children in Schools.* New York: Pergamon Press.

ICD-10 Classification of Mental and Behavioural Disorders (1992) *Clinical Descriptions and Diagnostic Guidelines.* Geneva: World Health Organisation.

Inamder, S.C. et al. (1982) 'Violent and suicidal behaviour in psychotic adolescents.' *American Journal of Psychiatry 134*, 932–935.

Itzin, C. (1993) (ed) *Pornography: Women, Violence and Civil Liberties.* Oxford: Oxford University Press.

Izzo, R.L. and Ross, R.R. (1990) 'Meta-analysis of rehabilitation programmes for juvenile delinquents.' *Criminal Justice and Behavior 17*, 134–142.

Jackson, D. (1995) *Destroying the Baby in Themselves: Why Did the Two Boys Kill James Bulger?* Nottingham: Mushroom Publications.

James, O. (1995) *Juvenile Violence in a Winner-Loser Culture: Socio-Economic and Familial Origins of the Rise in Violence Against the Person.* London: Free Association Books.

Johnson, R. (1979) *Juvenile Delinquency and Its Origins.* Cambridge: Cambridge University Press.

Johnson, R (1993) 'Intensive work with disordered personalities 1991–1993.' Unpublished report to the Reed Committee, January.

Johnson, R.N. (1972) 'Violence and society.' In (ed) *Aggression in Man and Animals.* Philadelphia, PA: W. B. Saunders Company.

Kappeler, S. (1986) *The Pornography of Representation.* Cambridge: Polity Press.

Kazdin, A.E. (1987) 'Treatment of antisocial behavior in children: current status and future directions.' *Psychological Bulletin 102*, 187–203.

Kazdin, A.E. (1994a) 'Psychotherapy for children and adolescents.' In A.E. Bergin and S.L. Garfield (eds) *Handbook of Psychotherapy and Behavior Change.* New York: Wiley.

Kazdin, A.E. (1994b) 'Antisocial behavior and conduct disorder.' In L.W. Craighead, W.E. Craighead, A.E. Kazdin, and M.J. Mahoney (eds) *Cognitive and Behavioral Interventions: An Empirical Approach to Mental Health Problems.* Boston: Allyn and Bacon.

Kazdin, A.E. (1994c) 'Interventions for aggressive and antisocial children.' In L.D. Eron, J.H. Gentry and P. Schlegel (eds) *Reason to Hope: A Psychosocial Perspective on Violence and Youth.* Washington: American Psychological Association.

Kazdin, A.E., Siegel, T.C. and Bass, D. (1992) 'Cognitive problem-solving skills training and parent management training in the treatment of antisocial behaviour in children.' *Journal of Consulting and Clinical Psychology 60*, 733–747.

Keilson (1979) *Sequential Traumatization in Children.* Jerusalem: Magnes Press.

Keith, C.R. (1984) 'Individual psychotherapy and psycho-analysis with aggressive adolescent: A historical review.' In C.R. Keith (ed) *The Aggressive Adolescent: Clinical Perspectives.* New York: Free Press.

Kelsall, M., Dolan, M. and Bailey, S. (1995) 'Violent incidents in an Adolescent Forensic Unit.' *Medicine, Science and the Law 8*, 21–36.

Kendall, P.C. (1993) 'Cognitive-behavioral therapies with youth: guiding theory, current status, and emerging developments.' *Journal of Consulting and Clinical Psychology 61*, 235–247.

Kendall, P.C. and Braswell, L. (1985) *Cognitive-Behavioral Therapy for Impulsive Children.* New York: Guilford Press.

Klapper, J. (1962) *Effects of Mass Communications.* New York: The Free Press.

Kleeman, J.A. (1967) 'The Peek-a-boo Game. Part I: Its origins, meanings and related phenomena in the first year.' *Psycho-analytic Study of Child 22*, 239–273.

Kleeman, J.A. (1973) 'The Peek-a-boo Game: Its evolution and associated behaviours especially bye-bye and shame expression during the second year.' *Journal of American Academy of Child Psychiatrists 12*, 1–23.

Klein, N.C., Alexander, J.F. and Parsons, B.V. (1977) 'Impact of family systems intervention on recidivism and sibling delinquency: a model of primary prevention and program evaluation.' *Journal of Consulting and Clinical Psychology 45*, 469–474.

Kluver, H. and Bucy, P.C. (1937) 'Psychic blindness and other symptoms following bilateral temporal lobectomy in Rhesus monkeys.' *American Journal of Physiology 119*, 352–353.

Kolvin, I., Miller, F.J.W., Fleeting, M., and Kolvin, P.A. (1988) 'Social and parenting factors effecting criminal-offence rates: findings from the Newcastle Thousand Family Study (1947–1980).' *British Journal of Psychiatry 152*, 80–90.

Krystal, H. (1988) *Integration and Self Healing.* Hillsdale, NJ: The Analytic Press.

Kurtz, Z., Thorne, R. and Wolkind, S. (1994) *Services for the Mental Health of Children and Young People in England. A National Review.* London: Department of Health.

Kydd, R.R. and Werry, J.S. (1982) 'Schizophrenia in children under 16 years.' *Journal of Autism and Developmental Disorders 12*, 343–358.

Labelle, A., Bradford, J.M., Bourget, D., Jones, B. and Carmichael, M. (1991) 'Adolescent murderers.' *Canadian Journal of Psychiatry 36*, 583–587.

Laermans, R. (1994) 'Leisure as making time: some sociological reflections on the paradoxical outcomes of individualisation.' In Actas do Congreso Mundial do Lazer, *New Routes for Leisure.* Instituto de Ciencias Socias, University of Lisbon, 61–73.

Laslett, R. (1982) 'A children's court for bullies.' *Special Education Forward Trends 9*, 1, 9–11.

Lavegin (1983) *Sexual Strands.* Hillsdale, NJ: Erlbaum.

Laws, D.R. and Marshall, W.L. (1990) 'A conditioning theory of the aetiology and maintenance of deviant sexual preference and behaviour.' In W.L. Marshall, D.L. Laws, and H.E. Barbaree (eds) *Handbook of Sexual Assault: Issues, Theories, and Treatment of the Offender.* New York: Plenum.

Lederer, L. (ed) (1980) *Take Back the Night: Women on Pornography.* New York: Morrow.

Le Doux, J.E. (1994) 'Emotion, memory and the brain.' *Scientific American.* June, 50–57.

Lee, J. (1979) 'Some treatment techniques with disruptive aggressive children.' *Association of Educational Psychology Journal 5*, 1, 29–32.

Lewis, D.O. (1983) 'Neuropsychiatric vulnerabilities and violent juvenile delinquency.' *Psychiatric Clinics of North America 6*, 4, 707–714.

Lewis, D.O., Mallouh, C. and Webb, V. (1989) 'Child abuse, delinquency, and violent criminality.' In D. Cicchetti and V. Carlson (eds) *Child Maltreatment: Theory and Research on the Causes and Consequences of Child Abuse and Neglect.* Cambridge: Cambridge University Press.

Lewis, D.O., Lovely, R., and Yeager, C. (1988) 'Intrinsic and environmental characteristics of juvenile murders.' *Journal of American Academic and Child and Adolescence Psychiatry 27*, 582–587.

Lewis, D.O., Moy, E., Jackson, L.D., Aaronson, R., Restifo, N., Sena, S. and Simos, A. (1985) 'Biopsychological characteristics of children who later murder. A prospective study.' *American Journal of Psychiatry 142*, 1161–1167.

Lewis, D.O., Pincus, J.H. and Bard, B. (1988) 'Neuropsychiatric psycho educational and family characteristics of 14 juveniles condemned to death in the United States.' *American Journal of Psychiatry 145*, 584–589.

Lewis, D.O., Shanok, S.S., Grant, M. and Ritvo, E. (1983) 'Homicidally aggressive young children: neuropsychiatric and experiential correlates.' *American Journal of Psychiatry 140*, 148–153.

Lewis, D.O., Shanok, S.S., Pincus, J.H. and Glaser, G.H. (1979) 'Violent juvenile delinquents: psychiatric, neurological, psychological, and abuse factors.' *Journal of the American Academy of Child Psychiatry 18*, 307–319.

Lewis, M., Lewis, M. and Schofield, D (1991) 'Dying and death in childhood and adolescence.' In M. Lewis (ed) *Child and Adolescent Psychiatry.* Baltimore, M.D.: Williams and Wilkins.

Levy, I.V. and King, I.A. (1953) 'The effects of testosterone propionate on fighting behaviour in young C57BL/ 10 mice.' *Anat. Rec., 117*, 562.

Liebert, J.A. (1985) 'Contributions of psychiatric consultation in the investigation of serial murder.' *Interpersonal Journal of Offender Therapy and Comparative Criminology 29*, 187–200.

Lindquist, P. and Allbeck, P. (1990) 'Schizophrenia and crime. A longitudinal follow up of 644 schizophrenics in Stockholm.' *British Journal of Psychiatry 151*, 345–350.

Little, M. (1990) *Young Men in Prison.* Aldershot: Dartmouth.

Lipsey, M.W. (1992) 'Juvenile Delinquency treatment: a meta-analytic inquiry into the variability of effects.' In T. Cook, D. Cooper, H. Corday, H. Hartman, L. Hedges, R. Light, T. Louis and

F. Mosteller (eds) *Meta-analysis for Explanation: A Casebook*. New York: Russell Sage Foundation.

Lipsey, M.W. (1995) 'What do we learn from 400 studies on the effectiveness of treatment with juvenile delinquents?' In J. McGuire (ed) *What Works: Reducing Reoffending: Guidelines from Research and Practice*. Chichester: John Wiley.

Lipsey, M.W. and Wilson, (1993) 'The efficacy of psychological, educational, and behavioral treatment: confirmation from meta-analysis.' *American Psychologist 48*, 1181–1209.

Lochman, J.E. (1985) 'Effects of different treatment lengths in cognitive behavioral interventions with aggressive boys.' *Child Psychiatry and Human Development 16*, 45–56.

Lochman, J.E., Burch, P.R., Curry, J.F. and Lampron, L.B. (1984) 'Treatment and generalization effects of cognitive-behavioral and goal-setting interventions with aggressive boys.' *Journal of Consulting and Clinical Psychology 52*, 915–916.

Lochman, J.E. and Lampron, L.B. (1988) 'Cognitive-behavioral interventions for aggressive boys: 7-month follow-up effects.' *Journal of Child and Adolescent Psychotherapy 5*, 15–23.

Lochman, J.E. and Lenhart, L.A. (1993) 'Anger coping intervention for aggressive children: conceptual models and outcome effects.' *Clinical Psychology Review 13*, 785–805.

Loeber, R. (1990) 'Development and risk factors of juvenile antisocial behavior and delinquency.' *Clinical Psychology Review 10*, 1–41.

Loeber, R. and Dishion, T.J. (1987) 'Antisocial and delinquent youths: methods for their early identification.' In J.D. Burchard and S.N. Burchard (eds) *Prevention of Delinquent Behavior*. London: Sage Publications.

Loeber, R. and LeBlanc, M. (1990) 'Toward a developmental criminology.' In M. Tonry and N. Morris (eds) *Crime and Justice (Vol.12)*. Chicago: University of Chicago Press.

Loeber, R. and Stouthamer–Loeber, M. (1987) 'Prediction.' In H.C. Quay (ed) *Handbook of Juvenile Delinquency*. New York: Wiley.

Lombroso, C. (1874) *L'uomo Deliquente*. Bocca: Turino.

Lösel, F. and Bliesener, T. (1994) 'Some high-risk adolescents do not develop conduct problems: a study on protective factors.' *International Journal of Behavioral Development 17*, 753–777.

Macleod, R.J. (1982) 'A child is charged with homicide. His family responds.' *British Journal of Psychiatry 141*, 199–201.

MacCleod, M. and Saraga, E. (1988) 'Challenging the orthodoxy towards a feminist theory and practice.' *Feminist Review, Special Issue: Family Secrets, Child Sexual Abuse*, 28, 16–55.

McCullough, J.P., Huntsinger, G.M. and Nay, W.R. (1977) 'Self-control treatment of aggression in a 16-year-old male.' *Journal of Consulting and Clinical Psychology 45*, 322–331.

MacCulloch, M., Snowden, P.R., Wood, P.J.W. and Mills, H.E. (1983) 'Sadistic fantasy, sadistic behaviour and offender.' *British Journal of Psychiatry 143*, 20–29.

McCarthy, J.B. (1978) 'Narcissism and the self in homicidal adolescents.' *American Journal of Psychoanalysis 38*, 19–29.

McDougall, C., Clark, D.A. and Fisher, M.J. (1994) 'Assessment of violent offenders.' In M. McMurran, and J. Hodge (eds) *The Assessment of Criminal Behaviours of Clients in Secure Settings*. London: Jessica Kingsley.

McGuire, J. (1995) 'Assessing self-control loss in violent offences committed by juveniles.' Paper presented at the 5th European Conference on Psychology and Law, Budapest, September 1995.

McGuire, J. and Priestley, P. (1985) *Offending Behaviour*. London: Batsford.

McMurran, M. and Hollin, C.R. (1989) 'Drinking and delinquency: another look at young offenders and their drinking.' *British Journal of Criminology 29*, 386–394.

McMurran, M. and Hollin, C.R. (1993) *Young Offenders and Alcohol-related Crime: A Practitioner's Guidebook*. Chichester: Wiley.

McNally, R.B. (1995) 'Homicidal youth in England and Wales 1982–1992: profile and policy.' *Psychology, Crime and Law, 1*, 333–342.

McShane, M.D. and Williams III, F.P. (1989) 'The prison adjustment of juvenile offenders.' *Crime and Delinquency 35*, 2, 254–69.

Maffesoli, M. (1994) *The Time of the Tribes.* London: Sage.

Main (1991) *A Typology of Human Attachment Organization, Assessed in Discourse, Drawings and Interviews.* Cambridge: Cambridge University Press.

Malamuth, N.M. and Donnerstein, E. (1982) 'The effects of aggressive-pornographic mass media stimuli.' In L. Berkowitz (ed) *Advances in Experimental and Social Psychology* (Vol. 15, 103–136). New York: Academic Press.

Marsh, P. (1978) *Aggro: the Illusion of Violence.* London: Dent.

Marsh, P. and Rosser, E. (1978) *The Rules of Disorder.* London: Routledge.

Mawson, A.R. (1987) *Transient Criminality: A Model of Stress Induced Crime.* New York: Praeger.

Measham, F., Newcombe, R. and Parker, H. (1994) 'The normalisation of recreational drug use among young people in North-West England.' *British Journal of Sociology 45*, 287–312.

Meichenbaum, D.H. and Goodman, J. (1971) 'Training impulsive children to talk to themselves: a means of developing self-control.' *Journal of Abnormal Psychology 77*, 115–126.

Meiselman, K.C. (1978) *Incest: A Psychological Study of Causes and Effects.* San Francisco, CA: Jossey-Bass.

Melzak, S. (1995) *Thinking About the Internal and External Experience of Refugee Children in Exile in Europe. Conflict and Treatment. War and Persecution.* Proceedings of the Hamburg Congress September 26–29th 1993. Osnabruck: Secolo Verlag.

Middleton, R. (1962) 'Brother–sister and father–daughter marriage in ancient Egypt.' *American Sociological Review 27*, 603–611.

Michelson, L. (1987) 'Cognitive-behavioral strategies in the prevention and treatment of anti-social disorders in children and adolescents.' In J.D. Burchard and S.N. Burchard (eds) *Prevention of Delinquent Behavior.* London: Sage Publications.

Miller, A. (1990) *The Untouched Key: Tracing Childhood Trauma in Creativity and Destructiveness.* London: Virago.

Miller, G.E. and Prinz, R.J. (1990) 'Enhancement of social learning family interventions for childhood conduct disorder.' *Psychological Bulletin 108*, 291–307.

Millham, S., Bullock, R., Hosie, K. and Little, M. (1988) *The Characteristics of Young People in Youth Treatment Centres.* Dartington Social Research Unit, University of Bristol.

Moir, A. and Jessel, D. (1995) *A Mind to Crime.* London: Michael Joseph.

Moran, J. (1984) 'Response and responsibility.' *Nursing Times*, April 4, p.28–31.

Morton, T.L. and Ewald, L.S. (1987) 'Family-based interventions for crime and delinquency.' In E.K. Morris and C.J. Braukmann (eds) *Behavioral Approaches to Crime and Delinquency.* New York: Plenum Press.

Moyer, K.E. (1971) 'The physiology of aggression and the implications for aggression control.' In J.L. Singer (ed) *The Control of Aggression and Violence.* New York: Academic Press.

Mrazek, F.J. and Kempe, C.H. (1981) *Sexually Abused Children and their Families.* New York: Pergamon.

Mungham, G. and Pearson, G. (eds) (1976) *Working Class Youth Cultures.* London: Routledge.

Murray, J. and Kippax, S. (1979) 'From the early window to the late night show.' In L. Berkowitz (ed) *Advances in Experimental Social Psychology.* New York: Academic Press.

Myers, W.C. and Kemph, J.P. (1990) 'DSM-III-R classification of Homicidal Youth – help or hindrance?' *Journal of Clinical Psychiatry 5*, 239–42.

Newburn, T. (1993) *Permission and Regulation.* London: Routledge.

Newburn, T. (1994) *Persistent Offenders.* London: PSI.

Newson, E. (1994) *Video Violence and the Protection of Children.* Nottingham: University of Nottingham.

Noble, P. and Rodger, S. (1989) 'Violence by psychiatric inpatients.' *British Journal of Psychiatry 155*, 384–390.

Noble, G. (1975) *Children in Front of the Small Screen.* London: Sage.

Novaco, R.W. (1975) *Anger Control: The Development and Evaluation of an Experimental Treatment.* Lexington, MA: D.C.Heath and Co.

Novaco, R.W. (1979) 'The cognitive regulation of anger and stress.' In P.C. Kendall and S.D. Hollon (eds) *Cognitive Behavioural Interventions: Theory, Research and Procedures.* New York: Academic Press.

O'Carroll, T. (1980) *Paedophila: The Radical Case.* London: Peter Owen.

Ogden, T.H. (1979) 'On projective identification.' *International Journal of Psychoanalysis 60,* 357–373.

Olweus, D. (1979) 'Stability of aggressive reaction patterns in males: a review.' *Psychological Bulletin 86,* 852–875.

Olweus, D. (1988) 'Environmental and biological factors in the development of aggressive behaviour.' In W. Buikhuisen and S.A. Mednick (eds) *Explaining Criminal Behaviour.* Leiden: E.J. Brill.

Paglia. C. (1992) *Sexual Personae: Art and Decadence from Nefertiti to Emily.* London: Penguin Books.

Palazzoli, M.S., Boscol, L., Cecchini, G. and Trata, G. (1978) *Paradox and Counter Paradox: A New Model in the Therapy of the Family in Schizophrenic Transaction.* New York: Jason Aronson.

Parry-Jones, W. (1984) 'Adolescent psychiatry in Britain. A personal view of its development and present position.' *Bulletin of the Royal College of Psychiatrists 8,* 230–233.

Patterson, G.R. (1986) 'Performance models for antisocial boys.' *American Psychologist 41,* 432–444.

Patterson, G.R. (1992) 'Developmental changes in antisocial behavior.' In R.D. Peters, R.J. McMahon and V.L. Quinsey (eds) *Aggression and Violence Throughout the Life Span.* London: Sage Publications.

Patterson, G.R. and Yoerger, K. (1993) 'Developmental models for delinquent behavior.' In S. Hodgins (ed) *Mental Disorder and Crime.* London: Sage.

Pearl, D., Bouthilet, L. and Lazar, J. (eds) (1982) *Television and Behavior.* Washington, DC: National Institute of Mental Health.

Pearson, G. (1983) *Hooligan: A History of Respectable Fears.* London: Macmillan.

Pecnik, N. and Stubbs, P. (1994) 'Working with refugees and Displaced Persons in Croatia: from dependency to development?' Unpublished, available from Paul Stubbs Social Work Department, University of Belgrade.

Perry B.D. (1993) 'The advisor.' *American Professional Society on the Abuse of Children 6,* 2, Summer 1993

Perry, B.D. (1994) 'Neurobiological Sequelae of Childhood Trauma: PTSD in Children.' In M. Murray (ed) *Catcholamines in Post-Traumatic Stress Disorder: Emerging Concepts.* Washington, DC: American Psychiatric Press.

Pffefer, C.R. (1980) 'Psychiatric hospital treatment of assaultative homicidal children.' *American Journal of Psychotherapy 34,* 197–207.

Phillips, C. and Dinitz, S. (1982) 'Labelling and juvenile court dispositions.' *Sociological Quarterly 23,* 2, 267–79.

Piontelli, A. (1992) *From Foetus to Child: An Observational and Psychoanalytic Study.* London: Routledge.

Plotnik, R. (1968) 'Changes in social behaviour of squirrel monkeys after anterior temporal lobectomy.' *Journal of Comparative Physiological Psychology 66,* 369–377.

Powers, E. and Witmer, H. (1951) *An Experiment in the Prevention of Delinquency: The Cambridge-Somerville Youth Study.* New York: Columbia University Press.

Prentice-Dunn, S. and Rogers, R.W. (1983) 'Deindividuation in aggression.' In R.G. Green and E.I. Donnerstein (eds) *Aggression: Theoretical and Empirical Reviews,* vol 2, Issues in research. New York: Academic Press.

Pratt, J. and Salter, N. (1984) 'A fresh look at football hooliganism.' *Leisure Studies 3,* 201–219.

Price, W.H. and Whatmore, P.B. (1967) 'Behavior disorders and patterns of crime among XYY males identified at a maximum security hospital.' *British Medical Journal 69*, 533–536.

Punamacki, R.L. (1987) 'Content of and facts affecting coping modes among Palestinian children.' *Scandinavian Journal of Development Alternatives 6 (1)*, 86–98.

Punamacki, R.L. and Suleiman, R. (1989) 'Predictors and effectiveness of coping with political violence among Palestinian children.' *British Journal of Social Psychology 29*, 67–77.

Pynoos, R.S. and Eth, S. (1985) 'Interaction of trauma and grief in childhood.' In S. Eth and R.S. Pynoos (eds) *Post Traumatic Stress Disorder in Children.* American Psychiatric Association.

Pynoos, R.S., Frederick, C., Nader, K., Arroyo, W., Steinberg, A., Eth, S., Nunez, F. and Fairbanks, L. (1987) 'Life threat and post-traumatic stress in school-age children.' *Archives of General Psychiatry 44*, 1057–63.

Pynoos, R.S. and Nader, K. (1993) 'Issues in the treatment of posttraumatic stress in children and adolescents.' In J.P. Wilson and B. Raphael (eds) *International Handbook of Traumatic Stress Syndromes.* New York: Plenum Press.

Quay, H.C. (1987) 'Intelligence.' In H.C. Quay (ed) *Handbook of Juvenile Delinquency.* New York: Wiley.

Rabiner, D.L., Lenhart, L. and Lochman, J.E. (1990) 'Automatic and reflective social problem solving in popular, average, and rejected children.' *Developmental Psychology 26*, 1010–1016.

Raffe, D. and Willms, J.D. (1989) 'Schooling the discouraged worker: local labour market effects on educational participation.' *Sociology 23*, 559–581.

Rantakallio, P., Koiranen, M. and Mottonen, J. (1992) 'Association of perinatal events, epilepsy and CNS trauma with juvenile delinquency.' *Archives of Childhood Disability 67*, 12, 1459–61.

Redhead, S. (ed) (1993) *Rave Off.* Aldershot: Avebury.

Regina vs Brown [H.L.(E)] 2 WLR 1993.

Reid, J.B. and Patterson, G.R. (1976) 'The modification of aggression and stealing behavior of boys in the home setting.' In E. Ribes-Inesta and A. Bandura (eds) *Analysis of Delinquency and Aggression.* Hillsdale: Lawrence Erlbaum Associates.

Ressler, R.K., Burgess, A.W. and Douglas, J.E. (1988) *Sexual Homicide Patterns and Motives.* New York: Lexington Books.

Richman, N. (1992) 'Annotation: children in situations of political violence.' *Journal of the Association of Child Psychology and Child Psychiatry 34*, 1286–1302.

Roberts, K. (1994), 'Young people and football in Liverpool.' In I. Henry (ed) *Leisure: Modernity, Postmodernity and Lifestyles.* Eastbourne: Leisure Studies Association Publication, 48.

Roberts, K. and Parsell, G. (1994) 'Youth cultures in Britain: the middle class take-over.' *Leisure Studies 13*, 33–48.

Roberts, K., White, G.E. and Parker, H.J. (1974) *The Character Training Industry.* Newton Abbot: David and Charles.

Robins, D. and Hobbs, D.B. (1990) 'The boy done good.' Paper presented to British Sociological Association conference, Guildford.

Rose, S.D. and Edleson, J.L. (1987) *Working with Children and Adolescents in Groups.* San Francisco: Jossey-Bass.

Rothbart, M.K., Derryberry, D. and Posner, M.I. (1994) 'A psychobiological approach to the development of temperament.' In J.E. Bates and T.D. Wachs (eds) *Temperament: Individual Differences at the Interface of Biology and Behavior.* Washington: American Psychological Association.

Rowland, W. (1983) *The Politics of TV Violence.* London: Sage.

Rubinstein, M., Yeager, C., Goodstein, C. and Lewis, D. (1993) 'Sexually assaultive male juveniles.' *American J. Psychiatry 150*, 2, 262–5.

Rutter, M. (1972) *Maternal Deprivation Re-assessed.* Harmondsworth: Penguin.

Rutter, M. (1985) 'Aggression and the family.' *Series Paedopsychiatrica 6*, 11–25.

Rutter, M. (1985) 'Resilience in the face of adversity. Protective factors and resistance to psychological disorder.' *British Journal of Psychiatry 147*, 598–611.

Rutter, M. (1989) 'Intergenerational continuities and discontinuities in serious parenting difficulties.' In D. Ciccheti and V. Carlson (eds) *Child Maltreatment Theory and Research on the Causes and Consequences of Child Abuse and Neglect.* New York: Cambridge University Press.

Rutter, M. (1989) 'Psychosocial risk trajectories and beneficial turning points.' In S. Doxiadis (ed) *Early Influences Shaping the Individual.* New York: Plenum Press.

Russell, D.E.H. (1984) *Sexual Exploitations: Rape, Child Sexual Abuse, and Sexual Harassment.* London: Sage.

Ryan, G. (1989) 'Victim to victimiser.' *Journal of Interpersonal Violence 4,* 325–341.

Ryder, R. (1991) 'The cult of machismo.' *Criminal Justice 9,* 1, 12–13.

Sané, P. (1993) *Childhood Stolen.*

Satten, J., Menninger, K.A. and Rosen, I. (1960) 'Murder without apparent motive: A study in personality disorganisation.' *American Journal of Psychiatry 117,* 48–53.

Sarason, I.G. (1978) 'A cognitive social learning approach to juvenile delinquency.' In R.D. Hare and D. Schalling (eds) *Psychopathic Behavior: Approaches to Research.* New York: Wiley.

Singer, J.L. (1966) *Day Dreaming.* New York: Random House.

The Scarman Report – The Brixton Disorders 10–12 April 1981. (1982) Harmondsworth: Penguin Books Ltd.

Scott, M.J. and Stradling, S.G. (1992) *Counselling for Post-traumatic Stress Disorder.* London: Sage Counselling in Practice Series.

Scott, P.D. (1977) 'Assessing dangerousness in criminals.' *British Journal of Psychiatry 131,* 127–42.

Scharff, J.S. and Scharff, D.E. (1994) *Object Relations Theory of Physical and Sexual Trauma.* New York: Jason Aronson.

Schlesinger, L.B. and Revitch, E. (1980) 'The criminal fantasy technique. A comparison of sex offenders and substance abusers.' *Journal of Clinical Psychology 37,* 210–218.

Schlesinger, P., Dobash, R.E., Dobash, R.P. and Weaver, C.K. (1992) *Women Viewing Violence.* London: British Film Institute.

Schlichter, K.J. and Horan, J.J. (1981) 'Effects of stress inoculation on the anger and aggression management skills of institutionalized juvenile delinquents.' *Cognitive Therapy and Research 5,* 359–365.

Schulman, M. (1973) *The Ravenous Eye.* London: Cassell.

Sears, Poplau, Freedman and Taylor (1988) *Social Psychology* (6th ed.). Englewood Cliffs, NJ: Prentice-Hall.

Seghorn, T.K., Pretsky, R.A. and Boucher, R.J. (1987) 'Childhood sexual abuse in the lives of sexually aggressive offenders.' *Journal of American Academy of Child and Adolescent Psychiatry 26,* 262–267.

Sgroi, S.M. (1982) *Handbook of Clinical Intervention in Child Abuse.* Lexington, MA: DC Heath.

Shah, S.A. (1970a) 'Recent developments in human genetics and their implication for problems of social deviance.' Paper presented at the American Association of the Advancement of Science, Chicago, Dec. 28.

Shah, S.A. (1970b) 'Report on the XYY Chromosome Abnormality.' *National Institute of Mental Health Conference Report.* Washington, DC: Government Printing Office.

Shepherd, S. (1993) *Prevalence of Sexual Abuse Amongst Juvenile Prisoners.* Report to Home Office. London: HMSO.

Shore, M.F. and Massimo, J.L. (1979) 'Fifteen Years after treatment: a follow up study of comprehensive vocationally oriented psychotherapy.' *American Journal of Orthopsychiatry 49,* 2, 240–245.

Short, R.J. and Simeonson, R.J. (1986) 'Social cognition and aggression in delinquent adolescent males.' *Adolescence 21,* 159–176.

Singer, S. and McDowall, D. (1988) 'Criminalizing delinquency: the deterrent effects of the New York juvenile offender law.' *Law and Society Review 22,* 3, 521–35.

Skinner, B.F. (1953) *Science and Human Behaviour.* New York: Macmillan.

Skynner, A.C.R. (1971) 'Group therapy with adolescent girls.' *Annual Review of the Residential Child Care Association 18*, 16, 16–32.

Slaby, R.G. and Guerra, N.G. (1988) 'Cognitive mediators of aggression in adolescent offenders: 1. Assessment.' *Developmental Psychology 24*, 580–588.

Slavson, S.R. (1940) 'Foundation of group therapy with children.' In M. Schiffer (ed) (1979) *Dynamics of Group Psychotherapy.* New York: Jason Aronson.

Smith, D. and Gray, J. (1983) *Police and People in London.* London: Policy Studies Institute.

Smith, P.K. and Sharp, S. (eds) (1994) *School Bullying: Insights and Perspectives.* London: Routledge.

Smith, S. and Pennells, M. (1993) 'Bereaved children and adolescents.' In K.N. Dwivedi (ed) *Group Work with Children and Adolescents.* London: Jessica Kingsley.

Snyder, J. and White, J.J. (1979) 'The use of cognitive self-instruction in the treatment of behaviorally disturbed adolescents.' *Behavior Therapy 10*, 227–235.

Snyder, J.J. and Patterson, G.R. (1987) 'Family interaction and delinquent behavior.' In H.C. Quay (ed) *Handbook of Juvenile Delinquency.* New York: Wiley.

Solomos, J. (1992) 'The politics of immigration since 1945.' In P. Braham, A. Rattansi and R. Skellington (eds) *Racism and Antiracism, Inequalities, Opportunities and Policies.* Buckingham: The Open University.

Sorrells, J. (1980) 'What can be done about juvenile homicide?' *Crime and Delinquency 26*, 2, 152–61.

Sparks, R. (1991) 'Reason and unreason in left realism.' In R. Matthews and J. Young (eds) *Issues in Realist Criminology.* London: Sage.

Sparks, R. (1992) *Television and the Drama of Crime.* Buckingham: Open University Press.

Spellacy, F. (1977) 'Neuropsychological differences between violent and nonviolent adolescents.' *Journal of Clinical Psychology 23*, 965–969.

Spielberger, C.D. (1991) *State-trait Anger Expression Inventory: Revised Research Edition.* Odessa, Florida: PAR.

Spivack, G. and Cianci, N. (1987) 'High-risk early behavior pattern and later delinquency.' In J.D. Burchard and S.N. Burchard (eds) *Prevention of Delinquent Behavior.* London: Sage Publications.

Stattin, H. and Magnusson, D. (1995) 'Onset of official delinquency: its co-occurrence in time with educational, behavioural and interpersonal problems.' *British Journal of Criminology 35*, 417–449.

Stewart, J.T., Myers, W.C. and Burket, R.C. (1990) 'A review of pharmacotherapy of aggression in children and adolescents.' *Journal of American Academic Child and Adolescent Psychiatry 29*, 269–277.

Steinem, G. (1980) 'Erotica and pornography: a clear and present difference.' In L. Lederer (ed) *Take Back the Night: Women on Pornography.* New York: Morrow.

Slotkin, J.S. (1947) 'On a possible lack of incest regulations in old Iran.' *American Anthropologist 49*, 612–617.

Stoller, R.J. (1986) *Perversion, the Erotic Form of Hatred.* Hemel Hempstead: The Harvester Press.

Straker, G. (1992) *Faces in the Revolution.* Athens, O.H.: Ohio University Press.

Straker, G. (1994) 'Integrating African and Western healing practices in South Africa.' *American Journal of Psychotherapy 48*, 3 Summer 1994.

Swartz, L. and Levett, A. (1992) 'Political oppression and children in South Africa: The social construction of damaging effects.' In N.C. Manganyi and A. du Toit (eds) *Political Violence and the Struggle in South Africa.* London: Macmillan.

Tarter, R.E., Hegedus, A.M., Winsten, S.T. and Alterman, A.I. (1987) 'Intellectual profiles of violent behavior in juvenile delinquents.' *Journal of Psychology 119*, 125–128.

Tate, (1996) 'Teach our children right from wrong, schools told.' Cathy Scott Clarke, Educational Correspondent, *The Sunday Times*, 14 January 1996.

Taylor, P. (1985) 'Motives for offending among violent and psychotic men.' *British Journal of Psychiatry 147*, 491–498.

Thomas, T. (1989) 'A cautionary tale.' *Criminal Justice* 7, 1.

Tremblay, R.E., Viatro, F., Bertrand, L., LeBlanc, M., Beauchesne, H., Boileau, H. and David, L. (1992) 'Parent and child training to prevent early onset of delinquency: the Montreal longitudinal-experimental study.' In J. McCord and R. Tremblay (eds) *Preventing Antisocial Behavior: Interventions from Birth Through Adolescence.* New York: Guilford Press.

Trepper, T.S. and Barrett, M.J. (1986) *Treating Incest. A Multiple Systems Perspective.* New York: The Haworth Press.

Trower, P., Bryant, B. and Argyle, M. (1978) *Social Skills and Mental Health.* London: Methuen.

Turner, R.H. (1964) *The Social Context of Ambition.* San Francisco: Chandler.

Turpin, R. and Lejune, J. (1969) *Human Afflictions and Aberrations.* Oxford: Pergamon Press.

Valentine, G.H. (1969) *The Chromosome Disorders.* Philadelphia, PA: Lippincott.

Van Beuren, G. (1994) 'The protection of children in armed conflicts.' *The International and Comparative Law Quarterly 43.*

Van Beuren, G. (1995) 'The international protection of family members' rights as the 21st Century approaches.' *Human Rights Quarterly.*

Varma, V. (ed) (1992) *The Secret Life of Vulnerable Children.* London: Routledge.

Varma, V. (ed)(1993) *How and Why Children Hate.* London: Jessica Kingsley Publishers.

Vizard, E. (1995 In press). 'The mind of the abuser: the dynamic origins of perversion.' Based on a talk given for the Sixth Flora Rheta Schreiber Memorial Lecture on 18.11.1995 in London.

Vizard, E., Hawkes, C., Wynick, S., Woods, J. and Jenkins, J. (1996) 'Juvenile sexual offenders: assessment issues.' *British Journal of Psychiatry 168,* 259–262.

Vizard, E., Monck, E. and Misch, P. (1995) 'Child and adolescent sex abuse perpetrators: a review of the research literature.' *Journal of Child Psychology and Psychiatry 36,* 731–759.

Walsh-Brennan, K.S. (1974) 'Psychopathology of homicidal children.' *R. Soc. Health – Journal 94,* 6, 274–277.

Wechsler, D. (1981) *Wechsler Adult Intelligence Scale: Revised.* San Antonio, Texas: The Psychological Corporation/Harcourt Brace Jovanovich.

Wechsler, D. (1992) *Wechsler Intelligence Scale for Children: Third Edition UK.* Sidcup, Kent: The Psychological Corporation/Harcourt Brace Jovanovich.

Welch, B.L. and Welch, A.S. (1969) 'Aggression and the biogenic amine neuro-humors.' In S. Garattinin and E.B. Sigg (eds) *Aggressive Behavior.* New York: Wiley.

West, D. and Farrington, D. (1973) *Who Becomes Delinquent.* London: Faber.

Whiteley, J.S. (1975) 'The psychopath and his treatment.' In T. Silverstone and B. Barraclough (eds) *Contemporary Psychiatry.* Ashford: Headley Brothers.

Widom, C.S. (1989) 'The intergenerational transmission of violence.' In N.A. Weiner and M.E. Wolfgang (eds) *Pathways to Criminal Violence.* London: Sage Publications.

Widom, C.S. (1989) 'The cycle of violence.' *Science 244,* 160–166.

Wilson, B. and Raphael, J.P. (eds) (1993) *International Handbook of Traumatic Stress Syndromes.* New York: Plenum Press.

Wilson, J.Q. and Herrnstein, R.S. (1985) *Crime and Human Nature.* New York: Simon and Schuster.

Wilson, S. (1995) *The Cradle of Violence: Essays on Psychiatry, Psychoanalysis and Literature.* London: Jessica Kingsley Publishers.

Williams, J., Dunning, E. and Murphy, P. (1984) *Hooligans Abroad.* London: Routledge.

Williams, G. (1990) *Interaztione Therapeutiche In Contesti Diversi.* Naples: L'Officina Tipografica.

Willis, P. (1990) *Common Culture.* Buckingham: Open University Press.

Willock, B. (1983) 'Play therapy with aggressive, acting out child.' In C.E. Schaffer and K.J. O'Connor (eds) *Handbook of Play Therapy.* New York: John Wley and Sons.

Willock, B. (1990) 'From acting out to interactive play.' *International Journal of Psychoanalysis 71,* 321–24.

Winnicott, D.W. (1956) 'The antisocial tendency.' In *Through Paediatrics to Psychoanalysis. Collected Papers.* London: Karnac Books and The Institute of Psychoanalysis.

Winnicott, P.W. (1986) *Home is Where we Start From.* Harmondsworth: Penguin.

Wolf, S.C. (1985) 'A multi-factor model of deviant sexuality.' *Victimology: An International Journal 10*, 359–374.

Wolfe, D.A. (1987) *Child Abuse: Implications for Child Development and Psychopathology.* New York: Sage.

Wooffitt, R. (1994) *The Language of Youth Sub-cultures: Social Identity in Action.* Brighton: Harvester Wheatsheaf.

Wright, C.W., Birney, V. and Smith, P.K. (1995) 'Security of attachment in 8 – 12-years-old: a revised version of the separation anxiety test, its psychometric properties and clinical interpretation.' *Journal of Child Psychology and Psychiatry 36*, 5, 757–774.

Wright-Watson, J. (1993) 'Group work with children and adolescents in a therapeutic community.' In K.N. Dwivedi (ed) *Group Work with Children and Adolescents.* London: Jessica Kingsley.

Young, J. (1987) 'The tasks facing a realist criminology.' *Contemporary Crises 11*, 337–56.

Young, J.E. (1990) *Cognitive Therapy for Personality Disorders: A Schema-focused Approach.* Sarasota, F.L.: Professional Resource Exchange.

Yoshikawa, H. (1994) 'Prevention as cumulative prevention: effects of early family support and education on chronic delinquency and its risks.' *Psychological Bulletin 115*, 28–54.

Yule, W. (1993) 'Children as victims and survivors.' In P.J. Taylor (ed) *Violence in Society.* Royal College of Physicians of London.

Zillman, D. (1979) *Hostility and Aggression.* Hillsdale NJ: Lawrence Erlbraum.

Zuckerman, M. (1994) 'Impulsive unsocialized sensation seeking: the biological foundations of a basic dimension of personality.' In J.E. Bates and T.D. Wachs (eds) *Temperament: Individual Differences at the Interface of Biology and Behavior.* Washington: American Psychological Association.

Zulueta, F. de (1993) *From Pain to Violence: The Traumatic Roots of Destructiveness.* London: Whurr.

Contributors

Susan Bailey is Consultant Adolescent Forensic Psychiatrist at the Adolescent Forensic Service at Mental Health Services of Salford.

Soni Bhate MBBS is a trainee psychiatrist at the City Health Trust and Newcastle University.

Surya Bhate MBBS DPM FRCPsych is Consultant/Senior Lecturer in Adolescent Forensic Psychiatry at the City Health NHS Trust and Newcastle University.

Gwyneth Boswell PhD is a Senior Lecturer in the School of Social Work at the University of East Anglia. She is a former Senior Probation Officer and co-author with Davies and Wright of *Contemporary Probation Practice* (1993). In recent years she has researched widely into violent young offenders and is the author of *Young and Dangerous: The Backgrounds and Careers of Section 53 Offenders*(1996).

Richard Davies Bsc MA CQSW AMBAP is Principal Adult Psychotherapist at and former vice chairman of the Portman Clinic, where he has treated patients who suffer from delinquency, sexual perversion or who perpetrate acts of violence. He is a course tutor for various courses for practitioners in the public and voluntary sector who work with the forensic patient. He also has a private practice and consults privately to various organisations and institutions concerned principally with risk management of dangerous offenders. He contributed to *Forensic Psychotherapy*, and is the editor of *Stress in Social Work*, to be published by Jessica Kingsley in 1997.

Kedar Nath Dwivedi, MBBS MD DPM FRCPsych,Consultant Child, Adolescent and Family Psychiatrist, Northampton and Clinical Teacher, Faculty of Medicine, University of Leicester.

Kevin Epps has been Principal Psychologist at Glenthorne Centre (Department of Health) since 1989. He has developed a particular interest in the management and treatment of aggressive and violent adolescents. He has published in various journals and contributed to edited books. He also teaches on several courses, runs workshops for various agencies, has contributed to national and local working groups concerned wiht young offenders, and acted as secretary to the British Psychological Society Division of Criminological and Legal Psychology Training Committee.

Nigel Fielding is Professor of Sociology and Deputy Dean of Human Studies at the University of Surrey.

Colin Hawkes BA (Hons) PGDipAppSocS CQSW began employment as a Probation Officer in 1971 after completing training as a lawyer. He has worked since then in the N.E. London Probation Service, establishing the Waltham Forest Throughcare Unit in 1974. In 1985 together with Dr Vizard, Dr G Mezey and Richard Austine he set up the N.E. London Sex Offenders Project for adult male child sexual abusers. Since 1991 he has been involved in the development of the Young Abusers project as Consultant Social Worker and subsequently Training and Development Co-ordinator.

Arthur Hyatt Williams is a psychoanalyst in private practice in London. He is a former Head of Adolescent Development at the Tavistock Clinic. He contributed to *Forensic Psychotherapy* (1996), published by Jessica Kingsley.

Jill Ann Jenkins BA MS AC Psy.D C.Psychol. moved to the UK in 1993, and has worked as a child psychologist both privately and for the NHS. As the Core Team Psychologist at the Young Abusers Project, Dr Jenkins has been responsible for the development of a cognitinve group treatment programme for young sex offenders. She has additionally developed and implemented a psychological assessment package for young sex offenders, adapting and revising many of the existing psychological assessment tools to suit the learning disabled British populations. Dr Jenkin's other responsibilities include treatment, research and programme planning.

James McGuire is Senior Lecturer and Course Director of the Doctorate in Clinical Psychology at the University of Liverpool. He studied psychology at the University of Glasgow, obtained a PhD at Leicester University and trained in clinical psychology at Leeds University. He has carried out research in prisons, probation services, adolescent units and special hospitals. Current research work includes projects on assessment of factors influencing violent offending by juveniles, and the design and evaluation of programmes of social problem-solving training. He is the author or co-author of a number of books, journal articles and other publications.

Sheila Melzak is Principal Community Child and Adolescent Psychotherapist at the Medical Foundation for the Care of Victims of Torture. Here she jointly co-ordinates the children and families consultation and treatment team, and is involved in individual, family and group psychotherapeutic work, consultation to professionals who work with refugee children and members of refugee communities and in training work. She is particularly interested in the community and psychological factors that mediate between the child's experience of organised violence and the internal representations of violence, scapegoating and secrecy.

Ken Roberts is Professor of Sociology at the University of Liverpool. He has written numerous books and articles on leisure, and was a founder member of the Leisure Studies Association. He is on the Executive Committee of the International Sociological Association Research Committee on Leisure, and is Chair of the Research Commission of the World Leisure and Recreation Association. He directed the Liverpool enquiries in the Economic and Social Research Council's 16–19 Initiative, conducted a comparative study of young people in Germany, and is currently investigating young people in Poland, Armenia, Georgia and the Ukraine.

Richard Sparks PhD (Cantab) teaches criminology at Keele University, having previously worked in the Open University and the University of Cambridge. He has written extensively on the depiction of crime and law enforcement in mass media, and is the author of *Television and the Drama of Crime*. Much of his other work has been about prisons and penal politics. He co-edited *Imprisonment: European Perspectives* and was co-author of *Prisons and the Problem of Order*. He is at present completing a study of people's fears and feelings about crime in an English town.

Ved P. Varma, PhD (London) was formerly an educational psychologist with the Institute of Education, University of London, the Tavistock Clinic, and for the London Boroughs of Richmond-Upon-Thames and Brent. He has edited or co-edited more than thirty books in education, psychology, psychiatry, psychotherapy and social work which includes, *How and Why Children Hate, How and Why Children Fail, Troubles of Children and Adolescents, Managing Manic Depressive Disorders* and, as co-editor with Professor Barbara Tizard, *Vulnerability and Resilience in Human Development*.

Eileen Vizard FRCPsych is Consultant Child and Adolescent Psychiatrist at the Young Abuser's Project. She has specialised in work with abused children and their families, dealing with the whole spectrum of child abuse cases. In 1986 Dr Vizard set up a community based group treatment programme for convicted child sexual abusers, and in 1992, an Assessment and Tratment Service for young sexual abusers of children. She has published, researched and taught widely within the field of child care and child abuse.

Subject Index

*References in italic indicate
figures or tables.*

ABC model 49
'abuse' definition 27
abuse prevalence, offenders'
    backgrounds 25–33, *27,
    36, 183*
activity group therapy 159
affective imagery training 167
age, and exposure to violence
    6–7
'age of criminal responsibility'
    41, 173
aggression, 'universality' of
    126
'aggression' definition 67
Aggression Replacement
    Training (ART) 56, 78–9
'aggressive–versatile' path
    71–2
'aggressiveness' definition 67
alcohol use 55
Anger Control Inventory 166
anger diaries 56, 166–7
Anger Inventory 166
anger management training
    77–8, 166–9
'antecedent' factors 49, 55
'Anti Social Tendency' 112
anthropological model 94
anxiety, television effects
    134–5, 140–3
archival sources 53
ART (Aggression
    Replacement Training)
    56, 78–9
art therapy 46–7
Asian immigrants 124,
    127–8, 130
assessment 8–10, 75
    case examples 10–16,
    116–17
    see also psychiatric
    assessment;
    psychological assessment
asylum law 3–4
attachment theory 8, 11–12,
    43, 101

distorted behaviour 161
Section 53 offenders 27–8
attention deficit hyperactivity
    disorder 169
avoidance problems 55

baselining 59–60
behavioural approaches
    48–50, *49,* 80
    behaviour modification
    169–71
    sexual violence models 91,
    100
bereavement, in offenders'
    backgrounds 27–8, *28*
biological models 157, 179
    of sexual violence 87–9,
    99, 101–2
'Bobo Doll' experiments 137
body language 157
bonding *see* attachment theory
brain chemistry models 157,
    179
    of sexual violence 87–9,
    99, 101–2
brutalization 104, 105, 108
bullying 64
bunde 152

Cambridge Study of
    Delinquent Development
    68, 183
career uncertainty 152–3
case examples 8, 10–16
    group work 164–5
    psychotherapy 111–22
    assessment 116–17
    family/personal history
    115–16
    theoretical background
    111–13
    racial violence 128–9
cautioning procedures, police
    175–6
charging procedures, police
    175–6
Child Behaviour Problem
    Profile 57
child care, offenders in 23–4,
    23
child development factors 6,
    8, 9, 70–1, 112–13
    case examples 15, 115–16,
    117–18

models 90, 97
Children and Young Persons
    Acts 22–3, 173, 174
Children's Anger Inventory
    57, 166
civilian casualties of war 5–6
'Clearing House' fighting
    game 170
cognitive-behavioural
    approach 48–50, *49,*
    74–5, 76
cognitive factors 73–4
    group work therapy 165–9
    sexual violence model 92,
    100
community level work 20
community policing 182
compensatory role of leisure
    154
Conners Teacher Rating Scale
    57
'consequences' (ABC model)
    49, 50
'contest' relations,
    police-gang 178
context of violence 2, 3–4, 9
    of television violence
    139–40
continuity of aggressiveness
    68–70
counter conditioning
    procedures 168
courts, youngsters' 170–1
Criminal Justice and Public
    Order Act 23, 24
Criminal Justice Acts 23
criminal responsibility, age of
    41, 173
criminology research 68
cue identification training 167
cultural factors 9, 18, 127–8
    sexual violence models 87,
    88, 93–4
    television violence 135–7
cultures, youth 144, 145–8,
    152

'dangerous play' 162
defensive strategies 161
de-individuation 167
delinquency rates 37
denial, parental 10

detention of offenders 46
S.53 offenders 23–4, 23
developmental factors see child development factors
developmental psychopathology research 68
deviance labels 184
Diagnostic and Statistical Manual of Mental Disorders 32, 34–5
diaries, anger 56, 166–7
diathesis-stress model 99
'digestion', psychic 104, 106–7, 108
discipline factors 71
discrimination, racial 125–6, 129
displacement theory 127
distal antecedents 49, 55
distorted proximity seeking behaviour 161
domination relationships 31
'dreaded feelings' avoidance 161
drugs culture 145–6
'duration' measurement 59

economic change, and leisure activities 147, 148–9
education
  moral role 130–1
  rise in post-compulsory 149
'effects' research, television 136–9, 140
emotional abuse, of S53 offenders 27, 27
emotional impact, of violence on children 2–21
  approaches and models 6–10, 16–20
  case studies 10–16
  context 3–4
  statistics 5–6
'escape club' incident 108
event sampling 60
examination stage 40
experiential group work 160, 161–5
  case study 164–5
expressive aggression 67
extent of aggression 65–7

'externalized' responses to abuse 31–3
extinction techniques 169

'fair fight training' games 170
families 2, 18–19
  interventions 10, 18, 19, 79–81
  group work compared 160
  interactions 70–2, 127, 183
  case study example 115–16
  uncertainty of 153
  sexual violence models 87, 88, 92–3
fantasy, role of 43, 44–5
fear conditioning 89, 101
feminist model of sexual violence 93
'fight training' games 170
finality, child's concept 42
'fingerprinting' example 175
follow-up 63–4
football violence 109
football youth culture 146–8, 156
'forensic enquiry' case study 111–22
frequency measurement 59
frustration hypothesis 16, 126
functional analysis 62–3
functional family therapy 80

gang behaviour 103, 104–5, 107–10
  order maintenance 176–9
  racial 125–8
gender differences, young offenders 31–3, 66
genetic factors 69–70
  sexual violence models 89, 99, 105
grief processes 46
group behaviour see gang behaviour
group membership, leisure activities 151–2, 154–5
group work 10, 19–20, 157–71
  experiential 161–5
  individual/family work compared 159–60
  psycho-educational groups 165–71

guilt feelings 42–3, 45–6

'Haircut' fair fighting game 170
'harsh' superego delinquents 158
'hassle logs' 56
Heysel disaster 146, 147
'HIA' syndrome 69
'helpless victim' identification 118
Hillsborough disaster 146, 147–8
historical factors, racial violence 124
historical information, collecting 53
historical model of sexual violence 94
'home' concept 16, 18, 19
hooliganism 146, 147
Hyperactivity-Impulsivity-Attention Deficit 69
hypothesis-testing 62–3

'identification with aggressor' 162–3
'impulse' v. 'power' violence 108–9
incentive-motivated aggression 169
incest 94
'individual' factors 105–6
individual models of sexual violence 87, 88, 88–92
individual-plus-family approach 80
individual treatment 19, 20, 75–9
  group work compared 159–60
individualization trends 150–2
individualized assessment 72
'induction' discipline 30–1
inevitability, child's concept 42
information-processing model 73
information sources, risk assessment 39–40
inherited characteristics see genetic factors
inner labelling 167–8

insecurity, television effects
134–5, 140–3
instrumental aggression 67
Integrated Perspectives
Model, YAP 84, 95–101,
95, 102–3
intellectual functioning tests
57–8
intergenerational violence
29–31
intermediate treatment
movement 159
internal representations,
child's 2–3, 11–13, 8, 15
'internalized' responses to
abuse 31–3
'inter-occasion interval'
variable 60–61
interventions *see* group work;
treatment approaches
interviewing 54–6
by police 181
inventories 56–7
irreversibility, child's concept
42

Juvenile Offender Law, New
York 174
'juveniles' 173

labelling
deviance 184
inner 167–8
law enforcement 172, 175,
176
'law of the jungle' behaviour
161–2
learning difficulties 57–8, 100
legal rights/responsibilities
172–3
leisure activities 144–56
bonding within tribes
154–6
recent youth cultures 145–8
youth's new condition
148–54
Liverpool, youth cultures
146–7
loss 6, 9, 17, 162
offenders' backgrounds
25–34, *28,* 36

macho values, police and
gang 178

malicious violence 112, 113,
120
masculinity, television
influences 134, 139–40
'mean world' outlook 141–2
measurement of behaviour 59

media influences 42, 95, 100,
127
see also television effects
medical models 157, 179
of sexual violence 88–90,
99, 101–2
Michael, group work example
164–5
monitoring 63–4
Montreal Longitudinal
Experimental Study 81
moral development 19, 41–2
television effects 135–7
multi-disciplinary assessment
50–1
multifactorial model of sexual
violence 92
multi-modal intervention
programmes 78–9
multiple deprivation 70
music, role in youth cultures
145

naturalistic v. simulated
situations 62
neurological models 157, 179
of sexual violence 88–90,
99, 101–2
New York, Juvenile Offender
Law 174
Newcastle Thousand Family
study 70
night time youth culture
145–6, 156
Nik (case study) 111–22
'non-aggressive' path 72
'non-social' superego
delinquents 158
non-specific narratives 61, *61*
non-verbal therapies 46–7

'observation interval' variable
60
observation methods 58–62
measuring behaviour 59–60
naturalistic v. simulated
situations 62

recording behaviour 60–1,
61
target behaviour 58–9
'observation occasion' 60
offenders 179
see also police relationships;
Section 53 offenders
'official' delinquency 66
'ontological security' 142
order maintenance 172, 175,
176, 182
Oregon Social learning
Center 79–80
organized abuse, of S.53
offenders 27, *27*
overlearning 168

parent training 79–80, 81
parental substitutes 17, 18
parental violence 2, 18–19,
112–13
parenting problems 70–1, 98
pedophilic disorder *see* sexual
violence
'peer group' models of sexual
violence 87, *88,* 93, 98
peer group reaction to
violence 104–5
'persistent' offenders 66, 176
physical abuse of children 5,
48–9, 157
of S.53 offenders 27, *27,* 71
physical models 157, 179
of sexual violence 88–90,
99, 101–2
police relationships 172–84
cautioning and charging
175–6
key issues 182–4
legal rights of children
172–3
methods 179–81
sentencing 174
subcultures/gang behaviour
176–9
political violence 2, 4, 5,
18–19
politicization of black
immigration 124–6, 130
pop music culture 145
pornography 94, 140
'post-adolescents' 150

post-traumatic stress disorder
(PTSD) 34–6, 46, 89, 96,
158
'power' v. 'impulse' violence
108–9
predictors of violence 33–4
prevention strategies 82
primary interventions 74
prison system, S.53 offenders
23–4, *23*
problem behaviour, defining
52–3
problem-solving training 77,
80, 81, 168
projective identification 163–4
protective factors 72, 162
proto-communities 152
proximal antecedents 49, 55
psychiatric assessment 37–47,
179–80
assessment of violence
39–42
role of fantasy 44–5
sadistic violence 42–4
safe intervention 45–7
psychic 'digestion' 103,
106–7, 109
psychodynamic approaches
158
experiential groups 161–5
sexual violence 90–91, 99,
105–6
psycho-educational group
work 160, 165–71
behaviour modification
169–71
cognitive therapy
approaches 165–9
psychological assessment
48–64, 74
assessment definitions
50–1, *51*
formulation 62–3
methods 52–62, *52, 61*
archival sources 53
intellectual functioning
57–8
interviews 54–6
inventories 56–7
observation 58–62, *61*
self-monitoring 56
monitoring 63–4

theoretical approach 48–50,
49, 126–7
psycho-social approaches
65–82
extent of aggression 65–6
management and treatment
74–81
understanding aggression
67–74
PTSD (post-traumatic stress
disorder) 34–6, 46, 89,
96, 158

qualifications, desire for 149
questionnaires 56–7

Race Relations Act 129
racial violence 123–31
case study 128–9
historical factors 124
politicization of
immigration 124–6
social determinants 127
suggestions 129–31
theories 126–8
raves 145–6, 148, 177
record-keeping 64
'recording interval' variable 60
recording techniques 60–1, *61*
refugee studies 3–4, 6
individual example 13–16
reinforcement approaches
169–70
relaxation training 77–8, 168
re-offenders 66, 176
resilience issues 7, 16–17, 72
'resistance' problems 55
response costing techniques
169–70
responsibilities, children's
legal 172–3
'right from wrong',
understanding 41–2,
130–1
rights, children's legal 172–3
risk factors 16, 40–1, 47, 74
in leisure activities 146,
147–8
youth's new condition
152–4, 156
ritual abuse, of S.53 offenders
27, *27*
road rage 112
Robert, S.53 offender 28–9

role play 62, 168
rule-governed violence 55–6

sadistic violence 37, 42–3
role of fantasy 44–5
safe intervention 45–7
sado-masochistic behaviour
113, 118, 119–20, 121
sampling 60
scapegoating 3–4, 9
schoolboy violence example
103–4
Seattle Social Development
Project 81
secondary interventions 74
secrecy issues 9, 10
Section 53 offenders 22–36
abuse and loss 25–6
family stressors 29–31
findings 27–9, *27, 28*
gender factors 31–3
legislation 22–3
population 23–5, *23, 24*
post-traumatic stress
disorder 34–6
predictors of violence 33–4
security needs 18
see also attachment theory
'selective incapacitation' 66
self-awareness training 167
self-instructional training
76–7
self-monitoring 56, 166–7
self-preservative violence
111–12, 113, 120
'sensitization' discipline 30–1
sentencing 174–6
Section 53 offenders
24–5, *24*
separation anxiety 162
see also attachment theory;
loss
sexual arousal disorder 85,
101–2
sexual development problems
96–7
sexual violence
by children 43–4, 44–5,
84–103
characteristics 83–5, *86*
police practice 183
theories 86–95, *88*

YAP Integrated
Perspectives Model
95–101, *96*
on children 5, 10
case study example 116,
118–19
S.53 offenders 27, *27,* 72,
91
shame, and sadistic violence
45–6
Simon, refugee case 13–16
simulated v. naturalistic
situations 62
situational factors 41, 73–4
'16–19 Initiative' 144
social anxiety, television
effects 134–5, 140–3
social-cognitive learning
theory *see* psycho-social
approach
social constructivist
framework 7–8
social development problems
71–2, 98
social factors 9, 183–4
racial violence 125, 129–30
sexual violence 87, *88,* 93–4
'youth's new condition'
149–50
social identities, and leisure
activities 153–4, 154–5
social problem-solving
training 77
Social Situations
Questionnaire 57
social skills training 75–6,
170–1
'society' based models of
sexual violence 87, *88,*
93–4
Spielberger State-Trait Anger
Expression Inventory
(STAXI) 56
'spill-over' links with leisure
154
stability of aggressiveness
68–70
statistics
delinquency rates 37
violence by children 65–7,
176
violence on children 5

stress inoculation training 77,
167–8
subcultural groups, order
maintenance 176–9
substitute carers 17, 18
superego functioning 158

target behaviour 58–9
teachers, role of 130–1
television effects 132–43
laboratory studies 137–8
pervasiveness 132–3, 134
research 136–7, 138
social anxiety 140–3
violence debate 133,
135–40
temperamental variables
69–70
ethnic differences 127–8
temporary communities 152
tertiary interventions 74
Theoretical Classifications
Diagram 87–95, *88,* 95,
102
family level 92–3
formal societal level 92–3
individual level 87–91
peer group level 92
wider perspectives level
94–5
therapeutic community
meetings 171
therapy *see* group work;
treatment approaches
three-term contingency model
49
time-out techniques 169
time sampling 60
Tom, family violence case
10–13, 15
transgenerational violence
29–31
trauma issues 6, 7, 9
trauma models 91, 96–7,
99–100
treatment approaches 4,
19–20, 45–7, 63–4,
74–81
family-based 79–81
individual 75–9
prevention 81
see also group work
treatment integrity 63

'tribes' 152
bonding within 154–6
triggers of violence 49, 55,
157–8, 166

uncertainty issues 152–4

'vagueness' problems 55
verbal meditation skills 168–9
victims 41
as future offenders 181
reporting needs 31
statements from 53
video-recording 61
violence definitions 1, 67
'Virginia Woolf' fighting
game 170
vulnerability issues 7, 16–17

warfare 5–6, 21
'weak-but-robust-
traditional-effects' view
138
Wechsler Intelligence Scales
57
West Indian immigrants 124,
130
West trial 3
'wider perspectives' models of
sexual violence 87, *88,*
94–5, 9100
witness statements 53
witnessing violence 103–4,
112–13, 157

YAP (Young Abuser's Project)
84, 85–6, *86*
YAP Integrated Perspectives
Model 84, 95–101, *96,*
102–3
Young Abuser's Project *see* YAP
'young adults' 150
young offenders *see* offenders;
Section 53 offenders
'young persons' 173
'youngsters' courts' 170
youth cultures 144, 145–8,
152
'youth's new condition'
148–54, 156
individualization 150–2
lengthening 148–50
risk 152–4

Author Index

Abel, G. 95
Able, G.G. 91
Achenbach, T.M. 57
Adams, J. 159
Adelman, H. 177
Adelson, E. 163
Adler, A. 127
Ageton, S.S. 93
Aichhorn, A. 158
Akhtar, N. 73
Alder, C. 93
Alexander, J.F. 80
Allebeck, P. 38
Allee, W.C. 89
Alterman, A.I. 58
American Psychiatric
    Association (APA) 32, 35,
    83, 100
Anthony, E.J. 159
APA (American Psychiatric
    Association) 32, 35, 84,
    100
Arbuthnot, J. 75, 80
Argyle, M. 57
Armstrong, L. 32
Aulich, L. 46
Austin, G.W. 166

Bach, G.R. 170
Bailey, S. 38, 43
Bandura, A. 67, 137
Bank, L. 79
Banks, M. 144, 149
Bard, B. 89
Barham, J. 83
Barker, M. 135
Baskin, C. 62
Bass, D. 80
Bates, J.E. 34, 48
Baum, C.G. 79
Beaumont, G. 165
Beck, S. 62
Becker, J.V. 72, 80, 82, 98
Beckett, G.E. 58
Bell, S. 159
Bellack, A. 62
Bender, L. 42
Benedek, B.A. and E.P. 42

Bentovim, A. 10, 18, 19, 91,
    92
Beres, D. 44
Berkowitz, L. 67, 73, 90, 94,
    126, 137
Bierman, K.L. 76
Bion, W. 105, 106, 107
Birney, V. 34
Blackburn, R. 67
Blake, W. 126
Blakely, C.H. 63
Blancero, D.A. 78
Bliesener, T. 72
Blom, G.E. 54
Bloomquist, M. 169
Boster, L. 183
Boswell, G. G.R. 22, 24, 25,
    31, 35
Bouthilet, L. 136
Bowlby, J. 8, 11–12, 27, 43
Bradley, E.J. 73
Braff, J. 180
Brandon, S. 165
Braswell, L. 76, 169
Brayne, E. 159
Bremer, J.F. 85
Brown, P. 149
Brown, R.V. 87
Browne 91
Bryant, B. 57
Bucy 89
Bullen, J.G. 167
Bullock, R. 41, 45
Burch, P.R. 76
Burgess, A.W. 42, 46
Burlingham, D.T. 18
Burket, R.C. 46
Busch, K.G. 42, 183

Calkins, S.D. 70
Camp, B.W. 54, 168
Carmen, E. 31
Carthan, W. 78
Cassity, J. 90
Cecchini, G. 92
Champion, D.J. 174
Chandler, M.A. 75
Chen, S.A. 83
Chess, S. 69, 70
Cianci, N. 68
Clark, D.A. 64
Cocozza, J. 180
Cohen, A. 177

Coie, J.D. 69
Cole, J.E. 46
Collias, N. 89
Colliver, J.A. 36
Commission on Obscenity
    and Pornography 93
Comstock, G. 138
Conners, C.K. 57
Cook, P. 159
Coppock, C. 159
Cornell, D.G. 42, 179, 183
Court-Brown, W.M. 89
Couture, M. 44
Craine, L.S. 36
Crepault, C. 44
Crick, N.R. 67, 73
Crittenden, P.M. 8
Cumberbatch, G. 139
Curran, F.J. 42
Curry, J.F. 76

Dangel, R.F. 78
Davar, E. 18
Davidson, W.S. 63
Davis, G. 85
Davis, D. 183
Davis, M 143
Dawes, A. 2, 7, 19
Denicola, J. 79
Department of Education and
    Science 27
Department of Health (DOH)
    5, 27
Derryberry, D. 69
Deschner, J.P. 78
Diamond, I. 94
Dicks, D. 89
Dienstbier, R.A. 30
Dinitz, S. 184
Disshion, T.J. 69
Dockar-Drysdale, B. 1
Dodge, K.A. 34, 48, 54, 67,
    73, 166
DOH (Department of Health)
    5, 27
Dolan, M. 38, 43
Donald, D. 2, 7
Donnerstein, E. 94
Doob, A. 141
Doorninck, W.J. van 54
Dore, R. 149
Douglas, J.E. 42
Douglas, M. 140

Dubey, D.R. 78, 169
Dumont, L. 124
Dunning, E. 156
Durlak, J.A. 77
Dwivedi, K.N. 159, 160–63, 165, 166
D'Zurilla, T. 54

Easson, M.B. 42
Eastman, E.S. 57
Economic and Social Research Council 144
Ecton, R.B. 56, 78, 169
Edelstein, B.A. 75
Edleson, J.L. 160
Egger, M.D. 89
Eggers, C. 39
El Sarray, E. 7
Elbedour, S. 7, 16, 21
Elder, J.P. 75
Elkin, F. 145
Epps, K.J. 64
Eron, L.D. 33, 67, 83
Eth, S. 34
Evans, B. 159
Evans, J. 159
Ewald, L.S. 80
Eygendaal, W. 146

Fagan, J. 97
Fahlberg, V. 33
Fanon, F. 4
Farrington, D.P. 33, 66, 68, 69, 70, 72, 183
Fehrenbach, P.A. 165
Feindler, E.L. 56, 78, 80, 169
Feinstein, 7
Felson, R.B. 54
Field, 19
Fielding, N. 174
Fields, R.N. 7
Finch, A.J. 57, 166
Finkelhor, D. 10, 34, 91
Fisher, M.J. 64
Fleeting, M. 70
Fleischman, M.J. 80
Flynn, J.P. 89
Fonegy, 7
Ford, M.E. 72
Forehand, R. 62, 79
Foucault, M. 94
Fox, N.A. 70
Fraiberg, S. 163
Fraser, 19

Frazer, M. 7
Freedman, 94
Fremouw, W.J. 78
Freud, A. 4, 16, 18
Freud, E. 126
Freud, S. 90
Friedman, C. 177, 178
Fuhrman, T. 77
Funkenstein, D.H. 89

Gallagher, B.J. 94
Garbarino, J. 16, 18
Garrett, C.J. 74
Garrison, S.R. 167
Gentry, M.R. 64
Gerbner, G. 141
Gibson, K. 7
Giddens, A. 135, 140, 142
Gilligan, C. 2, 7, 19
Ginott, H.G. 159
Glaser, G.H. 58
Glasser, M. 90, 111–12
Glendinning A. 151
Glick, B. 56, 78
Glover, E. 42, 158
Glueck, E. and S. 95
Godsland, J. 174
Gold, M. 70
Goldfried, M. 54
Golding, W. 108
Goldstein, A.P. 56, 76, 78
Goldstein, J. 4
Goodman, J. 76
Goodstein, C. 183
Gordon, D.A. 75, 80
Gottfredson, M.R. 69, 73
Grant, M. 58
Graves, K. 80
Gray, J. 181
Greco, C.M. 179
Green, R. 137
Gross, L. 141
Guardian 178
Guerra, N.G. 74, 77, 166
Gulbenkian Foundation 65, 67, 70, 71, 83
Gunter, B. 141

Hagell, A. 66, 139–40
Hains, A.A. 78
Hall, S. 139, 155
Hambridge, J.A. 46
Hamburg, D.A. 89
Hammond, W.R. 74

Hanmer, J. 140
Hawe, J.C.W. 46
Harington, J. 127
Harris, D.P. 46
Harrower, J. 159, 169
Hartman, C. 46
Hartstone, E. 180
Hawkins, J.D. 81
Hayes, J.R. 42
Heath, L. 42
Hebdige, D. 145
Hegedus, A.M. 58
Hellsten, P. 42
Hemsley, D.R. 167
Hendry, L.B. 151
Henggeler, S.W. 58
Henson, C.E. 36
Herbert, F. 54
Herbert, M. 54
Herman, J.L. 19
Herrenkohl, E.C. and R.E. 29, 30, 31
Herrnstein, R.S. 58, 69
Hersen, M. 62
Herzberger, S.D. 30
Hetherington, K. 152
Hindelang, M.J. 58
Hirsch, P. 135
Hirschi, T. 58, 69, 73
Hobbs, D.B. 147, 156
Hodge, R. 134, 139, 142
Hodges, J. 8, 11, 12, 13, 20
Holland, T.R. 58
Hollin, C.R. 43, 55, 62, 74
Holloway, J. 43
Home Affairs Committee 65, 66
Home Office 27, 93
Horan, J.J. 77
Hoshmand, L.T. 166
House of Commons 136, 139
Howard, A. 159
Howitt, D. 139
Hughes, J.N. 77
Huntsinger, G.M. 77
Hyman, C. 69

ICD (International Classification of Diseases) 84, 85
Inamder, S.C. 38
International Classification of Diseases (ICD) 84, 85

Itzin, C. 140
Iwata, M. 78
Izzo, R.L. 76

Jackson, D. 32
James, O. 66
Jefferson, T. 155
Jessel, D. 88, 98
Johnson, R. 179
Johnson, R.N. 94

Kaplan, M.S. 72, 98
Kappeler, S. 140
Katila, O. 42
Kazdin, A.E. 63, 74, 75, 77, 80
Keilson, 17
Keith, C.R. 158
Keller, H. 78
Kelsall, M. 38
Kempe, C.H. 91
Kemph, J.P. 42
Kendall, P.C. 73, 76, 77
King, I.A. 89
Kingsley, D. 78, 169
Kinston, W. 91
Kippax, S. 137
Klapper, J. 136
Kleeman, J.A. 162
Klein, M. 104
Klein, N.C. 80
Klings, A. 89
Kluver, H. 89
Koiranen, M. 179
Kolvin, I. and P.A. 70
Krystal, H. 161
Kurtz, Z. 39
Kydd, R.R. 39

Labelle, A. 43
Laermans, R. 152
Lamparski, P. 62
Lampman, C. 77
Lampron, L.B. 76
Langevin 90
Laslett, R. 170
Laws, D.R. 92
Lazar, J. 136
LeBlanc, M. 68
Lederer, L. 94
Le Doux, J.E. 89, 90, 101
Lee, J. 167
Lejeune, J. 89
Lenhart, L.A. 165, 168

Levi, M. 58
Levy, I.V. 89
Lewis, D. 183
Lewis, D.O. 58, 71, 157
Lewis, M. 42
Liebert, J.A. 43
Lindquist, P. 38
Linney, J.A. 72
Lipsey, M.W. 74
Little, M. 41, 45
Lochman, J.E. 69, 76, 165, 168, 169
Loeber, R. 68, 69, 71, 74
Lombroso, C. 88
Lösel, F. 72
Love, J.G. 151
Lovett, S. 159
Lutherman, C.Z. 89

MacCullock, M. 43
Macdonald, G. 141
MacLean, D.G. 36
MacLeod, R.J. 46
Maffesolli, M. 152
Magnusson, D. 71
Main, 8
Malamuth, N.M. 94
Mallouh, C. 71
Mann, F. 177
Marriott, S.A. 78
Marsh, P. 147
Marshall, W.L. 92
Massimo, J.L. 158
Mawson, A.R. 161
McCarthy, J.B. 42, 45
McCullough, J.P. 77
McDougall, C. 64
McDowell, D. 174
McGuire, J. 78, 169
McMurran, M. 55
McNally, R.B. 37
McShane, M.D. 174
Measham, F. 156
Meichenbaum, D.H. 76
Meiselman, K.C. 92
Melzak, S. 7, 16, 19
Menninger, K.A. 42
Michelson, L. 77
Middleton, R. 94
Miller, A. 32
Miller, C.L. 76
Miller, F.J.W. 70
Miller, G.E. 80

Millham, S. 25, 41
Misch, P. 72
Moir, A. 89, 99, 101
Monck, E. 72
Moran, J. 158
Morton, T.L. 80
Mottonen, J.J. 179
Mountcastle, V.B. 89
Moyer, K.E. 89
Mrazek, F.J. 92
Mungham, G. 155
Murphy, P. 156
Murray, J. 137
Myers, R.K. 89
Myers, W.C. 42, 46

Nader, K. 34
Narick, M.M. 75
Nay, W.R. 77
Neeper, R. 62
Nelson, W.M. 166
Newburn, T. 66, 135, 139–40, 176
Newcombe, R. 145
Newson, E. 136
Noble, G. 137
Noble, P. 38
Novaco, R.W. 166, 167

Observer 125
O'Carroll, T. 94
Ogden, T.H. 164
Olweus, D. 50, 68, 70
Ostapiuk, E.O. 64

Palazzoli, M.S. 92
Parker, H. 145, 148
Parry-Jones, W. 38
Parsell, G. 144, 152
Parsons, B.V. 80
Patterson, G.R. 71, 74, 79
Pearl, D. 136
Pearson, G. 135, 155
Pecnik, N. 20
Pennells, M. 159
Perry, B 89, 90, 99, 101
Perry, D. 5, 13, 20
Pettit, G.S. 34, 48
Pfeffer, C.R. 42
Phillips, C. 184
Pincus, J.H. 58
Piontelli, A. 105
Plotnik, R. 89
Poplau, 94

Posner, M.I. 69
Powers, E. 158
Pratt, J. 147
Prentice-Dunn, S. 167
Priestley, P. 169
Price, W.H. 89
Prinz, R.J. 80
Professional Social Work 3
Punamacki, R.L. 2, 7, 17
Pynoos, R.S. 34

Quay, H.C. 58

Rabiner, D.L. 168
Raffe, D. 148
Rantakallio, P. 179
Raphael, J.P. 34
Rasp, R.R. 78
Redhead, S. 145
Reid, J.B. 79
Ressler, R.K. 42
Revitch, E. 44
Richman, N. 7
Ritvo, E. 58
Roberts, K. 144, 148, 152
Robins, D. 147, 156
Rodger, S. 38
Rogers, R.W. 167
Rose, S.D. 160
Rosen, I. 42
Ross, D. 137
Ross, R.R. 76
Ross, S. 137
Rothbart, M.K. 69
Rowe, D. 89, 99
Rowland, W. 136
Rubinstein, M. 183
Russell, D.E.H. 93
Rutter, M. 7, 27, 29, 34, 70, 72
Ryder, R. 178

Salter, N. 147
Sandler, J. 79
Sané, P. 5
Sarason, I.G. 75
Satten, J. 42
Saunders, S. 140
Saylor, C.F. 166
Scarman Report 125
Scharff, J.S, and D.E. 90, 102
Schlesinger, L.B. 44
Schlesinger, P. 139
Schlichter, K.J. 77

Schreiner, D. 42
Schulman, M. 140
Scott, M.J. 34, 36
Scott, P.D. 39
Sears, 94
Sgroi, S.M. 91
Shah, S.A. 88
Shanok, S.S. 58
Shapiro, V. 163
Sharp, S. 64
Shepherd, S. 34
Shore, M.F. 158
Short, R.J. 166
Shucksmith, J. 151
Siegel, T.C. 80
Simeonson, R.J. 166
Singer, J.L. 44
Singer, S. 174
Skinner, B.F. 49
Skynner, A.C.R. 159
Slaby, R.G. 77, 166
Slavson, S.R. 159
Slotkin, 94
Smith, D. 181
Smith, P.K. 34, 64
Smith, S. 159
Snyder, J. 54, 71, 77
Solnit, 4
Solomos, J. 124
Solway, K.S. 42
Somberg, D.R. 54
Soriano, F.I. 78
Sorrells, J. 183–4
Sparks, R. 135, 136, 141
Spielberger, C.D. 56
Spivack, G. 68
Stabb, S.D. 76
Stattin, H. 71
Steinhilber, 42
Steinem, G. 93
Stewart, J.T. 46
Stolberg, A.L. 167
Stoller, R. 90
Stouthamer-Loeber, M. 68
Stradling, S.G. 34, 36
Straker, G. 2, 7, 19
Stubbs, P. 20
Sunday Times 130
Szykula, S.A. 80

Tanke, E. 97
Tarter, R.E. 58
Tartlin, A. 97

Taylor, P. 38, 94
Terry, R. 69
Theler, M.H. 165
Thomas, A. 69, 70
Thomas, T. 175
Thorne, R. 39
Thornton, L. 38
Times 125
Tolan, P.H. 74
Trata, G. 92
Tredoux, 7
Tremblay, R.E. 81
Tripp, D. 134, 139, 142
Trower, P. 57
Turner, R.H. 145
Turpin, R. 89

Valentine, G.H. 89
Van Beuren, G. 4, 6
van Kammen, W.B. 69
Vipond, E.M. 46
Vizard, E. 72, 84, 90, 101

Walsh-Brennan, K.S. 42
Weaver, A. 38
Webb, V. 71
Wechsler, D. 57
Welch, B.L. and A.S. 89
Welsh Office 27
Werry, J.S. 39
West, D. 33
West, D. 68, 183
Westley, W.A. 145
Wexler, S. 97
Whatmore, P.B. 89
White, G.E. 148
White, J.J. 54
White, M.J. 77
Whiteley, J.S. 171
Widom, C.S. 29, 33, 34, 71
Williams, F.P. 174
Williams, G. 107
Williams, J. 156
Willis, P. 152
Willms, J.E. 148
Willock, B. 162
Wilson, 74
Wilson, J.Q. 58, 69
Wilson, S. 34
Winnicott, D.W. 112
Winnicott, P.W. 16
Winsten, S.T. 58
Witmer, H. 158
Woffitt, R. 177

Wolf, S.C. 92
Wolfe, D.A. 29, 34
Wolkind, S. 39
Wright, C.W. 34
Wright-Watson, J. 159

Yeager, C. 183
Yoerger, K. 71, 74
Yoshikawa, H. 81
Young, J. 141
Young, J.E. 35
Yule, W. 29

Zillman, D. 165
Zuckerman, M. 70
Zulueta, F. de 8, 11, 33, 34